# THE PEOPLE
# OF AMERICA

PEOPLES OF THE WORLD SERIES

*Editor:* Sonia Cole

# THE PEOPLE
# OF AMERICA

## T. D. Stewart

*Emeritus Physical Anthropologist in the
National Museum of Natural History,
Smithsonian Institution, Washington D.C.*

Weidenfeld and Nicolson
*London*

ISBN 0 297 76520 5 cased
ISBN 0 297 76539 6 paperback

*Printed in Great Britain by*
Richard Clay (The Chaucer Press), Ltd., Bungay, Suffolk

# Contents

# Illustrations

# Acknowledgments

I am indebted in the first place to the series editor, Sonia Cole, for the invitation to author this book, and for her subsequent encouragement and sensitive editorial help. Her willingness to let me use my judgment in shaping the subject matter enabled me to proceed with the task more enthusiastically than would have been the case otherwise.

I did all of the writing during my last three years as an employee of the National Museum of Natural History with the rank of Senior Physical Anthropologist. Since in this rank I was free of administrative duties, I am indebted, secondly, to the Smithsonian Institution and its Secretary, S. Dillon Ripley, for allowing me to partake of a 'climate of science' designed for 'the increase and diffusion of knowledge among men'.

Converting a manuscript into a book must always strike an author as something entirely beyond his control. I am happy to say thirdly, however, that the editorial staff of Weidenfeld & Nicolson with whom I have worked at long distance – April Weiss and Benjamin Buchan – have been both courteous and efficient in offering counsel and acceding to my wishes. Weidenfeld & Nicolson helped me also by securing permissions to reproduce the illustrations and quotations which constitute a necessary part of a work of this sort.

Finally, I thank my wife for respecting my need for isolation during the long hours I spent at home typing the manuscript, correcting the page proofs, and preparing the index.

T.D.Stewart<br>January, 1973

# Preface

Some ten years ago I wrote a short handbook for the sub-department of anthropology of the British Museum (Natural History). This was in the days when the word 'race' was innocent of many of its present connotations and the booklet was entitled *Races of Man*. After it had been published, I realized that outside the major groups Caucasoid, Mongoloid and Negroid, there are no such things as 'races of man'. There are populations, there are ethnic groups, but they grade into one another to such an extent that races or sub-species, as normally defined in zoology, are really meaningless when applied to anthropology.

So, out with races, on with peoples. But call them what you like, there are obvious differences between them. You don't have to be a physical anthropologist to recognize that a Japanese, an Englishman and a Kikuyu don't *look* alike (probably they won't think alike either, but that is a question of culture and not genetics). Yet, as a statement drafted for UNESCO by fourteen physical anthropologists put it: 'Some biological differences between human beings within a single race may be as great as, or greater than, the same biological differences between races.'

There is no problem in finding a book on the birds of Europe or the mammals of Africa, but when it comes to human beings it is quite a different matter. Man is seldom included with other mammals, partly because of our conceit but mainly because the book would burst its binding. It was this lamentable lack which made me realize the need for world-wide coverage on people. To do justice to the subject, it would have to be in several volumes. As divisions based on 'race' presented such difficulties, the boundaries would have to be geographical.

The books would have to be written by specialists. Clearly they would have to be trained in physical anthropology, but they would need to be far more than just skull-measurers.

They would have to describe characteristics and relationships of the present populations of each continent, based on the latest findings of human biologists and geneticists. They would have to try and discover how people got where they are and how they coped with and were moulded by their environment. This would involve the whole pageant of migrations and invasions, conquest and trade, throughout history. It would also mean examining the hardware of preliterate societies, their tools, weapons, art and other artifacts. The origins of the diverse populations of today would have to be traced back to a handful of bones in the grey mists of prehistory.

The setting would also be important, taking in geology, climatology, ecology and many other -ologies. The animals man hunted, the vegetable foods he gathered and later cultivated, would all have to be brought in.

It would be hard enough to find authors competent to discuss all these varied aspects; but the geographical boundaries of the proposed volumes presented yet more difficulties. An anthropologist who had specialized, say, in the sophisticated cultures of Chinese or Indian civilizations might have little knowledge of, or interest in, the seal hunters and reindeer herders of northern Siberia; yet all these peoples, and many more, would have to be included in the one volume on Asia.

There was still another very important qualification that these paragons of authors would have to possess, perhaps more daunting for some than anything else. This was the ability to turn a mass of scientific data and statistics into a readable and stimulating book, of real value for serious students and at the same time appealing to non-specialists.

Naturally, each author would ride his favourite hobby-horse to a certain extent; indeed one would want them to, for enthusiasm is infectious. Each author in this series has in fact treated his subject with a different emphasis, one underlining the historical background, another the genetic aspects, and so on. These various approaches emphasize the wideness of the topics under discussion and perhaps enhance the interest.

SONIA COLE

xiv

# Introduction

Europe-orientated history books generally attribute the discovery of America to Columbus in the year 1492. In these books the possibility of earlier European discoveries of land across the Atlantic – by the Norse, by the agents of the Bristol merchants, or perhaps by others – is usually explained in more or less detail depending on the nationality of the intended audience, but then often dismissed on grounds that, even if these discoveries occurred, they exerted no substantial effect on the course of subsequent events. Thus, in the Western World – an expression which in itself reflects pre-Columbian thinking – American history is usually said to have begun when Columbus returned from his first voyage of discovery.

This view of a tremendously important event in human history is unidirectional and purblind, even if realistic, because it ignores, or at least minimizes, the fact that Columbus and the explorers who followed him found most of the new lands already inhabited. Obviously America had been discovered and settled by Asiatics in ancient times, long before Europeans developed the necessary means to do so; that is, ocean-going ships and reliable navigational aids. The original discoverers had entered North America on foot by a route unknown to Europeans until the eighteenth century. Because the movement out of Asia began so long ago, no one then could record the event for the future history books and only now are some of the facts being uncovered by archeologists.

It is evident also that the original discovery of America was far enough back in the past to allow time, not only for the settlement of a vast land area by the aborigines, but for the development of distinctive local cultures. Here and there in America cultural progress had advanced to stages that amazed their European discoverers. When shown some of Montezuma's gold pieces sent back to Europe by Cortés after his conquest of Mexico, Albrecht

Dürer is said to have exclaimed 'I have never seen in all my days what so rejoiced my heart as these things.'

Cultural developments of this sort take time. We are still not sure how much time, but in any case, enough to demand that some thought be given to the status of man in the Old World around the time of the first discovery of America. Finds of datable skeletal remains of the modern form of man – *Homo sapiens sapiens* – in Europe and the Near East (if the remains from the Skhūl cave at Mount Carmel, Palestine, are granted this status) indicate an age of only 30–35,000 years. Our variety succeeded a more primitive-looking man – *Homo sapiens neanderthalensis* – not known to have reached America. Where modern man came from is also unknown. Possibly this new human line developed in Asia but, if so, the evidence has not yet been discovered.

Ultimately, men of modern form reached all parts of the Eurasian continent and in the process those in the west lost all contact with those in the east and *vice versa*. The Atlantic Ocean was, of course, a barrier to further westward movement until relatively recent times. But, because of the Bering Strait, the Pacific Ocean is not a complete barrier to human migration eastward, and the men of the east continued on into America. Viewed in this way, and reckoned in the thousands of years of elapsed time since the men of the Old World parted company in their wanderings in opposite directions around the earth, the initial meeting of Columbus with the aboriginal Americans marks the end of an era in human biology during which mankind reached the height of racial differentiation.

The momentous meeting of East and West in 1492 also marks a new era in the peopling of America. Unlike the prehistoric era, when the aboriginal settlers found their way open to all parts of the hemisphere because no other humans were present to oppose them, the new era was characterized from the beginning by more or less redoubtable opposition from the natives who resented being displaced. Nevertheless, the period of exploration was soon followed mercilessly by settlement and ultimately by the greatest mass migration of peoples ever known. Mostly this human flood consisted of Europeans moving to America in search of more freedom and opportunity, but it also included large numbers of African Negroes forcibly transported there as slaves. Later, small numbers of Asiatic peoples arrived in response to a need for laborers. In short, the era of the peopling of America following Columbus involved population movements which represent an unprecedented change in the world's population balance and composition.

The foregoing is generally what this book is about. Its special point of view, however, is that of physical man – his numbers, his appearance and dimensions, his attempts to modify his body, his physiological processes, his diseases and his inheritance patterns. Most other anthropological books on America emphasize culture and relegate its possessor to the background as an insubstantial figure. This book is different in that it reverses this pattern; it attempts to give American man whatever physical substance has been discovered, without going into details of his cultural possessions.

I have pursued this course because I am a physical anthropologist and not a cultural anthropologist (archeologist or ethnologist). In any case, there is more than enough of interest in American physical anthropology to fill a book of this size. Necessarily, the selection of subject matter reflects my own personal interests and experiences within the Western Hemisphere. Otherwise, the selection simply extends the coverage and balances the different scientific approaches. All of this is aimed at maintaining a broad point of view, because only through perspective is it possible to understand the complex congregation of people that now inhabits America.

Although some geographical maneuvering is inevitable in dealing with such a large part of the earth's surface, the organization of the human subject matter is basically chronological. Of particular importance is the distinction between the prehistoric and historic aspects of the peopling process. This can be put in a different way. If the interface between the periods of history and prehistory, as they relate to America, is likened to the surface of the ocean, the process of the peopling of America resembles the well-known image of an iceberg, in that by far the larger part is but dimly discerned below the surface in the depths of prehistoric time. Like the iceberg, too, the part of the American story that looms above the surface, although comparatively small in the chronological sense, bulks large in the light of history.

3

# I

# Background:
# Anthropogeography

America means different things to different people. To many, particularly its inhabitants, it is simply the immediate place where they live (America: 'My country 'tis of thee'); to some it is no more than a constituent continent (North, Central or South America); and to others, perhaps mainly outsiders, it is a whole hemisphere, still often referred to as the New World. By geographical convention America is the Western Hemisphere. Our concern in this chapter, however, is with a special aspect of geography known as anthropogeography, which is the study of the distribution of man and his relationship to his physical environment. Because of this particular interest and the need to begin the story so far back in time, America will be considered to include only those parts of the Western Hemisphere which were settled by prehistoric man of Asiatic origin. This places Iceland outside the limits, but includes North America (with Greenland), Central America, the West Indies and South America.

### America's geographical isolation
The only place where America is visible from the Old World is at the Bering Strait between Siberia and Alaska just below the Arctic Circle. This is the key geographical feature in our story. Admittedly, it takes a clear day to see across the Strait, and then only the highest land is visible. In 1728 when Vitus Bering, for whom the Strait is named, sailed through here, he stuck so close to the Siberian coast that he saw no land on the American side and failed to detect the close approximation of the continents. At its narrowest part the Strait is only fifty-five miles wide. Yet the Diomede Islands in the

middle of the Strait serve as stepping stones to divide the distance into nearly equal parts.

South of Bering Strait the Aleutian Island chain stretches westward towards Asia from the Alaska Peninsula. Made up of some one hundred large and small islands arranged in a curving line 1,200 miles long, the chain marks the southern boundary of Bering Sea. Although none of these islands bears Bering's name, some of the western ones have as much right to this honor as the Strait and Sea, because Bering led the first expedition to sail by them and to see them from the south. The absence of his name here is due probably to the fact that the report of his voyage eastward from Kamchatka in 1741 gave map-makers the impression that he had skirted the southern coast of a western extension of the mainland (cf. plate 2). After this geographical error was corrected, the Aleutian Islands seemed like a natural passageway from Asia to the New World. However, the westernmost island, Attu, is separated from the Commander Islands off Kamchatka by about three hundred miles of open water, which is a sufficient barrier to people in a crude stage of culture to eliminate the chain as an eastward passageway. As will appear later, the first movement of man into the Aleutians was from the American side.

Across North America from Alaska the huge island of Greenland extends some 15° further north and is separated from a maze of islands, stretching westward and southward to the mainland of Canada, by relatively narrow water passages which are frozen much of the year. Some three hundred miles off Greenland to the southeast lies Iceland, far out of sight and never discovered, so far as is known, by the aboriginal inhabitants of Greenland. About three hundred miles southeast of Iceland are the tiny Faroes, remote outliers of Europe.

Except at the three places in the far north described above – Bering Strait, Attu and Greenland – America is widely removed from the Old World by broad oceans. The narrowest part of the surrounding oceans – from the bulge of Africa to the bulge of South America – is close to 1,800 miles. This in itself is a measure of the isolation that America once enjoyed.

America is said to have a greater north–south extension than any other continuous land area of the earth – roughly 10,000 miles measured as directly as possible over land. The even more indirect route that ancient man had to follow in going from Bering Strait to

Tierra del Fuego increases this mileage considerably. Yet the whole of this generalization depends pretty much for its validity on the qualification 'north–south'. Greenland does approach closer to the North Pole than any Eurasian land mass, and the tip of South America does extend further south than that of Africa (about 55° and 35° south latitude, respectively). However, in terms of pre-historic migrations, Bering Strait is close to 165° west longitude, whereas the tip of South America is close to 75° west longitude – about 90° further east, which is quite a bit out of a strictly north–south axis. By comparison, it is worth noting that the distance between the tip of Africa (at about 20° east longitude) and the narrow part of northeastern Siberia 145° further east can be measured directly over land and also amounts to around 10,000 miles. Moreover, this Old World land area is not discontinuous to the extent that man could not pass from one end to the other in ancient times.

Although America may not be as unique in extent as in degree of north–south orientation, it is still a vast land to have remained undetected until very late in human history. North and South America together are said to comprise an area of over 15 million square miles. Ignorance of the existence of such a vast New World had nothing to do with the size, extent or global orientation of the area; it was primarily due, as already explained, to geographical isolation. Europeans had to develop their conception of the world as a whole, as well as their technology, to a point where they could venture on to the Atlantic Ocean out of sight of land before they could think of going in the direction of America. Yet because of the circumstance that America and Asia approach one another closely at one point in the far north, early Asiatics had only to develop their still primitive technology to the point of protecting themselves from intense northern cold in order to reach on foot the inter-continental connection.

### A biological cul-de-sac

The geography of America presents another aspect from the stand-point of its earliest discoverers. Once across Bering Strait in that ancient time, man had no way of knowing he had entered a place from which he could escape only by retracing his steps. Whatever impelled him to move northward and eastward through Asia must have continued to move him onwards into America, but probably seldom backwards. Was it simply his curiosity as to what was over the next hill, on the other side of the lake, beyond the forest or the desert? Or was he being led by the instincts of a hunter following the movements of animal herds? Whatever the nature of the drive, man seems always to have been an explorer. Today, having exhausted most of the mysteries of the world's land masses, and having accelerated his technological progression almost beyond belief, man is turning his attention to the depths of the oceans and to outer space. Given the means to do this, he can no more refrain from descending to the bottom of the ocean or ascending to the moon than the early Asiatics could stop at the threshold of America.

Since the region of Bering Strait occupies such an important place in this story, it deserves further consideration from the geographical standpoint. Was there a water passage between the Old and New Worlds at this point when the first man arrived on the scene, or were the two Worlds then connected by land? A satisfactory answer to this question is not yet possible, simply because the date when man first crossed over is still unknown. By good fortune, however, much new information about the region, mainly of a geological nature, became available in 1967 in a book provocatively entitled *The Bering Land Bridge* [77]. The book is an expansion of a symposium organized for the VII Congress of the International Association for Quaternary Research held in Boulder, Colorado, in 1965. The organizer of the symposium and editor of the book (himself a contributor to both) was David M. Hopkins of the US Geological Survey. Had Hopkins not spent twenty years doing his share of the research culminating in this book, any answer at the present time to the above question would be perforce even less satisfactory than the one that will be given here.

Hopkins stresses the fact that the Bering Strait and much of the seas on both sides – Bering Sea to the south and Chukchi Sea to the north – are relatively shallow. Depths over thirty fathoms are rare in the Strait and for long distances out to sea on either side. Near shore the figures drop to four fathoms and less. On learning this fact I recalled the time in 1927 when I was a member of a Smithsonian Institution expedition to Nunivak Island on the Alaskan side of Bering Sea. The US Coast Guard Service had turned down a request for transportation of the expedition members and equip-

8

ment to the island in one of the Coast Guard cutters stationed in the Aleutians. The excuse was that the waters around Nunivak were too shallow for vessels of the cutter's size. Actually, this is not so, as the Coast Guard itself proved, after we reached the island, by sending one of the cutters there on a survey mission. Although the unexpected appearance of the cutter slowly feeling her way into Nash Harbor (the headquarters of the expedition on the eastern end of Nunivak) was convincing evidence that the Coast Guard placed little faith in existing charts, I was not aware then that it also implied a respect for the shallowness of the whole northern part of Bering Sea.

Later that season I left Nunivak on a small trading schooner homeward bound separately via the mouths of the Yukon River to St Michael and ship-passage to Seattle. While we were going along the Alaskan coast below the southern mouth of the Yukon, out of sight of land, we struck bottom and bumped along on it for a while until the rising tide freed us. There is nothing quite like the peculiar shudder of a vessel when it strikes bottom, especially under such circumstances, for creating a lasting impression of the occasion on the mind of a landlubber at sea for the first time. For me, at least, there is more to the shallowness of the Bering Sea than meets the eye.

As most maps of the region show, the shallowness of the Bering Sea ends abruptly along a line running from just beyond the tip of the Alaska Peninsula (from which the Aleutian Islands chain extends) northwest past the Pribilof Islands to the vicinity of Cape Navarin on the Siberian side. Along this line away from land the depths drop off suddenly from around a hundred fathoms to three to four hundred fathoms and deeper. In reality, therefore, the line marks the edge of a submerged platform. North of Bering Strait in the Chukchi Sea the platform ends in a similar fashion, but the details are unimportant here. What is important is that the Bering–Chukchi platform, as it is called, extends some five hundred miles on either side of Bering Strait, and, if the sea level were lowered 150 feet or more, would appear as a vast and rather featureless lowland.

9

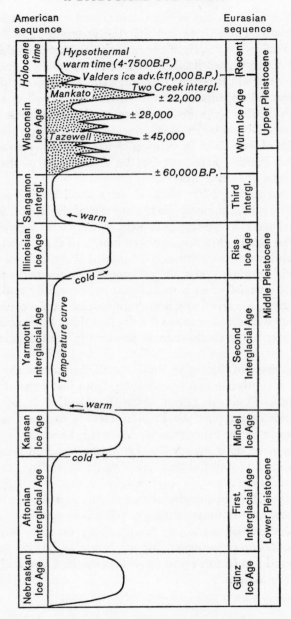

Fig. 1 Pleistocene chronology, After Dunbar and Waage [50a].

## Ice-free borders of the Bering Strait

Changes of sea level of 150 feet or more are not just hypothetical; they have occurred in the past, as will be shown, when great amounts of water accumulated in the northern continental areas in the form of glaciers (fig. 1). At such times the Bering–Chukchi platform actually constituted an intercontinental land bridge connecting large unglaciated areas in northeastern Siberia and western Alaska. Geologists refer to the whole of this low-lying, ice-free region as 'Beringia'. Figure 2 shows Hopkins' concept of Beringia

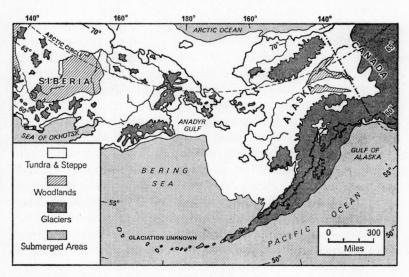

Fig. 2 Geography of Beringia during the height of the Wisconsin or Würm glaciation. After Hopkins [77]

during the height of the last glaciation. Viewed as a continuous region utilizable for the movements of animals (including man, if he showed up there while it was in existence), Beringia was accessible most of the time only from the west. Eastward the way was blocked most of the time by ice, everywhere except through central Alaska where the Yukon and Koskokwim Rivers now drain to just beyond what is now the boundary between the United States and Canada in the vicinity of the Arctic Circle. Clearly, then, when Beringia existed as continuous land, it seldom provided a throughway into the heart of America, but only into a small part of what is now Alaska.

If Beringia lasted as an uninterrupted land area only during the height of continental glaciation, and Bering Strait reappeared periodically with the sea level rise following the melting of the glaciers, so too did a connection between Alaska and the heart of America reappear almost simultaneously, putting an end to the small Alaskan *cul-de-sac*. The connection took the form of a north–south aligned ice-free corridor along the eastern side of the Canadian Rockies. This means that the previously glaciated region, extending all the way across northern North America, parted, leaving a Cordilleran ice sheet on the western side of the corridor and a Laurentide ice sheet on the eastern side. With the amelioration of the climate that accompanied the recession of the glaciers it was natural, presumably, for a corridor to form in the lee of the high mountains due to their ability to capture most of the moisture from the eastward moving air currents.

The existence of Beringia as an ice-free region surrounded by glaciers probably had one thing in common with the process that resulted in the opening of the corridor, namely, low precipitation. Some dryness persists today in Siberia, as well as in central and northern Alaska. In glacial times the colder air masses moving in these directions may have had a lower moisture capacity and may have been less successful than now in crossing the intervening mountain barriers without dropping their moisture, especially since the mountains had additional height owing to the presence of great ice fields and ice caps. In any case, low precipitation and low temperatures combined to inhibit forest growth in Beringia and to encourage the formation there of tundras and grasslands. These in turn attracted a variety of herbivorous animals, along with the carnivorous animals that preyed upon them. Once these animals were in the Alaskan part of Beringia, of course, they could and did take advantage of the corridor leading further into America, when it opened up.

Students of living and extinct animals have spent much time studying the relationship between the mammals of Eurasia and America and working out the movements that led to the present distributions. Figuring in terms of kinds of animals – or taxa, to use the technical term – scientists have calculated that during roughly the last seventy-five million years about twice as many taxa dispersed from the Old to the New World as in the reverse direction. Moreover, the movement appears to have rather steadily accelerated throughout this long time period so as to reach a climax in the last million or so years. Among the mammals especially prominent during the last stage were the horse, bison and mammoth, these having been found to compose 85-95 per cent of certain fossil mammal faunas collected in central Alaska.

The picture of Beringia as a distinct, if transient, geographic entity, and as an attractive habitat for migratory animal life, has been presented here in extremely simplified form. Still to be examined are the estimates of the times when Bering Strait dried up and a land bridge developed between the continents. At this point, however, nothing summarizes what has already been said better than one sentence from the book cited above and forming part of the synthesis written by Hopkins himself (p. 476):

The complex chronological sequence of openings and closings of a land bridge from Siberia to Alaska and of closings and openings of an ice-free corridor from Alaska to central North America has evidently operated increasingly as a set of one-way valves, allowing unrestricted flow of biota in one direction and extremely limited flow in the other [77].

This simile conjures up a vision of a long line of animal species slowly developing over eons of time in Eurasia and being drawn relentlessly by the one-way Beringia valve system into America. And following after the horse, bison and mammoth came the latest species to develop, the only one walking upright and making tools – man.

In this context the timing of man's crossing of the bridge assumes an importance unlike that of any other animal. Man was bringing with him a special acquisition – culture – that had eluded all the other animals preceding him in the long intercontinental trek. By means of culture he could adjust to a variety of environments so as to increase his chances of survival. With the aid of tools and weapons made by flaking stones or sharpening sticks he could kill and cut up animals for food, prepare clothing and shelter and defend himself against his enemies. The control of fire enabled him to cook his food and keep himself warm. Beyond this basic inventory of cultural acquisitions, which most certainly he had to possess in order to venture so far north, very little is known at present about the capabilities of the first Americans. With dates in hand, however, for the times when the land bridge and corridor were present, cross-checking can be instituted between man's cultural progress in Asia, on the one hand, and the oldest evidence of human occupation in America, on the other. It is mainly in this way that a judgment can at present be made regarding the most likely time of man's first crossing.

At this point the cold climate that early man encountered in this northern part of the world needs to be considered. Did it seriously handicap him in moving from the Old World into the New? John M. Campbell of the University of New Mexico, who has worked for a number of years in the interior of Alaska, argues that even in winter the cold was in no way a handicap and may even have been an advantage [28]. He cites as an example the long and wide Arctic Coastal Plain of northern Alaska – the now famous 'North Slope'. This is an area pockmarked with uncounted thousands of lakes. 'For all practical purposes,' Campbell says, 'it is impossible during the warm season for a man afoot to traverse [this area]. But from October to June he can go afoot in any direction across it at a rate of twenty to thirty miles a day, and if he can keep a compass heading, he can travel it in a straight line, for there are no terrain features which he must avoid.'

Campbell adds (p. 43), 'If primitive man is to live at all in the cold regions, he must learn to live in them the year around, and I suspect that in the open lands of the north, [early man] as well as [recent] Eskimos learned to exploit the advantages of winter . . .' 'This does not mean,' he continues, 'that the northern summer is prohibitively formidable either, although mid-summer for some far northern hunting societies is a time of relative want. But in many far northern regions warm season overland travel is severely inhibited, and I am thereby led to the conclusion that the long winters and short summers of the arctic and subarctic were nearly essential to the earliest explorations and colonizations of much of northern Asia and northern America' [28].

## Periodical land bridges

Dating of the land bridge and corridor will be discussed separately, beginning with the bridge. Geologists have attacked this problem

14

indirectly; that is, by concentrating on the rises of sea level – they call them 'marine transgressions' – that opened up Bering Strait. When the sea remained at some elevated level for a period of time, traces of the former beaches were left along the coasts, in this instance the coasts of Alaska and Siberia, in the form of deposits of marine sediments. Except where the land has subsided recently, the deposit representing a transgression is located, of course, at some point above the present sea level. In addition, each deposit often contains fossils that, by themselves or in combinations, enable geologists to distinguish the age of one deposit from that of another in terms of long time-periods.

Rather recently closer dating of the fossils from the old beach deposits became possible because of an important by-product of the atomic age in which we now live, namely, the process of utilizing the rate of decay of the isotopes of certain naturally-occurring radioactive elements for the determination of lapsed time since the death of the organisms. Although these new techniques permit dating in terms of years (absolute dating) instead of in relation to something else (relative dating), and thus represent a great advance over all previous dating methods, the techniques are so new and complicated that the available figures are still few in number and some may not be trustworthy. All of this is reason for considering the reconstructions of Beringia as still tentative.

After establishing the characteristics of an old marine deposit – especially its elevation, fossil assemblage, and exact age – the identification of other remnants of the same deposit at other coastal points is then possible, because each marine transgression was a worldwide phenomenon. Obviously this is a simplified statement of the laborious and time-consuming process by which the sequence of sea-level oscillations has been worked out.

Up to the middle of 1966, Hopkins had identified seven successive transgressions on the coasts of Alaska covering a period of over two million years, beginning some time around the end of the Pliocene epoch and coming up through the Pleistocene, or ice-age, to the Recent. Only the last three transgressions have a bearing on the present story. The oldest of the three is called 'Pelukian', derived from Peluk Creek near Nome, where it is represented by fossiliferous gold-bearing sand and gravel. The oldest age obtained from the shells is 100,000 $\pm$ 8,000 years before the present (BP). This is a radiometric or isotopic determination from the $Th_{230}/U_{238}$ ratio.* Other Pelukian deposits have been reported from low-lying coastal areas throughout northern and western Alaska and on St. Lawrence Island in Bering Sea. The ancient shore line was around seven to ten meters above the present sea level.

The second oldest of the last three transgressions bears the name 'Woronzofian', after a clay deposit located near Point Woronzof in the Anchorage area at the head of Cook Inlet. The $Th_{230}/U_{238}$ ratio for a shell from this deposit indicates an age between 48,000 and 33,000 years. Other Woronzofian deposits have been recognized at Point Barrow on the northern coast of Alaska, at several other places in southern Alaska, and also possibly in southeastern Alaska. Relative to the present sea level, this ancient shore line was probably a few meters lower, since it has been found in areas of the Alaskan coast believed to have been uplifted lately.

The most recent of the last three transgressions is named 'Krusensternian', after Cape Krusenstern on the northern side of the entrance to Kotzebue Sound. Old shore deposits near the Cape consist of sand and gravel making up a sharply curving barrier bar separating a large lagoon from the Chukchi Sea. A series of some 114 beach ridges is defined on the wider areas of the barrier, those nearest the present shore being occupied by present-day Eskimo camps, and each more-distant ridge yielding successively older kinds of cultural artifacts. Some of the ridges furthest from the present shore have yielded artifacts estimated to be 4,000–5,000 years old. Most of these deposits represent shore lines within two meters above present sea level.

Hopkins' speculative reconstruction of the history of sea-level

* $Th_{230}$ (ionium) is produced from the decay of $U_{234}$ and $U_{238}$ and hence is referred to as a daughter product of uranium. Its half life is 76–80,000 years. The $Th_{230}/U_{238}$ ratio provides a direct approach for determining age in the time range of 40,000 to 250,000 years. The method is complicated and does not require explanation here. However, according to John N. Rosholt, Jr., of the US Geological Survey, an authority on this form of dating, 'If the [calculated age] is to represent the true age [of the material analyzed], three assumptions must be valid: (1) The uranium was introduced into the nonuraniferous material over an interval of time that was short compared to the age of the daughter products; (2) no measurable amount of external contamination by daughter products occurred; (3) measurable uranium or daughter products were not subsequently leached from the material. These conditions are rarely fulfilled in natural environments.' [174]

changes in the Bering Strait area during the last 30,000 years, based on all the data relating to the last two transgressions, is shown in Figure 3. Here the transgressions are the parts of the curve above the line labeled 'land bridge open'. Accordingly, Hopkins thinks that the bridge was open over the long period from just before 25,000 years ago to about 15,000 years ago, and

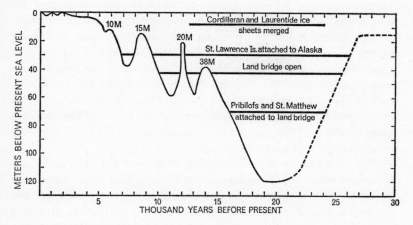

Fig. 3 Speculative reconstruction of the history of sea levels during the last 30,000 years in the Bering Sea area. After Hopkins [77]

that between about 14,000 and 10,000 years ago the bridge was twice open briefly. Not shown in the figure, of course, is the sea level in the interval between the Pelukian and Woronzofian transgressions. Information is insufficient for the period prior to 30,000 years ago to make the same sort of reconstruction, but if the bridge opened during that time, the suggested date is somewhere around 50,000 years ago.

Turning now to the ice-free corridor between northeastern Alaska and central North America, the available information is best presented indirectly just as in the case of the land bridge. In other words, the land bridge was viewed in terms of interruption (marine transgression) and the corridor will be viewed in terms of ice barrier (continental glaciation). This is because, as with the marine transgressions, the evidence for the glacial advances can be

readily studied. As compared with the evidence of marine transgressions at Bering Strait, however, that for the glacial advances in
the area of the corridor has received much less attention.

Authorities seem to agree that glaciers generally reached their
late Pleistocene maximum about 20,000 years ago. For this reason
it is assumed that the Cordilleran and Laurentide ice sheets
coalesced from as early as 23,000 years ago until as late as 14,000–
10,000 years ago. These suggested times for the last merging of the
continental ice do not quite coincide with those for the marine
transgressions at Bering Strait, so there may have been two short
intervals, one around 25,000 years ago and the other around
13,000–11,000 years ago, when continuous land communication
was possible eastward through Beringia and down the corridor
east of the Rockies into central North America. Again, as in the
case of the bridge, the information about the status of the corridor
prior to about 25,000 years ago is unsatisfactory for the purpose of
generalizations of this nature.

The significance of the foregoing geological findings and their
historical reconstructions now must be reviewed from the standpoint of human migrations. According to present evidence, the
ice-free corridor connecting Alaska and central North America
opened up during the waning of the last major glaciation, somewhere around 14,000 to 10,000 years ago. This would have
permitted any men who had reached Alaska, and perhaps even
those who were crossing the land bridge just as it was in the last
closing, to move southward. If man reached central North America
earlier than this, he had to come either at the time the corridor and
bridge were open, between about 28,000 and 23,000 years ago, or
at an uncertain date much earlier, perhaps in the neighborhood of
50,000 years ago. Anyway, the opening and closing of the corridor
are the critical factors.

Conceivably, early man entered Alaska even when the bridge
was closed by crossing over Bering Strait on the ice. The modern
Eskimos are known to do this. But, except when the corridor
opened up, early man could not have moved on into the heart of
the continent. Crossing the high ice-covered mountains and the
vast ice sheets to the south and east of the lowland parts of Alaska
was out of the question, as was escape southward along the Pacific
coast. The extension of the glacial ice to the ocean would have

made an otherwise rugged coast impassable, except in boats, which the early technology presumably did not afford.

## Cold-screening of diseases

The frequent mention of ice and of the important role the glaciers played in limiting early man's movement into North America is a reminder that within historic times Alaska has been a healthy place in which to live. So long as the inhabitants remain isolated, they stay free from colds and infectious diseases. The rare occurrence of epidemics usually can be traced to contacts with newcomers at ports of entry. This suggests that in isolated regions of the far north the cold is unfavorable to the spread and perpetuation of disease germs.

A 1965 epidemic of mumps on St George Island of the Pribilof group in the Bering Sea dramatizes this aspect of the geography of disease. Following the return of some students from the mainland for summer vacation, 119 of 212 native residents of the island came down with clinical signs of mumps in a fifteen-week period. Thirty-seven other residents were found to have serologic evidence of subclinical infection. All age groups were involved, from infants (57% of 37) to adults fifty years of age and over (77% of 26) [164]. According to the records, no case of mumps had been reported on St George since 1907. This was only the second such epidemic to occur in Alaska in eight years.

Mumps is not the only disease that has appeared suddenly somewhere in Alaska after an unusually long interval. Polio, rubella, influenza and measles also have been implicated in this way. The rare occurrence of epidemics in Alaska today, in spite of easy, rapid and frequent communication, leaves little doubt that such epidemics must have occurred even more rarely back in the days when the Territory of Alaska was being settled.

These health considerations have a bearing on the original peopling of the New World. Out of them has developed a concept of Beringia, and the northern regions leading to and from it, as a germ filter that served to hold back the diseases of the people who passed through it. To appreciate this concept fully one has to take several things into account: the northern populations in those ancient times probably consisted of small isolated bands; population movements had no planned goal, but simply represented an eastward drift along with that of the other animal life, and hence must have moved very slowly – perhaps sometimes at the rate of a relatively few miles in a generation; the distance ultimately covered on the way into the New World is vast and hence the time required must be reckoned in terms of many generations; and, lastly, only the fittest survived the harsh northern climate that existed over the whole distance. Viewed in this way, it is not unreasonable to think that because the location of the land entrance to the New World is so far north, the men who passed through this cold zone in effect passed through a germ filter, leaving behind whatever disease germs there were in the Old World. Information about the aboriginal population of the New World that seems to support this concept will be presented in due course.

## Ecological challenge to man's adaptability

Thus far this broad view of American anthropogeography has involved mainly the features that affected prehistoric men approaching from the west and that determined how and when they entered. The point has also been made that once past the northern continental ice sheets, ahead of these early men lay a tremendous land mass that extends further south and is orientated more nearly north–south than the Old World. The great southward extent of this land mass in itself implies the existence of all the climatic zones known in the Old World – sequentially, subarctic, temperate, subtropic, tropic, and then again in reverse order subtropic, temperate and subarctic. These zones in turn imply the existence of a variety of other features – forests, plains, deserts, jungles. All of these features are present, of course, as are hills, mountains and plateaus. Moreover, most of the mountains and other uplands course in a north–south direction, thus offering little impediment to the southern movement of peoples.

Probably the most serious impediment to the movement of humans in an early state of culture from one end of the Western Hemisphere to the other was a geographical feature not previously mentioned, namely the narrow isthmus, known to us as Central America, connecting North and South America in the subtropics above the equator. In the Darien part of Panama the width of the isthmus is only thirty-one miles. Such a constriction of the continental land masses suggests that, given the right conditions, a real bottle-neck existed here so far as migrations are concerned. Not only were there jungles; but also the narrowness of the isthmus would have made defence easy for inhabitants bent on opposing continued migration southward. Indeed, the distributions of American animals, both living and extinct, include many instances of restriction to either North or South America. Apparently, therefore, the isthmus was playing a role of this sort long before the arrival of man. Even today travel through the isthmus is extremely difficult, due in part to the difficulty of building this stretch of the Pan-American highway. Yet in spite of whatever difficulties existed, prehistoric man found a way to get through.

These climatological and physiographic features of the interior of America have been mentioned in anticipation, not only of the human distributions to be considered later, but of certain physical and physiological characteristics of the aboriginal peoples noted in historic times. According to the present concept of Darwin's theory of evolution, population change is brought about mainly by some form of selection. The environment, be it the thin cold mountain air, the dry desert heat, the moist heat of the tropical rain forest, or some other set of circumstances, provides the selection mechanism. When people encounter one of these environments, the individuals who are best able to cope with it will have the best chance to survive and reproduce. Slowly through long exposure to a particular environment a population acquires a genetic system featuring the characteristics that are often referred to as adaptive. Thought of in reverse, in other words from the standpoint of the extent of the population changes that took place in prehistoric America as a result of selective pressures, the element of time comes to the fore. Had the American population by 1492 become distinct enough from the Asiatic population from which it was derived to indicate whether or not its arrival dates back less than 20,000 years or more than 20,000 years? This is an important question when considering the details of the American population.

# 2

# Background:
# Paleoanthropology

Up to this point man has been subordinated to geography. Where, how and when prehistoric man first entered America, and what he and his descendants found in this new world in the way of environments exerting selective pressures, are important for understanding the peoples now recognized as American Indians. But equally important for this purpose is the reservoir of mankind in Eurasia, particularly the groups most likely to have reached Beringia when the route into America was open. Not much can be learned, unfortunately, about the physical types of these ancient peoples, because the recovered skeletons are few in number, poorly dated and difficult to interpret. On the other hand, the evidence of cultural development, as shown by associated stone and bone artifacts, pottery and so on, exists in greater quantity and is more readily dated and interpreted. An outline of the early cultural stages in Eurasia will help at least in deciding later which of the cultural influences reached America and when.

### Early Asiatic representatives of modern man
The nature of the information afforded by the finds at early-man sites in Asia is illustrated by those from Choukoutien, China. At this locality, about twenty-six miles southwest of Peking, the remains of two distinctly different types of men were recovered. The earlier and more primitive-looking one is a close relative of the famous 'Pithecanthropus' (*Homo erectus*) found eighty years ago in Java and believed to have lived in the Middle Pleistocene, some half a million years ago. The Chinese representative, also *Homo erectus*, was given the name 'Sinanthropus'. The later type of man

at Choukoutien belongs to our own species, *Homo sapiens*, and seems to have lived, judging from the cultural evidence, in the late Upper Pleistocene, exact time unknown. The 'Upper Cave' where this second type was found still serves as its name.

Of the two human types found at Choukoutien, 'Upper Cave man' alone falls within the time range being considered. Therefore, 'Sinanthropus' will be dismissed, but with one noteworthy comment. Already half a million years ago, this primitive form of man had reached a point close to the Pacific coast of Asia at 40° north latitude where it is cold in winter. There is evidence that he had achieved control of fire, and that this is one of the reasons he was able to survive this far north. Also, there is evidence that already he was making stone tools in a pattern that has a distribution limited to northeastern India, southeast Asia and China (fig. 4).

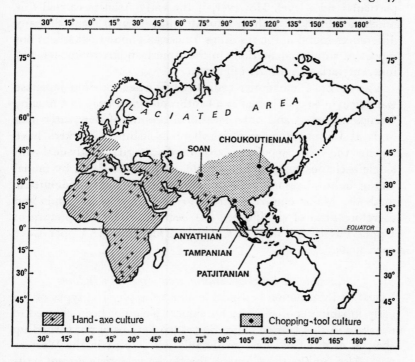

Fig. 4 The distribution of handaxe and chopping-tool cultures in the Old World during the Middle and early Pleistocene. After Movius [134]

23

This pattern includes forms, called 'choppers and chopping tools', which are lacking from the Old Stone Age cultures of this time in the West.

The Upper Cave skulls illustrate the difficulty of saying anything useful about the physical appearance of the prehistoric Asiatics, beyond the fact that by perhaps 30,000 years ago they were, generally speaking, essentially of the modern form. Franz Weidenreich, the famous anthropologist who in 1939 meticulously described most of the Upper Cave skeletal remains, reported one of the Upper Cave skulls as resembling an early European, a second as resembling a Melanesian and a third as resembling an Eskimo [236]. Since Weidenreich assigns all three skulls to a single family group, the high amount of physical variability here is discouraging to the hope of finding a distinctive physical type at a particular time level. However, if the early Asiatics carried this much variability with them into America, it could mean that any differences found in the resulting American populations might not represent simply adaptations to the American environments, but inherent variations in the migrants.

The work at Choukoutien came to a halt when the Sino-Japanese war began in 1937. Thereafter all anthropological work in China by foreigners ceased and only occasional reports of new early-man finds at Choukoutien and elsewhere by Chinese workers have reached the West. Reports of post-war discoveries mostly deal with single skeletons, usually incomplete, and always dated by faunal and/or cultural associations rather than by the new radiometric methods. Major emphasis seems to be on the oldest finds and therefore little of significance has been added to the picture of Upper Pleistocene man in China provided by the Upper Cave specimens.

### Resemblance between Asiatics and American Indians
Even less information is available about the physical types of the early inhabitants of Siberia. Foreigners have not been allowed to excavate in this vast area and Soviet workers have not turned up skeletal material of any considerable age, except in the Western part. Also, unlike the Chinese, the Soviet scientists do not write their reports in English and hence information about new finds is slow in reaching the outside world. So far the largest and best

described collections are those from 'Neolithic' sites in the Angara River and Upper Lena River regions. The American physical anthropologist, Aleš Hrdlička, was able to measure a good number of these specimens in the museums of Moscow and Irkutsk during 1939 in connection with his survey of Siberian skeletal remains. Having spent a lifetime studying American skeletal material, Hrdlička gained the impression that 'The Neolithics of eastern Siberia show a close relation to the oblong-headed lower vaulted tribes of America, the southern Siberian Eneolithics range closely with the high-vaulted Algonkin type'. Of the peoples still living in Siberia whose skulls he examined, he was able to say: 'The Chukchi connect definitely with the Bering Sea Eskimos, the [round-headed] Tungus relate evidently with the Aleuts' [92].

These statements based upon skulls recall others about living men made by Hrdlička a quarter of a century earlier (1913) following his first visit to southeastern Siberia and northern Mongolia. Again, having seen many living American Indians, he could say:

Among all these people there are visible many and unmistakable traces of admixture or persistence of what appears to have been the older population of these regions, pre-Mongolian and especially pre-Chinese, and those best representing these vestiges resemble to the point of identity the American Indian. These men, women and children are brown in color, have black straight hair, dark brown eyes, and facial as well as bodily features which remind one most forcibly of the native Americans. Many of them, especially the women and children, if introduced among the Indians, and dressed to correspond, could by no means at the disposal of the anthropologist be distinguished apart [83].

### Eurasian tool traditions

Unlike the people themselves or their skeletal remains, their surviving cultural materials are not only more plentiful, but embody combinations of elements or traits which vary in easily recognized ways. The combinations or patterns of cultural traits changed rather slowly in ancient times, while spreading widely. This is the basis, of course, for the cultural periods – Paleolithic, Neolithic and their sub-divisions – which have been used for many years and still have a definite utility in spite of the increasing availability of absolute dates. In this connection reference has been made to the 'chopper/chopping tool' tradition already present in southern and eastern Asia in Middle Pleistocene times. At the same time level in western Eurasia and Africa these distinctive tools are absent and instead the hand axe, a tool missing in the East, is present. Basic cultural differences between East and West, as typified by the few tools that have been named, continued up through time. By the middle Upper Pleistocene the predominant culture in the West was distinct enough from that preceding it to warrant the designation 'Mousterian', after the name of the town, Le Moustier, in the Dordogne region of France where it was first observed. It is not important here to describe the intricate details of the stone work, which are referred to as a bifacial retouching tradition.

The Mousterian is associated with a primitive type of *Homo sapiens*, known as Neanderthal man. This association has been found in many places in southwestern Europe and as far east as Shanidar Cave in northeastern Iraq and Tashik-Tash Cave in southern Uzbekistan, both located in southwestern Asia. At Shanidar the top of the Mousterian layer has been dated by $C_{14}$ at around 43,000 years ago.* Modified Mousterian elements ('Mousteroid') are found in cultures widely spread over northeastern Asia. Thus, Chester S. Chard of the University of Wisconsin in a review of recent archeological developments in the Soviet Union notes that:

Mongolia was settled, presumably during the [early part of the last glaciation], by populations with Mousteroid industries of western affinities who evidently came from Soviet Central Asia. There is as yet no evidence that they penetrated Siberia. Subsequently, Mongolia is characterized by industries with heavy tools made from split pebbles. This tradition, plus a strong survival of Mousteroid elements, forms the

---

* $C_{14}$ is an isotope of carbon formed in the atmosphere as a result of atomic bombardment from outer space. Because of the dependence, either directly or indirectly, of all living things on the atmosphere, $C_{14}$ becomes incorporated in living matter. Following death, no more of the isotope is added and that present decomposes at the rate indicated by its half-life. Up to 1961 the half-life of $C_{14}$ was taken to be 5,568 years; since then the more accurate figure of 5,760 years has been used. This means that after 5,760 years half is gone; after another 5,760 years, one half of this; and so on by halves until there is too little to measure. By this method absolute dates, with only small probable errors, have been obtained from various forms of organic carbon. They range back in time from only a few hundred years before the present to something over 50,000 years ago. Where historical dating is also possible in the early part of this range, agreement between the two methods is generally good.

major component of the Siberian Paleolithic and hence points to Mongolia as the primary source of the latter [33].

The Mousterian was followed in Europe by another distinctive culture known as Aurignacian, a name derived as usual from the type site, which in this instance is near the town of Aurignac in the Haute-Garonne region of France. Among its distinctive features are bone points with split bases and a high percentage of blade tools showing workmanship superior to that of the Mousterian. Since this new development occurred late in the Upper Pleistocene, the bearers of the Aurignacian culture were, of course, the modern form of *Homo sapiens*. As in the case of the preceding culture, however, Aurignacoid traits spread eastward and probably reached Beringia by the end of the Upper Pleistocene.

These generalizations about what was going on in Eurasia before the first discovery of America give no indications of the vast amount of archeological work that underlies and supports them. Each new discovery in eastern Asia, coming ever more frequently, changes the picture, sometimes by yielding a new date, sometimes by changing a cultural distribution. Theories about population movements during these early times change accordingly. A good example of this is supplied by Chester Chard in a paper published in 1963. The purpose of this paper was to admit to a change of opinion as to 'Old World roots' after an interval of only two or three years. Chard's ability to follow the Russian literature closer than most people makes his re-analysis of the situation, even after such a short period of time, especially pertinent to the present account.

He states his original position thus: 'It had been the general assumption that all of the oldest New World cultures were direct importations from Asia – more specifically, from Siberia – and that the prototype for their distinctive features must be sought in the latter area. I think this notion has now been sufficiently dispelled and needs no further comment' [32].

In his 1959 paper, Chard pointed out the conspicuous division of northeastern Asia into two major culture areas: the Pacific coastal zone and the interior. Since the earliest American cultures seemed to antedate the oldest interior sites then known, he came to the conclusion that the primary New World roots must lie in the

Pacific coastal zone. He postulated a single movement from the Manchuria–Amur region early in Wisconsin times (the last glaciation, see fig. 1) of a people with a simple stone industry in the chopper/chopping tool tradition as a sole basis for all subsequent New World developments down to about five thousand years ago. The nature of the available migration routes through northeast Asia indicated that such a movement was feasible only during times of lowered sea levels associated with glaciations.

By contrast, Chard's position in 1962, changed to account for evidence appearing in the meantime, was that there were two basic early movements from the Old World reservoirs. The first was along the Pacific shore, bringing an industrial tradition of choppers, bifacial implements, amorphous flakes and a Mousterian-like technique, perhaps about 40,000 years ago, early in the last glaciation. A secondary movement from the interior of Siberia, he believed, brought a crude blade technique, possibly the germ of Aurignacian-like bifacial flaking, via the Lena-Arctic coastal region about 25,000 years ago. He saw no reason to postulate any subsequent population movements until the appearance of the Arctic Mongoloids, perhaps five thousand years ago.

A more recent (1967) and somewhat different opinion is that of Hansjürgen Müller-Beck of the University of Freiburg, Germany, who, although primarily an Old World archeologist, spent several years travelling about the world for the purpose of studying this problem [135]. He seems unimpressed with the chopper/chopping-tool tradition as a component of the cultures brought to America. Indeed, he would have the first discoverers enter around 28,000 years ago and bring with them a culture containing Mousteroid elements. Not until after 15,000 years ago would he recognize Aurignacian-like elements entering America.

No one should be surprised that two eminent authorities differ in their independent interpretations of the archeology of northeastern Asia; differences of this sort are bound to exist in such a poorly developed field as this one. On the contrary, it can be taken as indicative of the future better understanding that their views are so similar in certain fundamental respects and so changed as against the prevailing view of a decade ago.

# 3

# The American Population
# in 1492

The reader may think it is strange to jump from a vague time in the past, an unknown number of millenia ago, to a specific year in the Christian era. Yet this is not very different from the jumps across continents and through glacial periods which he has experienced in the preceding chapters. In addition to background on the first Americans, an overview of them at their peak is necessary. This chapter, therefore, focuses on America as a human population entity in the year 1492 when Columbus' first expedition ushered in a new era for the world. At this point in time, so very recent as human history goes, the aboriginal Americans were the product of isolation in a land mass containing many different environments. From this date onward the isolation was to break down; first, naturally, along the coasts, and then in the interior. Biologically speaking, when peoples thus shorn of their isolation come into contact with other peoples, it can have serious consequences on both sides. Moreover, when the peoples concerned are of different races, the resulting mixtures differ from the original strains. In effect, therefore, information on the American population of 1492 and shortly thereafter serves as a baseline for judging the extent and nature of previous and subsequent changes in this population.

### Traditional population estimates

One of the important attributes of a population is its density, expressed either in total numbers or in numbers per unit of area. Surprisingly, this is something that is not known accurately for many populations even today, especially the big ones. For example, the Chinese have never been counted carefully and they are always reported as an estimate. Also, it is less than two hundred years since the United States took its first official census. And this was preceded by only one other national census, that of Sweden. But consider how much more difficult it is to get a head count when there is a delay of 400–500 years, as in the case of aboriginal America.

European travelers to the different parts of America in the early days never really saw all of the people of any one part, and they may have gained false impressions as to the density of inhabitants. On the other hand, in some places the population was reduced so rapidly that subsequent visitors could not tell how large it had once been. Moreover, some feel that the early records cannot be depended upon because the military men possibly exaggerated the number of their enemies, the administrators the number of their tribute-payers and the missionaries the number of their converts. All such things have made estimates of native American populations a matter of controversy.

Julian H. Steward, the editor of the *Handbook of South American Indians* [193], ran into this situation when he reviewed [192] the estimates of aboriginal American populations in an attempt to produce for South America a map of population densities comparable to Kroeber's [111] for North America (fig. 5). He was struck by the extent of the discrepancies in the results of studies by reliable scientists. In his words (p. 655),

The hemisphere totals vary from Kroeber's 8,400,000 (a figure less than Ricketson's 13,000,000 for Yucatan alone) to Rivet's . . . and Sapper's . . . 40–50,000,000 and Spinden's . . . 50–75,000,000. South American totals range from Kroeber's 4,300,000 to Rivet's 25,000,000; Means . . . arrives at 16–32,000,000 for the Andes alone. . . . It is obvious that either the data or the methods were at fault [192].

After examining the methods of his predecessors, Steward decided on one that utilized the earliest data that appeared to be reliable – in some cases missionary or administrators' reports, in others, travelers' accounts. He then extended the density calculated for the tribe in question to others who had similar cultures and lived in similar areas. As the tribes had probably declined somewhat by the time these estimates were made, he concluded that the densities calculated from them were, even allowing for exaggeration, likely to be too small.

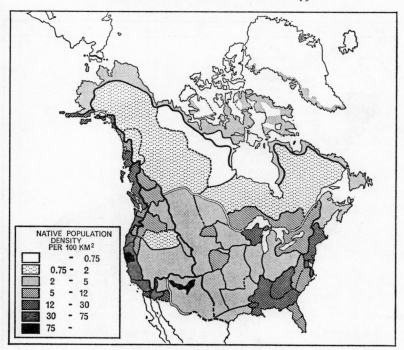

Fig. 5 Native population densities north of Mexico in 1492, by cultural areas. After Kroeber [111]

Steward's resulting map of South America, the West Indies and the southern part of Central America (fig. 6) follows the scheme used by Kroeber, except that the categories of population density per 100 km² are reduced from seven to five by the elimination of the two smallest. So far the population of Middle America has not been plotted in this way.

The studies of Kroeber and Steward are cited here, not because they have the highest claim to accuracy, but because they provide the only population maps that are reasonably comparable. Although they may err in estimates of total numbers, they are not likely to be very wrong in relative densities. Granting this, a noteworthy feature of both maps is the concentration of population on the western side of both continents. A similar map of Middle America, were it available, would undoubtedly show a connecting high

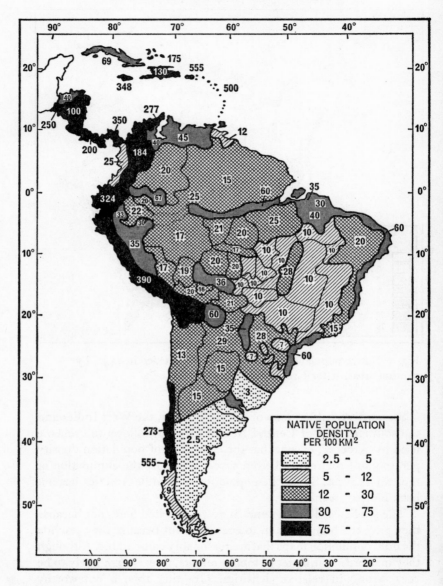

Fig. 6 Native population densities of the West Indies, Central and South America in 1492. After Steward [192]

density pattern, particularly in central Mexico. Undoubtedly the coastal and other lowlands here were the most attractive parts, but the neighboring highlands and mountains were not unpopulated. Very likely this narrow, north–south trending, high-density pattern reflects a long-traveled migration route. Also, the fact is noteworthy that all of the hemisphere, except the interior of Greenland, was occupied to some extent by the native population. In general, the regional variations in population density reflect differences in climate, flora and fauna, soil, topography, and the technology known to the local inhabitants.

Getting back to the matter of total population size, one way to show this is by reproducing Steward's figures as in Table 1,

TABLE I

Estimates of native American population ca. 1492*

(Figures in millions)

| Area | Population estimate according to: | | | |
| | Sapper [179] | Rosenblat [173] | Kroeber [111] | Steward [192]† |
| --- | --- | --- | --- | --- |
| North of Mexico | 2·00–3·50 | 1·00 | 0·90 | 1·00 |
| Mexico | 12·00–15·00 | 4·50 | 3·00 | 4·50 |
| West Indies | 3·00–4·00 | 0·30 | 0·20 | 0·22 |
| Central America | 5·00–6·00 | 0·80 | —‡ | 0·74 |
| Andes (from Colombia to Chile) | 12·00–15·00 | 4·75 | 3·00 | 6·13 |
| Remainder of South America | 3·00–5·00 | 2·03 | 1·30 | 2·90 |
| Hemisphere total | 37·00–48·50 | 13·38 | 8·40 | 15·49 |

* From Steward [192]
† The North American estimate follows Kroeber; Mexico is from Rosenblat; others are Steward's
‡ Central America is included with South America

comparing his estimate for the hemisphere with those of Kroeber [111], Rosenblat [173] and Sapper [179]. Kroeber's total figure, by far the most conservative, works out to a density index of 0·2 per km² (or one person per 5 km²); Rosenblat's to 0·3 per km²; Steward's to nearly 0·4 per km²; and Sapper's to 0·9 – 1·2 per km².

## Newer population estimates

These figures do not give any indication of the controversy going on over this subject at the present time in anthropological circles. The scholars who have investigated the evidence are divided into two schools: those who accept as factual the reports of the conquerors, early missionaries and others, of very dense American populations in places where rapid reduction soon occurred; and those who reject this early testimony and insist that native technology could not support the high densities indicated. The latter group is represented by the authorities already cited; the other group is best represented at the moment by Sherburne F. Cook of the University of California (Berkeley) and associates and by Henry F. Dobyns of the University of Kentucky. Those taking a new look at this subject, stimulated mainly by reanalysis of all available data for central Mexico, have come up with estimates ranging upward to around a hundred million for the hemisphere as a whole. One such estimate by Dobyns (Table 2) assumes the

TABLE 2

### Estimated aboriginal population*
(Figures in millions)

| Area | Nadir population | Date of nadir | Projections ×20 | ×25 |
|------|------|------|------|------|
| North America | 0·49 | 1930† | 9·80 | 12·25 |
| Mexican civilization | 1·50 | 1650 | 30·00 | 37·50 |
| Central America | 0·54 | 1650 | 10·80 | 13·50 |
| Caribbean Islands | 0·02 | 1570 | 0·44 | 0·55 |
| Andean civilization | 1·50 | 1650† | 30·00 | 37·50 |
| Marginal S. America | 0·45 | ? | 9·00 | 11·25 |
| Western Hemisphere | | | 90·04 | 112·55 |

* From Dobyns [48]
† The sources of these figures are too extensive to quote

validity of a 'standard' hemispheric depopulation ratio of either 20 to 1 or 25 to 1 [48]. The use of this ratio requires the location in time of the point of greatest decline (nadir) in the population total for each area. The original population estimate is obtained by multiplying the nadir population figure by the depopulation ratio.

The resulting totals yield an index of density for the hemisphere population of between 2·1 and 2·7 per km². In taking this extreme stand, Dobyns characterizes it as 'an antidote to previous overly low estimates of aboriginal American population, and as a working hypothesis to stimulate research into this question'.

Obviously, all that can be said at present about the approximate size of the native American population of 1492 is that it was between ten and a hundred million, which is indeed a very broad approximation. Since there is no way as yet of being sure whether the true figure was nearer one extreme or the other, and since also there is no sure indication yet of when this population began proliferating, very little can be deduced about the pattern of population growth.

When reasonably firm figures for the size of a human population at different periods of time are plotted as a graph, an S-shaped, or sigmoid, curve results; that is, assuming one has a full life history of a population, an initial stage of long gradual increase in numbers is followed by a stage of swift up-turn or acceleration, and ultimately by a stage of deceleration or leveling-off. The shorter the time and the larger the final size figure, the more the pattern of the graph resembles an elongated S (cf. fig. 31, p. 228). This pattern of growth is said to be 'explosive'. There is reason to believe that the growth of a relatively disease-free human population in the geographical situation that America once represented – a place offering no opposition to settlement by other humans and affording a wide choice of acceptable environments – should have been explosive. Be this as it may, some of those who favor a native American population in 1492 approaching a hundred million seem to feel that this must be close to the limit of density that the technologies of that time could sustain. This is something to keep in mind when the individual American groups are looked at closely.

### Lack of immunity to disease

Dobyns' use of depopulation ratios as high as twenty to one and twenty-five to one by itself tells nothing of the causes of the depopulation that began after 1492. The slaughter that marked ruthless conquests, especially that by the Spaniards, is well known because it was reported by a number of reliable observers. Less well known is the extent of the deaths due to the introduction of new diseases and to the cultural disruption in one form or another, including famine, brought on by both the battles and the diseases. Disease and famine kill less ostentatiously than warfare and epidemics, and hence are detectable mainly through indirect signs such as the decline in numbers of inhabitants listed in tribute rolls.

In the latest study of evidence of this sort for central Mexico, Borah and Cook present population estimates that indicate a different nadir from that used by Dobyns in Table 2 [20]. As plotted in a graph (fig. 7), these latest figures show that the most

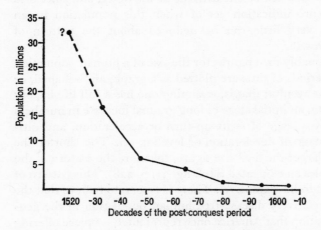

Fig. 7 Decline of the population of central Mexico according to the estimates of Borah and Cook [20]

intensive depopulation occurred between 1519, when the conquest of this region began, and 1548. The more gradual decline after 1548 is not explained. Stating the indications of the graph in more readily understood terms, by 1548 only one Indian was living in central Mexico for every five who had lived there thirty years before, and by 1605 only one Indian was living in central Mexico for every thirty-two who had lived there eighty years before.

Although the respective roles of slaughter, famine and disease in producing such a rapid and marked population decline cannot be disentangled with certainty, there is a growing feeling that disease was the leading cause of death after the immediate impact of the conquerors had been felt. The medical historian P. M. Ashburn lists three imported diseases – 'in order of frightfulness, smallpox, typhus and measles' – which he designates 'the shock troops of the conquest' [6]. He goes on to explain (p. 80) that 'Famine and scurvy were slow and placid [in their attack], but these three white man's diseases were swift, violent, mutilating. Their very character made one think of the shock and terror of war.'

Bernal Díaz del Castillo, a foot soldier of Cortés during the conquest of Mexico, wrote down his recollections of that event forty-eight years later [98]. Historians are wont to remark on the phenomenal memory of Díaz and cite in this connection the fact that in his old age he remembered the number of steps in the ascent to Montezuma's great temple in Mexico City as being not just a large number, but specifically 114. Speaking of Narváez, who landed in Mexico in 1519 hoping to supersede Cortés, Díaz says (p. 235): 'Let us return now to Narváez and a Negro he brought with him who was full of smallpox, and a very black dose it was for New Spain, for it was because of him that the whole country was stricken, with a great many deaths.'

Cuba, from where Narváez had come, is believed to have had an epidemic about this time, since Las Casas reports an epidemic in nearby Santo Domingo in the years 1518–19 [114]. Of the latter epidemic Las Casas stated in the 1550s when he wrote his *Historia de las Indias* (III, p. 270): 'I do not believe that there remain alive a thousand who escaped this misery of all the immense multitude of people that was formerly in this island and which we had seen with our own eyes.'

Las Casas, like Díaz, had a good memory, especially for anything involving the welfare of his beloved Indians. He had been among the first to come to America and later as Bishop of Chiapas he was to become known as the 'Apostle of the Indians'. His famous *Historia* contains so much evidence of the mistreatment of the Indians that he charged the rector and chapter of the San Gregorio monastery in Valladolid, Spain, with whom he deposited the manuscript, not to allow it to be generally read for forty years. Even then political influences in Spain prevented its publication until 1875.

There is no need here to document further the epidemics known to have ravaged the native American population from shortly after 1492 onward. Necessarily the documentation spreads over a long period of time as the isolation of the natives broke down in more and more remote places. What has been given for the period of initial contact is the most important and is enough to make the point that another characteristic of the American population, besides its large size, was its lack of immunity to the Old World diseases introduced by the Europeans and their Negro slaves.

Today we know of two ways a person may acquire immunity to a specific disease. One of these is by becoming ill of, and recovering from, this disease; this is the 'active' or 'natural' way. The other is by being injected or inoculated with a product of the disease which has been rendered harmless and yet induces the body to develop the immune state; this is known as the 'passive' or 'artificial' method.

The natural immunities of a population are maintained by the constant presence of the diseases producing them. Exposure to the same diseases, generation after generation, seems to give a population a level of immunity which keeps the diseases from being as virulent as they would be in a population lacking a long history of disease exposure.

Two populations with very different patterns of immunity are clearly represented by the peoples of the Old and the New Worlds in 1492. Observers at the time repeatedly noted that the smallpox, which the Spaniards and their Negro slaves transmitted to the American natives, scarcely affected the former while being highly virulent for the latter. The rapidity with which this and probably other infectious diseases spread over America after 1492 had such a devastating effect on the native population that the diseases involved must presumably have been new to the Western Hemisphere. The American population lacked even a minimum level of immunity and people of all ages, not just the young, were struck down.

### Evidence of malaria

Among the diseases whose presence or absence in the aboriginal New World has produced the most controversy are malaria, syphilis and tuberculosis – all chronic diseases. Malaria, which produces an intermittent fever, has a limited distribution depending on the range of the particular species of mosquito that transmits the causative agent, which is a parasite. All of this was learned quite recently; malaria was not differentiated from other fevers by fifteenth- and sixteenth-century observers. Also, malaria does not directly affect the skeleton of its human victim, so there is no help from this source in discovering whether the disease afflicted prehistoric man.

Although investigation of the history of malaria has been handicapped in this way, a solution of the problem has come recently from an unexpected source, namely, the other animals that carry the malarial parasites and hence are referred to (along with man) as 'hosts'. In the Old World most of the primates – man, the great apes and the monkeys – and a number of other mammals constitute the hosts. By contrast, today in the New World only man and the cebid monkeys of Central and South America serve in nature as hosts [51]. No other American mammals play this role. Moreover, the malarial parasites in America are virtually identical with those of the Old World. Only two questionable new species have been reported in the American monkeys and they have very limited distributions.

The South American monkeys, of which the cebids are one of only two families, are so distinct from the corresponding primates of the Old World that they are classed as a separate superfamily (Ceboidea). Among other things, the ceboids have a flat instead of a sharp nose, three premolar teeth instead of two, and often a grasping or prehensile tail instead of an ordinary tail. The Old and New World groups are believed to have parted company perhaps as much as seventy-five million years ago. About sixty million years ago the ancestors of the ceboids first reached South America from North America where they have no living descendants. Considering the extent of the differentiation these monkeys have undergone in the New World compared with that of the malarial parasites now found with them, a very different time of arrival is indicated. Could it be that man brought the malarial parasites with him from Asia a few thousand years ago? This is hardly likely in view of what was said earlier about the 'cold filter' through which he had to pass. Indeed, the only reasonable explanation is that the parasites were introduced from Europe after 1492.

Incidentally, one former reason for not including malaria among the diseases imported by Europeans was the American natives' supposed traditional knowledge of the curative properties of chinchona bark (quinine). Further studies of the history of quinine have shown that there was no such native tradition prior to the seventeenth century, when the value of chinchona bark was accidentally discovered by Europeans.

## Origins of syphilis

Syphilis is the second of the three important diseases whose presence in America before 1492 is disputed. Many historians and medical writers of the late fifteenth and early sixteenth centuries claimed that syphilis appeared suddenly and spread rapidly in Europe following the return of Columbus' expeditions. Eventually when the concept of immunity was understood, the accounts of the initial rapid spread of the disease over Europe seemed to support the view that syphilis was new to the people of that continent and was therefore an American disease. Eventually, also, anthropologists reinforced this view when they began looking at collections of European skeletons from before 1492 and failed to find lesions that could be called bone syphilis. In America, on the other hand, the anthropologists found that skeletons of the native population often exhibited lesions that they interpreted as being caused by syphilis. Unfortunately, the value of these finds was impaired by the recurring uncertainty as to whether the American skeletons so involved were truly of pre-Columbian age and whether the lesions could have been caused by some other disease besides syphilis.

In the course of my own research on American Indian skeletal remains, I have been impressed by the frequent occurrence of putative syphilitic lesions in certain bones, especially the shin-bones, in collections definitely of post-Columbian date and also by the marked decrease in frequency of these lesions in collections of late-pre-Columbian date. Moreover, the almost complete absence of such lesions from many collections dating back unquestionably into the early part of the Christian era has always struck me as significant. However, the failure to find these peculiar bone lesions in America less than two thousand years ago, like so much negative evidence, is seldom mentioned. Can it be that syphilis is one of the world's newest diseases?

These considerations, combined with the knowledge that syphilis and yaws are closely related diseases and that yaws is now prevalent in some parts of the American tropics, led me, with

Alexander Spoehr, to propose in 1952 a theory to account for the situation that appears to have existed in 1492 [218]. We suggested that if, just prior to 1492, the organism causing syphilis had differentiated locally in the West Indies from the closely related organism causing yaws, Columbus arrived at the right time to carry the new disease to Europe. Once this had happened, every expedition leaving Europe for America or other parts of the world would have been manned by sailors, some of whom had picked up the disease in the brothels of the port cities, and were potential spreaders of the disease. The main fault with this theory is that yaws, although now present in America, is not certainly a New World disease; pre-Columbian skeletons from the West Indies are not notable for pathological lesions resembling those of either syphilis or yaws.

Since the 1950s a different point of view, which places the origin of syphilis in the Old rather than the New World, has come to the fore [65, 94]. This recognizes the fact that syphilis exists today in two forms: venereal and non-venereal or endemic. The former is the disease that first became known in European urban centers at the end of the fifteenth century; it is transmitted primarily by the venereal route and can have serious consequences for its victims. The latter occurs typically in human groups living essentially a nomadic life in an *arid*, warm climate. Endemic syphilis and yaws are both transmitted mainly in infancy and childhood by non-venereal routes and usually run a shorter and milder course than the venereal form. Yaws differs from endemic syphilis in its preference for a *humid*, warm climate.

The causative organisms for all three diseases, known as treponemes, are impossible to tell apart microscopically; in fact they are so much alike in every way that the diseases they cause are now commonly referred to collectively as treponematoses. The implication here is that the differences between the three diseases depend on the interaction between the treponeme(s), the environments and the ways in which men live. A further implication is that at least three evolutionary stages are represented: yaws → endemic syphilis → venereal syphilis.

Some medical authorities argue that pinta – a treponemal disease identified mainly with America – represents a stage prior to yaws in the evolution of the treponematoses. For this to be so it is

41

necessary to assume that pinta once had a world-wide distribution and that it gave rise to yaws in the Old World before disappearing there. C.J.Hackett, lately of the World Health Organization and an authority on yaws, subscribes to this view, as becomes apparent from his reconstruction (fig. 8) of the world situation regarding

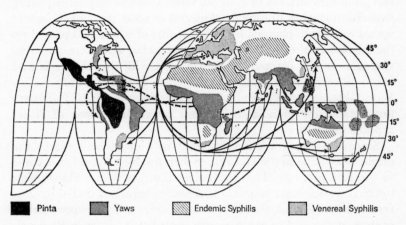

| Pinta | Yaws | Endemic Syphilis | Venereal Syphilis |

Fig. 8 Hypothetical world distribution of human treponemal diseases of the sixteenth century. Solid lines indicate spread of venereal syphilis; broken lines, spread of yaws. After Hackett [65]

the treponematoses in the sixteenth century [65]. On the other hand, E.H.Hudson, an authority on 'bejel', a form of syphilis endemic in the Near East, sees the American pinta as essentially a variety of yaws somehow derived from the Old World in prehistoric times [94].

Be this as it may, both Hackett and Hudson are in agreement about the Old World origin of venereal syphilis from yaws through the intermediacy of endemic syphilis.

### Tuberculosis and the 'hunchbacks'

As compared with the foregoing long discussion of syphilis, much less needs to be said about tuberculosis – the third important disease whose presence in prehistoric America is disputed. Unlike syphilis, tuberculosis has no particular association with the European discovery of America; but like syphilis, it attacks the bones, although in a different way. A frequent and characteristic skeletal site for the lesions of tuberculosis is located in the spinal column, usually involving one or more vertebrae in the lower part of the rib-bearing section. Often as a result of these spinal lesions a backward-bowing deformity develops, sometimes referred to as 'hunchback'. When the condition of hunchback has been present long enough for the disease to have 'burned out', the part of the spine that is involved – originally a series of separate segments – appears distorted and grown together in a solid mass of bone.

Solid, deformed spines of the sort described have been observed from time to time in the skeletal remains of putatively prehistoric Americans. Also, representations of human beings on rock faces and in pottery decorations in America occasionally include hunch-backed figures. The same is true of pottery vessels and figurines made in the human form. All such things have been interpreted to mean that tuberculosis was present in America before the arrival of Columbus. Generally speaking, there was scarcely any dissent from this long-accepted view until recently. The main dissenter, Dan Morse, has had much experience with the disease at the Municipal Tuberculosis Sanitarium of Peoria, Illinois. In a review of all the evidence in 1961 he found fault with most of it, either because the dates were doubtful or because the depicted deformity and bone involvement were not typical enough to represent pre-sumed cases of tuberculosis [131]. Nevertheless, he does not regard the matter as settled; on the contrary, he is optimistic that eventu-ally someone may find better evidence or even come up with some sort of tuberculin test for dried bone.

The foregoing considerations of the health status of the American population in 1492 emphasize the absence of prior exposure by this population to the diseases that occur today in epidemic form all over the world, and also the absence in this population of the parasites causing malaria. As for the treponematoses in America at this time, only pinta (yaws?) can be said certainly to have been present, because clear evidence is lacking that it had given rise either to endemic syphilis or to venereal syphilis. Evidence of the presence of tuberculosis in prehistoric America is still difficult to evaluate, but in any event does not suggest a serious health hazard. By contrast with the contemporary health situation in the Old World, that in America was undoubtedly very different. Under-standably, some of the first explorers and missionaries looked upon this difference with admiration. Indeed, only through the medical advances of the past century has it been possible for any part of the modern world to arrive at a comparable state of freedom from disease.

Population health depends, of course, upon other things besides the diseases mentioned. What about malnutrition, intestinal parasites, arthritis, tooth decay in prehistoric America? Judging from skeletal evidence, individual cases of malnutrition certainly existed, but at the same time the general level of nutrition was good, although varying somewhat with environment, as will be shown later. In this connection, the negative evidence again is too often ignored. Aleš Hrdlička frequently recalled in my presence how much childhood rickets he had seen in New York City just before the turn of the century when he was practising medicine there. His reason each time for remarking on this was his renewed awareness of the complete absence of any signs of rickets in the remains of the American natives.

*Intestinal parasites*

The presence of intestinal parasites in the prehistoric population can be established only from the remains of intestinal contents, either *in situ* in mummies or after having been expelled in life as feces (coprolites). Unfortunately, specimens in either form well enough preserved for study are scarce at best, and practically nonexistent in many of the warmer areas where parasites were most likely to have existed. The mummies of prehistoric Americans owe their existence mainly to natural desiccation, a process which turns the skin to a leathery consistency while allowing the internal organs to disintegrate. Thus, nothing much besides connective tissue is found in the abdominal cavities of dried mummies.

Ancient bodies in which the intestinal tract has survived have been found in South America, either well sealed off under the desert sands along the coast of Peru or perpetually frozen in the high Andes of Chile. Surprisingly, little effort has been made to preserve and study those discovered in the coastal region, so nothing is known about their parasites. On the other hand, great effort was expended in preserving and studying an Andean specimen discovered in 1954, the only one for which information is available [132]. Greta Mostny, Director of the Museo Nacional de

Historia Natural in Santiago, Chile, to whom most credit should go, reported that the body in question is that of a boy, eight to nine years of age, who died – judging from the clothing and ornaments – in late pre-Hispanic times. He may have frozen to death.

She reported also that a parasitologist of the University of Chile, T.Pizzi, found eggs of *Trichuris trichiura* in the boy's intestine. This is a species of nematode known as 'whipworm' because of its hair-like form. Usually parasites of this species produce no symptoms, but occasionally may cause diarrhea, vomiting and nervous disorders. The finding of eggs alone in this case may not signify a general health hazard for the peoples living in the high altitudes of the Andes in pre-Hispanic times.

Archeologists have only recently begun to realize the possibilities of learning more about the diets and diseases of prehistoric peoples from the dried excreta or coprolites they left at their habitation sites. Studies of this sort, which are appearing with increasing frequency, usually cite E.O.Callen and T.W.M.Cameron of McGill University, Canada, as having pioneered the method in the Western Hemisphere. They began their work about 1955 at the request of a curator of the American Museum of Natural History in New York, Junius Bird, who had recovered a series of coprolites in 1946–7 from different levels in a habitation mound on the north coast of Peru [27]. The mound, known locally as Huaca Prieta, is now famous, in large part because it gave the first indication of the existence in this part of the world between 3500 and 1200 BC of people living in a pre-ceramic stage of culture. Also, they were in the incipient stage of true agriculture, with seemingly some production of beans, peppers, gourds and squash.

I visited Huaca Prieta two years after Bird finished working there and found his trenches into the side of the mound still just about as he had left them. Standing in one of the trenches and looking closely at the layered deposits – the accumulation of rubbish and debris from human encampments – I happened to see at eye level some threads sticking out of the wall between pebbles. Careful removal of the pebbles revealed a small piece of loosely-woven cotton cloth, which was easily extracted intact. Knowing that my museum in Washington had nothing of the sort in its collections, I decided then and there to become a looter to this extent and take the bit of textile back home with me. The recovery of such an ancient piece of textile – its position in the mound suggests a date around 2000 BC – after a couple of years of exposure to the air demonstrates as well as anything else the dryness of much of the north coast of Peru. It is this dryness, of course, that preserved the feces and other wastes which the inhabitants added to their living site generation after generation.

According to Callen and Cameron the coprolites recovered by Bird from one layer near the bottom of the mound were found to contain numerous objects believed to be the eggs of a species of tapeworm (*Diphyllobothrium*) [27]. A definite identification was not possible and little is known about the possible life of the eggs of parasitic worms in feces which have been subjected to rapid desiccation. Although the life cycle of the tapeworm includes animal intermediaries, some of which are present in South America, and although the ancient inhabitants of Huaca Prieta ate some of these intermediaries seemingly without cooking them, the limited and uncertain finding of tapeworm eggs in only one layer of coprolites is an unsatisfactory incrimination of man even as an accidental host.

Callen was called upon again more recently to study ancient human coprolites from caves in the Tehuacan Valley of Mexico [26]. He blames the massed vegetable matter in these coprolites for his failure to find any eggs of parasites.

Frederick Dunn of the Hooper Foundation, University of California Medical Center in San Francisco, was also unsuccessful in finding true parasites in coprolites from Lovelock Cave in Nevada [72]. He did find non-pathogenic larval nematodes of the genus *Rhabditis* and regarded this as evidence that helminths can survive in recognizable form after desiccation. However, he took the total absence of true parasites – hookworms, whipworms, roundworms, etc – as indicating a parasite-free human population.

Other recent studies of North American coprolites have yielded more positive results, although the implications are not grave from the health standpoint. As might be expected in view of the present interest in the subject, coprolites were recovered in Mug House, a cliff-dweller ruin in the newly explored Wetherill Mesa section of Mesa Verde National Park, Colorado. All earlier investigators of cliff-dweller ruins had missed the opportunity to get information from this source. R.Samuels of Meharry Medical College in Nashville, Tennessee, to whom the coprolites were entrusted for study, found one identifiable animal parasite of man in a single specimen about a thousand years old [178]. As usual the evidence was in the form of eggs – 'seen in low numbers' – but in this case they were the eggs of *Enterobius vermicularis*, the ubiquitous pinworm. Such scanty evidence again tells nothing of the organism's prevalence in the population. This is to be expected because the pinworm is seldom an inhabitant of the intestine and usually produces only mild irritation in the perianal region that is more of a nuisance than anything else.

The last investigation along this line which I will mention relates to Danger Cave and Hogup Cave in Utah [58, 130]. Danger Cave was filled with cultural debris and refuse, including coprolites, to a depth of eleven feet. A $C_{14}$ date of 9503 ± 600 BC was obtained from organic material at the lowest level. In a sample of forty coprolites representing all levels no protozoan parasites were detected. However, in twenty-one of the twenty-six specimens from the two lowest levels eggs of a worm of the phylum Acanthocephalia were found. Species differentiation was not possible from the morphological characteristics of the eggs, so it is assumed simply that the species is the one occurring today in the vicinity, namely *Moniliformis clarki*, commonly referred to as a 'thornyheaded worm'. Infestation in man by *Moniliformis clarki* has not been reported, and one thus would have to assume that the early inhabitants of Danger Cave whose feces contained the eggs were the victims of false parasitism, ie, they had eaten the intermediate or definitive hosts of the parasite – crickets and rodents, respectively. The effect of this sort of parasitism on community health and individual life expectancy is uncertain. Human infestation by a related form, which also has a formidable proboscis, is said to cause diarrhea, weight loss, anemia, emaciation and, not uncommonly, death from perforation of the intestinal wall.

Only one specimen from Danger Cave, dating from around 7837 BC, contained eggs of an exclusively human parasite, namely, of the pinworm *Enterobius vermicularis*. Yet in Hogup Cave, which was occupied from about 6400 BC to AD 1400, four specimens, ranging in age from around 4010 BC to 650 BC contained eggs of this parasite. Except for extending the time range of the infestation some nine thousand years back of the date from Mesa Verde, the find does not change the health picture.

If the foregoing extended discussion of human diseases in pre-Columbian America has been tedious in its detail, it has served at least to show that in those times disability from such sources was not a severe restriction on population growth. Even though this area of study, which is called paleopathology, is not yet well developed and much remains to be discovered, nevertheless the conclusion that the ancient Americans were a relatively healthy lot is probably correct.

### Variation of body size

Although disease may not have had a major deleterious effect on pre-Columbian American populations, the environment in general, being diverse throughout the hemisphere as already noted, can be expected to have produced regional differences in body size by 1492. The available evidence, even though partly indirect, bears out this expectation. Moreover, this evidence presents a surprisingly orderly geographical pattern. That the evidence, if orderly, has been derived somewhat indirectly, is due obviously to the fact that measurements of body size were not taken in prehistoric times. Of course, one is not entirely dependent on such measurements, because size can be determined also from skeletal remains; but in many areas, particularly in the tropics, skeletal remains have not survived. Fortunately, however, many of the Indians observed in post-Columbian times were relatively free from European admixture, and were living much as their ancestors had lived in the past, so it seems safe to conclude that they had retained the body proportions of their ancestors. On this assumption certain widely observed body dimensions, such as stature, sitting height, head size and face size, have been plotted on maps of the hemisphere. The results show a consistent pattern. For instance, Indian stature (fig. 9) is generally highest in the temperate zones of North and South America and diminishes from there both northward and southward, but especially towards the tropics. Thus the lowest statures are found in Central America and in northern South America.

Prehistoric man was not alone among American mammals in reacting to the environment in this way. The puma, that tawny-

Fig. 9 Distribution of four categories of Indian stature in the
Western Hemisphere. After Newman [143]

brown member of the cat family whose hemispheric range is almost
as wide as man's, has a regional distribution of body size strikingly
similar to that for man's stature (fig. 10). Indeed, this phenomenon
is so widely recognized zoologically that it is called 'Bergmann's
rule' in honor of Carl Bergmann (1814–65), a German comparative
anatomist and physiologist, who was the first to bring it to attention.

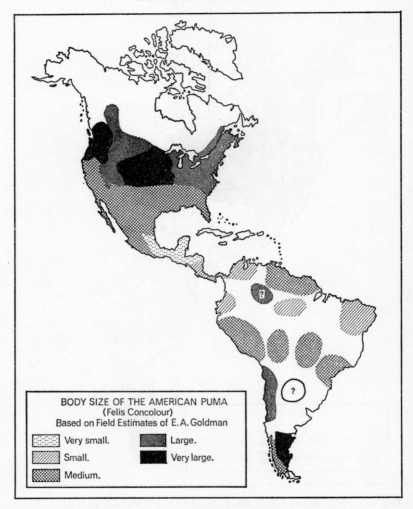

Fig. 10 Distribution of five categories of puma body size in the Western Hemisphere. After Newman [143]

Plainly, therefore, a bodily response of this sort is too general to be attributable to something unique to man, such as his culture.

What is it about the tropical regions that depresses body size in animals, and particularly in man? Basic to this complex process is the fact that warm-blooded animals, including man, generate more energy for existence and growth than they use. Much of the excess is dissipated in the form of the waste heat of cellular combustion. However, loss of heat from the body depends on the climate and becomes more difficult as external temperature and humidity increase, as in the tropics. This in turn necessitates a lowered tissue combustion rate and shows up as reduced energy and growth. For example, Clarence A. Mills, the great student of environmental medicine, has noted that 'On the cattle ranches of Panama it takes four to five years to produce a nine hundred-pound steer ready for slaughter [whereas] in Iowa or nearby areas of the United States a thousand-pound steer is usually marketed one and a half to two years after birth' [128].

The main source of body energy is the diet, together with the vitamins, especially the B vitamins, which enable the animal to convert the food into energy. But in the tropics the natural foods have low vitamin contents, for various reasons which I will not go into except to note that the extra rainfall of the tropics tends to leach the nutritive elements from the soil. Thus, turning again to Mills' work in Panama, he writes (p. 5):

Using thiamin excretion in the urine as a good index of a subject's status with respect to this vitamin, it was found that people living there on native foods (native meats particularly) were thiamin-deficient . . . Tropically grown meats produced much less rise in thiamin excretion than did those imported from the United States.

Since the diets poor in vitamins yield less energy, this leads again to suppression of activity and growth.

Obviously this explanation does not account for all the size reduction of a population. In addition to everything else, there must be a selection process favoring individuals who are best able to cope with the environmental handicaps and to reproduce their kind. Because the end result is small size, probably this in itself is an advantage in the tropics.

### The blood-group pattern

Indirect evidence shows also that in 1492 the American population had distinctive regional patterns of ABO blood groups. Unlike body size, these blood groups are inherited as separate genes not directly affected by the environment. Thus, every individual from birth belongs to one of the four groups A, B, AB and O. Consequently, the population to which the individual belongs has the blood groups present in different proportions. For example, a typical Spanish population has 46·5% A, 9·2% B, 2·2% AB, and 41·5% O. By contrast, a typical north Chinese population has 25·1% A, 34·2% B, 10·0% AB, and 30·7% O [24].

Particularly striking in these two examples is the much higher percentage of blood group B in the Chinese: 34·2% vs. 9·2% in the Spanish. These figures bear out the fact that for the world at large the highest frequencies of blood group B occur in Asia. Considering that America was first settled from Asia, one would expect to find a continuation of the high percentages of B east of Bering Strait and on southward to Tierra del Fuego. But this is not the case. Only small amounts of B have been found in the recent native populations on the eastern side of the Strait, and practically none south of what is now Alaska (fig. 11).

One of the problems of trying to deduce an ancestral blood-group pattern from that of the modern descendants of the same population relates to the effect of racial intermixture. People of mixed racial ancestry tend to have a blood-group pattern somewhere between the patterns of the two ancestral groups. This is true of the present city populations of Latin America, where mixture of Indians and Spaniards is particularly heavy. Typical figures for the mestizos of Mexico City are 28·6% A, 10·6% B, 2·5% AB, and 58·3% O [133]. Obviously, places where the population is so heavily mixed are of little help in unraveling the ancestral blood-group patterns. If, instead, one looks only at the Indian groups that have had the least contact with outsiders, one can expect to see little change from the original patterns.

Blood-group studies made on the most remote and least acculturated American Indians show, with few exceptions, from eighty to a hundred per cent group O, with the remaining percentage being mostly group A. Actually, so often does the percentage of group O approach 100 in the remote populations of Central and South America that the total absence of A, B and AB here, at least in late prehistoric times, can be accepted as highly probable. Considering that Indian isolation has been breaking down for nearly five hundred years, it is not surprising to find now an occasional

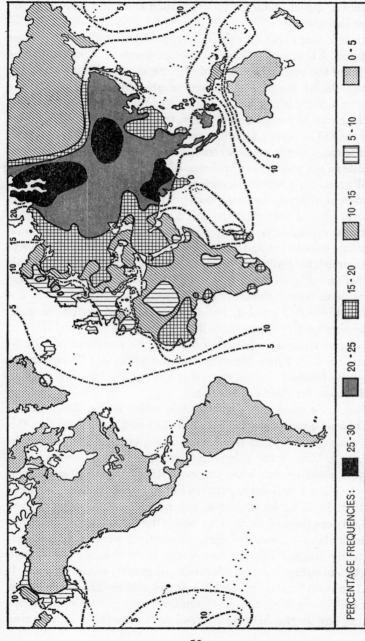

Fig. 11 Distribution of blood group gene B in the aboriginal population of the world. After Mourant et al. [133]

PERCENTAGE FREQUENCIES: 25 - 30 | 20 - 25 | 15 - 20 | 10 - 15 | 5 - 10 | 0 - 5

individual with a blood group other than O among seemingly the purest Indians.

Nor is it surprising that the most significant amounts of groups A, B and AB occur in North America north of Mexico. In the process of the original settlement of America, people seem to have crossed Bering Strait and pushed southward in more than one wave, as already indicated. Certainly the Eskimos were still crossing the Strait in recent times. Thus, the presence of blood groups other than O in North America, and especially on the western side, bears witness to these late events. Unfortunately, it has not been possible to get confirming evidence of the settlement sequence by blood grouping prehistoric skeletons. The ability of the organic constituent of bone to give a blood-group reaction of the usual sort is lost or altered soon after the soft parts decay.

In any event, it is now generally accepted that the original American population had a combination of blood-group characteristics sufficiently distinct to warrant the classification of this population solely on the basis of gene frequencies as a separate race. In his definition of the American genotype, Boyd [24] refers not only to the ABO groups, but to certain blood factors as well: 'Possessing varying (sometimes high, sometimes zero) incidence of gene $A_1$, no $A_2$, and probably no $B$ or $rh$. Low incidence of gene $N$. Possessing $Rh^{z'}$'. Since the details of the additional blood factors have little bearing on the present story, the reader is referred to Boyd's book for their explanation.

What does need explaining at this point is the difference in ABO blood-group patterns between Asia and America. Does this difference cast doubt on the Asiatic origin of the first Americans? Not at all. One of the things that emerges from the world-wide study of blood groups is the extent to which the continental areas have developed distinctive patterns in proportion to their degree of isolation. In fact, the genotypic races based on blood groups are primarily continental races. Apparently the separation of the major habitable land masses by seas, mountains, deserts and forests effectively limited human movement in prehistoric times and thereby encouraged the development of genetic differentiation. If blood group B was late in reaching America, it appears to have been later still in reaching the more remote parts of Europe, perhaps even as late as the historic Mongol invasions [29]. This timing suggests that the *B* gene appeared by mutation in Asia late in human history; that is, after the initial migrations to America. To believe otherwise would require that the first Americans had the gene when they moved eastward but lost it somehow subsequently. Although this is possible theoretically, and especially when populations are small and scattered, the likelihood of it having happened in America is less believable than the alternative explanation. Be this as it may, the resulting blood-group pattern, so unique in its deficiency of group B, indicates that the expanding population of the American *cul-de-sac* retained a high degree of genetic isolation until 1492.

### Uniformity of physical type

I will conclude this overview of the American population in 1492 by citing an opinion often expressed in one form or another by widely-traveled observers, beginning with the Spaniard Antonio de Ulloa in 1772 [230]. The Spanish version of the famous statement reads as follows: '*Visto un Indio de qualquier región, se puede decir que se han visto todos en quanto al color y contextura.*' (Variously translated: 'If we have seen one American, we may be said to have seen all, their color and make are so nearly alike.' Or more simply: 'He who has seen one tribe of Indians, has seen all.') Though not unchallenged, this opinion still seems to reflect a considerable element of truth [216].

In spite of varying in bodily proportions, as pointed out above, all observed American Indians have exhibited straight black hair, swarthy skins (the term 'redskin' is a misnomer), a tendency to the Mongoloid eyefold and prominent cheek bones. These external features have relatively low variability and it is for this reason, of course, that the Indian physical type seems so uniform and readily recognizable. At the same time, it is my opinion that more variation, even of the facial features, would be expected if the forerunners of the present Indians had been in the hemisphere for a longer period than 20–30,000 years [209].

# 4

# Theories and misconceptions about American origins

The information in the preceding chapters provides some of the perspective needed to understand certain geographical and anthropological misconceptions that entered into Columbus' interpretation of his discovery and certain other interpretations that were offered during the post-Columbian period. For additional perspective it is necessary to take into account the European state of knowledge and view of the world at the end of the fifteenth century.

Medieval geography centered around the Mediterranean, particularly the bible lands. The then-known world was usually represented in the few existing maps as being circular or oval in shape and often surrounded by water (cf. plate 3). Peripheral land details were scanty and unreliable, suggesting the hearsay nature of the places and distances with which the cartographers had to work. Although the idea that the world was round, instead of flat as most people believed, was gaining in acceptance, the need for, and means of, representing this on a globe was still to come.

### Marco Polo's geography of Asia

One of the eastern continental areas but recently brought to European attention in some detail was the part of Asia then referred to as Cathay and the Indies. Chiefly responsible for this new information was Marco Polo, a member of a Venetian trading family, who returned home about 1295 after an extended overland trip to the territory of the Mongols, where he had met and become a favorite of the 'Great Khan' (Ghengis Khan). Marco Polo had made this trip with his father and uncle, both of whom had visited the Khan before (between 1260 and 1269). The second trip, which probably lasted about twenty-five years, had been made to inform the Khan that the Pope had refused his request for missionaries to be sent to his country. Soon after the three Polos returned to Venice, Marco became involved in the war between the Venetians and Genoese and was captured by the latter. In spite of this misfortune, his fame as a traveler was such that he was induced, probably in 1298, to dictate his 'story' to a scribe who was a fellow prisoner. The resulting *Book of Marco Polo* was spread around rapidly by means of numerous copies, at first in Latin and then in other languages [156].

One of the copies of the *Book* reached Spain and was seen there by Columbus before he started on his first voyage of discovery. We know this because a library in Seville has a copy with marginal notes in Columbus' handwriting. His acquaintance with the *Book* apparently explains a statement in the prologue (p. 19) to the log or journal of his first voyage [37]:

... through information given by me to Your Highnesses [King Ferdinand and Queen Isabella] of the countries of India, and of a Prince called the Great Khan, which means in our language, King of Kings; how that many times, he and his predecessors had sent to Rome to solicit doctors of our holy faith that he might be instructed in the same; and that the Holy Father had never furnished them, and thus so many people were lost, believing in idolatry, and receiving among them doctrines of perdition; therefore, Your Highnesses, as Catholic Christians, and princes, lovers of the holy Christian faith, and promoters thereof, and enemies of the Mahometan sect, and of all idolatries and heresies, determined to send me, Christopher Columbus, to the said parts of India, to see the said Princes, people and territories, and to learn their nature and disposition, and the means to be employed in converting them to our holy faith; and commanded that I should not go by land to the East, by which route it had been customary to go in safety, but by a Westerly route, by which there is until now no certain evidence that anyone has gone.

The daily entries in the log or journal give further indications of the effect of Marco Polo's *Book* on Columbus' thinking. For example, on 13 October, the day after the first landfall, the entry (p. 36) includes the following statements:

At break of day the shore was thronged with people all young . . . and all of good stature, fine looking; their hair not crisped but straight and coarse like horse hair, head and forehead broader than I have ever seen in any other people; eyes fine and large: none are dark hued, but of the color of the inhabitants of the Canaries . . . Their limbs are strait, and not with prominent bellies, but were well formed . . .

I was anxious to learn whether they had any gold, as I noticed that some of the natives had rings hanging from holes in their noses, and by signs they gave me to understand that to the south there dwelt a king who had large vessels of wrought gold, and that he had a great quantity. I tried to get them to go for some, but they could not understand they were to go . . .

. . . not to lose time, I have determined to see if I cannot find the island of Cipango.

Columbus' 'Cipango' seems to be Marco Polo's 'Chipangu', which some authorities believe to be Japan. Marco Polo described (II, p. 253) Chipangu as

. . . an island toward the east in the high seas, 1500 miles distant from the continent; and a very great Island it is.

The people are white, civilized and well-favoured . . . And I can tell you the quantity of gold they have is endless; for they find it in their own islands . . . You must know that [the Lord of the Island] hath a great Palace which is entirely roofed with fine gold, just as our churches are roofed with lead, insomuch that it would scarcely be possible to estimate its value. Moreover, all the pavement of the Palace, and the floors of its chambers, are entirely of gold, in plates like slabs of stone, a good two fingers thick; and the windows also are of gold, so that altogether the richness of this Palace is past all bounds and all belief.

Clearly, on the one hand, Marco Polo was exaggerating, and on the other, Columbus was engaging in wishful thinking, except in his descriptions of the people and their setting. Columbus truly wanted his landfalls to be the Indies, the people to be Indians and the gold to be where this geographical identification seemed to indicate it should be. Yet before long only names, such as 'West Indies' and 'Indians', survived as reminders of Columbus' geographical misconception. The discovery of gold in spectacular quantities fell to the lot of others.

Columbus' geographical misconception is easily accounted for. He had become convinced by Marco Polo's *Book* and other sources that the world was smaller than it is and that Asia extended so far eastward that it could be reached by a relatively short voyage westward across the Atlantic. Thus, when he encountered land in the form of islands more or less where he expected to find it, he saw no reason to doubt that he had reached the Indies known to Marco Polo and therefore the inhabitants were Indians. The geographical error was not fully corrected until the Magellan expedition of 1619–22 completed the circumnavigation of the world. This extraordinary feat proved that Columbus had discovered a new world – already called America after Amerigo Vespucci, who seems first to have sensed the truth [4] – and that this new world was separated from Asia and the true Indies by a vast expanse of ocean. Now for the first time the world could be represented on a sphere with a scale approaching reality.

### The anthropological mystery intensified

The exposure of Columbus' geographical misconception revealed his anthropological misconception. Since he had not reached the East Indies, the peoples of the new-found lands could not be East Indians. Who then were they? How did they get there?

A ready answer to the second of these two questions would likely have suggested an early and acceptable answer to the first. But as we have seen, nearly three centuries were to elapse before the discovery of the proximity of northwestern North America to Asia, and until then the New World seemed completely isolated from the Old. During this interval attempted answers to both questions had perforce to be tied into accepted beliefs, especially religious beliefs, because anything to the contrary would not have been tolerated.

According to the Bible, the truth of which was seldom questioned in those days, all human beings are descended from one pair, Adam and Eve. Rationalization of this belief had led to the placement of Paradise – the abode of Adam and Eve – somewhere on the eastern fringe of the known world. Such geographical vagueness might have proved a handicap in accounting for the New World inhabitants, except that of all the descendants of Adam and Eve, only Noah's family survived the biblical flood. So it was necessary only to trace existing mankind to the sons of Noah – Shem, Ham and Japheth. This could be done more or less directly through events occurring either immediately following the flood or at various times thereafter and in different parts of the Old World.

Most of the non-scientific explanations of the original peopling of America can be accounted for under this scheme, if due allowance is made for gradually advancing knowledge and simultaneous gradually declining religious domination over intellectualism. For instance, to cite an extreme case, the Egyptians were judged by the ancients to be descended from Noah, probably through Ham. In America the occurrence here and there of various Egyptian-like customs, such as the construction of pyramids and the representation of the human body in profile, naturally reminded explorers of the surviving ancient Egyptian monuments. This led to the concept of contact between Egypt and America in times past, either directly by boat or indirectly by way of a mythical island (Atlantis) in the Atlantic Ocean.

What makes this case extreme among explanations of American origins is not so much its inherent unlikelihood as the fact that some people still believe it, as witness the 1969–70 voyages across the Atlantic by Thor Heyerdahl and associates in replicas of ancient Egyptian reed boats [75ᵃ]. Of course, no one could accuse Heyerdahl of trying to prove the Egyptian origins of American Indians as a whole. He was merely trying to show that a boatload of Egyptians could have reached America and that cultural and physical influences could have been introduced in this way. This is not the same thing as proving that a boat did make the crossing. Indeed, in my estimation, any modern effort of this sort smacks of pseudoscience.

### The 'lost tribes of Israel'

The Jews figure in the early explanations much more often than do the Egyptians. In their case it is not necessary to go back into biblical history as far as Noah. According to a passage in the second book of Kings (17:6) [125]:

In the ninth year of Hoshea the king of Assyria captured Samaria, and he carried the Israelites away to Assyria, and placed them in Halah, and on the Habor, the river of Gozan, and in the cities of the Medes.

For the further history of this group it is necessary to turn to the apocryphal fourth book of Esdras (13:40–5), the key part of which reads:

... they formed this plan for themselves, that they would leave the multitude of the nations and go to a more distant region, where mankind had never lived, that there at least they might keep their statutes which they had not kept in their own land. And they went in by the narrow passages of the Euphrates river. For at that time the Most High performed signs for them, and stopped the channels of the river until they had passed over. Through that region there was a long way to go, a journey of a year and a half; and that country is called Arzareth [Hebrew for 'Another Land'].

This combination of scriptural sources provided sixteenth-century writers with an explanation of how America was populated that was acceptable to the Church, an important consideration at that time. Since many of the writers giving attention to this subject were churchmen, usually members of the religious orders involved in missionary activities in America, perhaps the explanation represents some sort of ecclesiastical concord. If not, it was sufficiently convincing within the limits of existing knowledge to warrant repeating over and over. As we shall see, the explanation has survived in modified form into recent times.

In support of the claim that the Indians were the lost tribes of Israel, some of the sixteenth-century writers went to great lengths to show that the Indians resembled the Jews in many respects. Father Gregorio Garcia, a member of the Order of Teachers (*Orden de Predicadores*) in Peru, is a case in point, as witness the third of the five books constituting his *Origen de los Indios de el Nuevo Mundo* [59]. Bancroft [8] has retained something of the flavor of Garcia's original argument in his summary thereof, a part of which follows (p. 79):

... The opinion that the Americans are of Hebrew origin is further supported by similarities in character, dress, religion, physical peculiarities, condition, and customs. The Americans are at heart cowardly, and so are the Jews; the history of both nations proves this. The Jews did not believe in the miracles of Christ, and for their unbelief were scattered over the face of the earth, and despised of all men; in like manner the people of the New World did not readily receive the true faith as preached by Christ's catholic disciples, and are therefore persecuted and being rapidly exterminated. Another analogy presents itself in the ingratitude of the Jews for the many blessings and special favors bestowed on them by God, and the ingratitude shown by the Americans in return for the great kindness of the Spaniards. Both Jews and Americans are noted for their want of charity and kindness to the poor, sick, and unfortunate; both are naturally given to idolatry; many customs are common to both, such as raising the hands to heaven when making a solemn affirmation, calling all near relatives brothers, showing great respect and humility before superiors, burying their dead on hills and high places without the city, tearing their clothing on the reception of bad tidings, giving a kiss on the cheek as a token of peace, celebrating a victory with songs and dances, casting out of the place of worship women who are barren, drowning dogs in a well, practicing crucifixion.

And on and on in the same vein for another page or so.

Although it is difficult now to understand how such bizarre things could have been said in seriousness, anyone who has explored the literature of the period will recognize that they were a widely accepted part of the existing 'climate of opinion'. Indeed, instead of presenting original views on the subject, Garcia was reporting what others had been saying and was debating only the points to which exception had been taken.

But if 'the Spanish father's learned ignorance and pedantry', as Bancroft calls it, is amazing, consider the somewhat similar case of Viscount Kingsborough's nineteenth-century version of the theory and his nine magnificent imperial folio volumes offered in proof [108]. Moved up in time two centuries and given some scholarly dignity, Kingsborough's *Antiquities of Mexico* (1831–48) is still the story of the 'lost tribes', but in a different format. This young nobleman became involved with what he conceived to be a strong resemblance between the religion of the ancient Mexicans and that of the Jews. From the day when as a student at Oxford he became enamored with a Mexican manuscript in the Bodleian Library, until his premature death in 1837 only about twenty years later, he concentrated on presenting every Mexican analogy he could find, much of it in hand-colored facsimile form. Considering that he spent his fortune on this hobby and died in a debtor's prison, it is lamentable that the results of his fanatic labors are more appreciated now by bibliophiles than by scholars.

I have singled out Garcia and Kingsborough from all those who have advanced the 'lost tribes of Israel' theory of the peopling of America largely because of the influence their books have had on shaping opinion. Also, these two examples are enough to make the point that the theory was well established in the century after the discovery of America and was still being taken seriously in the first half of the nineteenth century. The wide knowledge of the theory and its appeal to the religious-minded probably had a bearing on the important variation of the theory that appeared in North America while Kingsborough was deeply engaged in his project in England.

### The Book of Mormon

Joseph Smith, Jr., of the village of Manchester, some twenty miles southeast of the City of Rochester, in New York State, was in his early twenties when he received a call to found a new religion. (Kingsborough also was in his early twenties when he first saw religious analogies in a Mexican manuscript.) As reported subsequently, Smith claimed to have had a series of visits from the angel Moroni between the years 1823 and 1827, during which Moroni revealed to him the location of a set of inscribed plates on a nearby hill. On 22 September 1827 Moroni permitted Smith to remove the plates for the purpose of translation, which was facilitated by an accompanying code of some sort. Translation proceeded rapidly and resulted in the publication in 1830 of *The Book of Mormon* upon which the Church of Jesus Christ of Latter-day Saints is founded. Unfortunately, the plates are no longer in existence, because Moroni returned them to heaven on 2 May 1838 after Smith became fearful for their safety on account of aroused public curiosity.

In the official description of *The Book of Mormon* given on the title page, a distinction is made between two sections of the abridged record [184]: (1) that 'of the people of Nephi, and also of the Lamanites – Written to the Lamanites, who are a remnant of the house of Israel'. . .; and (2) that 'taken from the Book of Esther. . ., which is a record of the people of Jared, who were scattered at the time the Lord confounded the language of the people, when they were building a tower to get to heaven – Which is to show unto the remnant of the House of Israel what great things the Lord hath done for their fathers; and that they may know the covenants of the

Lord, that they are not cast off forever . . .' This distinction is important from the standpoint of dates: the former (involving the Nephites and Lamanites) extends from 600 BC to AD 421; the latter (involving the Jaredites) is earlier, but not actually dated. Ferguson [55] places the Jaredite era between 2800 BC and 500 BC.

Note, too, that in the above quotations from the title page of *The Book of Mormon*, the expression 'remnant of the House of Israel' is used, instead of 'the lost tribes of Israel'. Of course, since the Nephites and Lamanites (the Jaredites are thought to have been Sumerians) had wandered by boat, not by land, all the way from Israel to America, for all practical purposes they were lost; and it is on this basis that Mormonism is being considered in the present context.

The historical account of the Israelites in America unfolded in *The Book of Mormon* is too complicated to go into fully here. By AD 421, the date of the last inscriptions on the plates, the Jaredites are said to have disappeared long ago, and all but a few of the Nephites are said to have just been slaughtered by the Lamanites. The few remaining Nephites, including Moroni – the son of Mormon – had joined the Lamanites. This suggests that the following 1,000 years would have been all the time available for the Lamanites to develop into the American Indian population that occupied the entire Western Hemisphere in 1492. If this were indeed the case, it would constitute a record population explosion.

I cannot leave this subject without noting that *The Book of Mormon* exhibits the appropriate limitation of geographical knowledge of the assigned time-period, in that it reports the Israelites as having come to America by ship, rather than overland via a route not then known to exist. Father Garcia was more plausible in this respect, even though he too could have had no knowledge of the geographical relationship between North America and Asia [59]. The good Father simply fell back on Marco Polo's report of a narrow strait in northeast Asia separating the kingdom of 'Anian' from the mainland. This geographical idea had been perpetuated by at least two sixteenth-century cartographers: Jacopo Gastaldi and Bolognino Zaltieri [158]. Indeed, Zaltieri's 1566 imaginary map of North America (plate 1) shows a Strait of Anian almost in the same position as Bering Strait on modern maps.

On the other hand, after Columbus proved that the newly discovered land was within ship reach of the Old World, many people must have started wondering whether earlier navigators from the Mediterranean area and western Europe had also reached this land directly and whether they were responsible for its being peopled. We know that there are vague accounts in the ancient literature of Phoenician and Carthaginian navigators sailing westward through the 'Gates of Hercules', as the two promontories at the eastern end of the Strait of Gibraltar were called, and returning with reports of land in that direction. And even before Columbus set sail rumors are reported to have been passed around in the seaports of Britain and Scandinavia of discoveries of land to the west. It is not surprising, therefore, that, in addition to the Egyptians and Jews, other Old World peoples have been credited with being the ancestors of the New World population.

### The Atlantis theory

It would have been as unreasonable probably in the sixteenth century as it is today to believe that the Phoenicians or Carthaginians, without something more than their small ships, could have peopled a land area as large, and as far away, as the New World. The extra thing that gave the idea credibility was the fabled island of Atlantis mentioned as existing in the Atlantic somewhere east of the New World and hence within possible reach of Europe. Supposedly, this island was the land which the earliest navigators had discovered and colonized. Then, in turn, it was supposed that when the colonists had multiplied, they were able to make the short trip westward to the New World. At this point the explanation has a cataclysm overtaking Atlantis and causing it to sink beneath the ocean without leaving a trace. Modern scholars believe instead that the fable of Atlantis reflects the eruption of a volcano on the island of Thíra, in the Greek archipelago, in prehistoric Minoan times. According to archeological evidence, the eruption caused submergence of part of Thíra and heavy loss of life.

### Voyages of the Vikings

If Atlantis had no reality as a way station to the New World, another bit of land, represented in various parts of the north Atlantic on some fifteenth- and sixteenth-century nautical charts, probably was real. This is an island named Brasil – not to be confused with the modern country similarly named in South America. Discussions regarding a recently uncovered letter from an Englishman in the archives at Simancas (Valladolid), Spain, in which the discovery of Brasil prior to Cabot's 1497 voyage is mentioned, raise the possibility that ships from Bristol, England, had visited the Newfoundland Banks before 1492 [161]. Since the letter is addressed to a Spanish official with the title 'Almirante Mayor' (Columbus was often referred to by this title), and the addressee is said to have previous knowledge of the discovery, there is the additional possibility that Columbus knew of the existence of land on the western side of the Atlantic before he embarked on his first voyage. This interpretation tends to confirm a statement by Francis Bacon published in 1622 (p. 188):

And there had beene before that time [1492] a discouerie of some *Lands*, which they tooke to be *Islands*, and were indeed the *Continent of America*, towards the *Northwest*. And it may be that some Relation of this nature comming afterwards to the knowledge of COLUMBUS, and by him suppressed, (desirous rather to make his Enterprise the *Child* of his *Science* and *Fortune*, then the *Follower* of a former *Discouerie*) did giue him better assurance, that all was not at *Sea*, from the *west* of *Europe* and *Africke* vnto *Asia* [7].

Attesting to still earlier voyages and landfalls in the northern Atlantic by Scandinavian sailors is another recent literary find, this time of a previously unknown map of the world (plate 3) accompanying a portion of a manuscript about a mission to the Mongols in 1245–7 [183]. The map, which is now at the Yale University Library, has been designated 'The Vinland Map' because it presents the earliest cartographic evidence in the northern Atlantic of land identified as Vinland and situated west of Greenland. Although the new map cannot be definitely dated, it seems to have been based upon a model similar to the world map in Andrea Bianco's 1436 *Atlas*. Thus, in keeping with maps of this period, as already noted, the known world is represented here in circular fashion and surrounded by water. Vinland, which appears in the upper left-hand corner as an island and has been given the number '66' for purposes of description, is in the position of eastern North America.

The inscription on the map just above Vinland (given the number '67') has been translated as follows (p. 140):

By God's will, after a long voyage from the island of Greenland to the south toward the most distant remaining parts of the western ocean sea, sailing southward amidst the ice, the companions Bjarni and Leif Eiriksson discovered a new land, extremely fertile and even having vines, the which island they named Vinland. Eric [Henricus], legate of the Apostolic See and bishop of Greenland and the neighboring regions, arrived in this truly vast and very rich land, in the name of Almighty God, in the last year of our most blessed father Pascal, remained a long time in both summer and winter, and later returned northeastward toward Greenland and then proceeded [i.e., home to Europe?] in most humble obedience to the will of his superiors [183].

The indicated date of the bishop's visit to Vinland is AD 1117. There is some evidence from other Scandinavian sources that Vinland had been discovered first in the eleventh century.

The literature is full of accounts of discoveries in northeastern North America – extending as far west as Minnesota and as far south as Massachusetts – attributed to the presence of Vikings. These include stone structures, bronze swords, 'mooring stones', and 'runic' inscriptions. To date, however, only the site of L'Anse au Meadow in Newfoundland, excavated by Helge Ingstad [100], is accepted by competent archeologists as genuine. In any case, there does appear to be archeological support for the existing historical documents.

Was Vinland another name for Brasil? Did both names refer to the part of North America now known as Newfoundland? Did Columbus have foreknowledge of the Norse and British discoveries in this part of the world? Increasingly the answers to these questions are coming to be convincingly affirmative. Yet from the standpoint of the origin of the aboriginal American population, these affirmative answers mean little or nothing. The dates are far too late for any considerable population to accumulate as a result of the European–American contacts. Besides, the British navigators of this period seem to have been more intent on finding good fishing grounds than on colonizing the nearby land. The Norsemen, on the other hand, while colonizing Greenland, seem to have been content simply to visit Vinland in search of timber. The fact that all the parties involved failed to take advantage of a golden opportunity could indicate that the people already occupying the coastal areas developed a resentment to the intrusions. We know that this is what happened in the case of the later historically documented colonization efforts.

It should be mentioned that Bristol was not the only part of the British Isles from which early westward voyages are said to have begun. Those from other ports are semi-legendary in character and nothing further has been discovered as yet to give them substance. For example, the abbeys of Conway and Strat Flur in northern Wales are said to preserve accounts of the twelfth century voyages westward by a Welshman named Madoc. He is reported to have reached and colonized a large fertile country across the ocean. This was learned when he returned and outfitted for a more ambitious second voyage from which nothing was ever heard. The possibility that contact actually occurred between the Welsh and American Indians has received support from time to time from those who have claimed the discovery of Welsh words in various Indian languages. According to reputable linguists, however, such word resemblances often occur by chance and by themselves are seldom to be taken seriously.

All of the attempts to explain the origin of the aboriginal American population considered thus far are totally unconvincing in the light of present knowledge, despite their often extended – and, in a few instances, continuing – popularity. At most, a few sporadic contacts across the north Atlantic, beginning in the eleventh or twelfth century, can be given any credence. Even these left no detectable cultural and physical imprints on the American Indians. On the other hand, activity of this sort between Asia and America is in another class, and I will have something to say on this subject when I get to American archeology. It is mainly in connection with the developing archeological picture that the possibility of trans-Pacific contacts have become a matter of anthropological concern.

## The Antarctic hypothesis

Of more pertinence to the present discussion is a rather different theory about the peopling of America which takes us back to the concept of a migration ultimately from Asia. The difference is that it envisions a southern instead of a northern route. Also, it was only lately advanced by a world-famous anthropologist, Paul Rivet (1876–1958), Director of the Musée de l'Homme in Paris from 1928 to 1940, and one of the leading Americanists of his day.

Like many of the pioneering anthropologists of the early twentieth century, Rivet was largely self-taught in anthropology, his formal training having been in medicine. That he failed to follow a career in medicine was due to his having accepted appointment in 1901 as a medical officer on a French geodesic mission to Ecuador. The six years spent in that country, in close association with American Indians, converted him to anthropology and made him an Americanist. From that time onwards he was to return again and again to Latin America, occasionally for long periods of time. There he became widely known and was held in high esteem for his anthropological views. I was witness to this fact at conferences in Lima and São Paulo late in his life.

Like some other contemporary anthropologists working in America, Rivet did not limit himself to one aspect of the field. He was best known, however, for his work in linguistics and physical anthropology. His experiences in these lines led him to see, on the one hand, analogies between dialects of the peoples of the South Pacific and of South America (mainly in word lists) and, on the other hand, resemblances between human skulls from the same two areas. From 1924 onwards this led him to publish a series of papers detailing the evidence for Melanesians, Polynesians and Australians in America and attempting to account for their presence there.

Although Rivet conceded that the peopling of America must have been primarily by way of Bering Strait, he could not see at first how a migration from as far away as Australia could have reached South America by the northern route and still retained any vestige of its original identity. A trans-Pacific crossing for the Australians seemed to him out of the question. The solution to this puzzle was supplied in 1925 by a noted Portuguese anthropologist, A. A. Mendes Corrêa, in the form of a hypothetical route across Antarctica [127]. By this southern route the distance, which is still at least some 6,000 miles, is decreased over that via the Bering Strait route somewhere in the order of one to three. Yet the southern route requires the crossing of stretches of ocean between tiny islands up to eight hundred miles apart and the traversing of a large continent covered with ice and snow (unless the climate had ameliorated at the time). In spite of such improbabilities, Rivet held to his point of view to the end of his life. This is indicated by the issue a year before his death of a new edition of his little book entitled *Les Origines de l'Homme Américain* [167].

## The mystery cleared

Most serious students of the last two centuries have not been misled by the explanations reviewed in this chapter. They would probably all agree, furthermore, that any addition to the aboriginal American population by routes other than Bering Strait would have amounted to little more than a trickle. By way of example, I can do no better than quote the opinion of a very wise eighteenth-century American, Thomas Jefferson, as expressed in his *Notes on the State of Virginia*, written in 1781–2 [102]:

Great question has arisen from whence came those aboriginals of America? Discoveries, long ago made, were sufficient to show that a passage from Europe to America was always practicable, even to the imperfect navigation of ancient times. In going from Norway to Ireland, from Ireland to Greenland, from Greenland to Labrador, the first traject is the widest: and this having been practised from the earliest times of which we have any account of that part of the earth, it is not difficult to suppose that the subsequent trajects may have been some-times passed. Again, the late discoveries of Captain Cook, coasting from Kamschatka to California, have proved that if the two continents of Asia and America be separated at all, it is only by a narrow straight. So that from this side also, inhabitants may have passed into America; and the resemblance between the Indians of America and the eastern inhabitants of Asia, would induce us to conjecture, that the former are the descendants of the latter, or the latter of the former: excepting indeed the Eskimaux, who, from the same circumstances of resemblance, and from identity of language, must be derived from the Groenlanders, and these probably from some of the northern parts of the old continent.

# 5

# Living Indians encountered by the explorers: the high civilizations

Many of the arguments that the scholars advanced in their misguided and premature efforts to account for the aboriginal New World population were the result of the course of exploration and discovery; and to a considerable extent the New World peoples themselves directed this course. I have quoted Columbus' statement in the log of his first voyage about the inquiries he made of the West Indian natives regarding the location of cities reported by Marco Polo. Columbus was looking for richer land, particularly gold-bearing land, and the natives' reaction, whether or not they fully understood his desire, was to point southward and westward. We know now that the contacts of these island peoples had always been in those directions and never to the north. Their ancestors – Ciboney, Arawak, and to a lesser extent, Carib – had arrived in ages past mainly, if not entirely, from South America along the chain of islands known now as the Lesser and Greater Antilles. Whether or not the Ciboney came from Florida instead of South America is debatable, but there is little doubt about this movement of peoples from South America never having continued beyond the Greater Antilles and the Bahamas to Florida [222]. All of this probably explains why Columbus continued his explorations to the south and west.

## The Spaniards and Mexican gold

In general, low-lying islands and continental coasts are not the best gold-bearing lands. Not having reached further than the coasts of South and Central America, Columbus brought back to Spain little in the way of gold. He was soon followed, however, by others who established more intimate contacts with the natives of the coasts of Central America. Again it is clear that these natives, like those of the West Indies, directed the further course of exploration and discovery. For example, Bernal Díaz remembered that when the 1518 expedition, under Juan de Grijalva, arrived at a river which had been named Tabasco earlier, and which was promptly renamed Grijalva (p. 30),

. . . more than thirty Indians came with their chief to the place under the palm trees where we were camped and brought roast fish and fowl, fruit and corn bread. They spread out mats, which they call *petates*, put cloths over them, and presented some trinkets of gold that were not worth more than two hundred pesos. They also brought some native cloths and shirts which they asked us to accept, as they had no more gold, but they said that farther on, where the sun set, there was a great deal of it. They repeated the words 'Colua' and 'Mexico'. None of us knew what Colua or Mexico meant, and although there was not much value in the presents they had brought, we now knew for certain that they possessed gold. Captain Grijalva thanked them and gave them green beads, after which we embarked, as the ships were in danger in case of a north wind. Also, we wanted to reach the place where they said there was gold [98].

As it turned out, of course, the Spaniards were being directed to a great city, called Tenochtitlán, in the mountainous interior on the site of present-day Mexico City. This was the heart of the Aztec civilization and empire. For the Spaniards to reach there required another expedition in 1519 under the leadership of Hernando Cortés. As his small army advanced towards this goal, evidence increased that the primitive ways of life on the islands and along the coasts were giving way to a remarkably elaborate form of civilization. Tenochtitlán almost defied Bernal Díaz' powers of description. Four days after arriving there, he was one of those who joined the emperor Montezuma in viewing the city from the top of the largest pyramid-temple. As he remembered it (p. 158),

There we stood looking, for that large and evil temple was so high that it towered over everything. From there we could see all three of the causeways that led into Mexico . . .

We saw the fresh water that came from Chapultepec, which supplied the city, and the bridges on the three causeways, built at certain intervals so the water could go from one part of the lake to another, and a multitude of canoes, some arriving with provisions and others leaving with merchandise. We saw that every house in this great city and in the others built on the water could be reached only by wooden drawbridges or by canoe. We saw temples built like towers and fortresses in these cities, all whitewashed; it was a sight to see. We could look down on the flat-roofed houses and other little towers and temples like fortresses along the causeways.

After taking a good look and considering all that we had seen, we looked again at the great square and the throngs of people, some buying and others selling . . . There were soldiers among us who had been in many parts of the world, in Constantinople and Rome and all over Italy, who said that they had never before seen a market place so large and so well laid out, and so filled with people [98].

Thus, with the natives pointing the way to the gold, the Spaniards were able to come rapidly and almost directly to the center of the high civilization in the New World most accessible to them. In the course of reaching that center and subsequently of subduing the tribes under its domain, the area comprising this civilization became evident. In terms of modern Mexico the Aztecs held sway over the States of Morales, Mexico, Guerrero, Hidalgo, Puebla, most of Veracruz and Chiapas, and, of course, the Federal District of Mexico. How much further into Central America their influence effectively extended is uncertain. This is not to say, however, that the same high level of civilization existed everywhere in this large area; as usual, the rural and remote areas must have experienced a cultural lag. Estimates of the size of the population involved vary from near three million to over thirty-seven million, as already noted (pp. 33–44).

Judging from surviving evidence, much of it semi-legendary in character, the Aztecs had built up their empire relatively rapidly. They are believed to have been a rather insignificant tribe at the time they wandered down from the north and into the Valley of Mexico around the beginning of the fourteenth century. Ambitious leadership and careful political maneuvering enabled them to take advantage of their neighbors and swiftly gain the upper hand. A confusing element in this story is the fact that they are known also as Tenochcas and Mexicas. The name Tenochca lent itself to the designation of their principal sixteenth-century city in the Valley of Mexico – Tenochtitlán – located on an island in Lake Texcoco. It was here that their emperor Montezuma was living when Cortés arrived. The name Mexica has survived mainly as the designation of the succeeding modern nation and its capital city located on the site of Tenochtitlán – Mexico and Mexico City, respectively. In view of all this, and of the fact that the original people spoke a Nahua language, and ultimately gave this language currency over most of their empire, the term 'Aztec' has no precise meaning.

### The Spaniards and Peru

After the discovery of the Aztec civilization and the downfall of Tenochtitlán in 1520, only a few more years were required by another group of Spaniards to reach the second American center of high civilization, again by the same means and by the most direct course. Indeed, a major step had already been taken along that course: nearly ten years earlier Vasco Núñez de Balboa had learned from the coastal Indians of Darien about an ocean to the west and about gold in a place called 'Peru'. This had led him to the discovery of the Pacific Ocean in 1513 and to the planning of an expedition southward along the Pacific coast of South America to Peru. Balboa's death put an end to that plan and postponed the discovery of Peru until 1527, when an expedition from Panama under the leadership of Francisco Pizarro got as far as the northern coast of Peru. It was not until 1533, of course, that Pizarro, on another expedition, entered the city of Cuzco, the heart of the Inca civilization and empire.

The Spaniards' approach to Peru, and their reaction to what they found there, was not recorded by an eyewitness in a manner comparable to that of Bernal Díaz for Mexico. However, something of their amazement as they neared Peru and received reports about that country is portrayed, probably rather accurately, by William H. Prescott [159] in his famous *History of the Conquest of Peru*. During Pizarro's first expedition to Peru, for example, he

decided at one point to explore ashore while his pilot Ruiz recon-
noitered southward by ship. Upon reaching the Bay of St Matthew,
just north of the Equator (p. 242),

. . . Ruiz, standing off shore, struck out into the deep sea; but he had not
sailed far in that direction when he was surprised by the sight of a vessel,
seeming in the distance like a caravel of considerable size, traversed by a
large sail that carried it sluggishly over the waters. The old navigator
was not a little perplexed by this phenomenon, as he was confident no
European bark could have been before him in these latitudes, and no
Indian nation yet discovered, not even the civilized Mexican, was
acquainted with the use of sails in navigation. As he drew near, he found
it was a large vessel, or rather raft, called *balsa* by the natives, consisting
of a number of huge timbers of a light, porous wood, tightly lashed
together, with a frail flooring of reeds raised on them by way of deck.
Two masts or sturdy poles, erected in the middle of the vessel, sustained
a large square-sail of cotton, while a rude kind of rudder and a movable
keel, made of plank inserted between the logs, enabled the mariner to
give a direction to the floating fabric, which held on its course without
the aid of an oar or paddle . . .

On coming alongside, Ruiz found several Indians, both men and
women, on board, some with rich ornaments on their persons, besides
several articles wrought with considerable skill in gold and silver, which
they were carrying for purposes of traffic to the different places along the
coast. But what most attracted his attention was the woollen cloth of
which some of their dresses were made. It was of a fine texture, delicately
embroidered with figures of birds and flowers, and dyed in brilliant
colors. He also observed in the boat a pair of balances made to weigh the
precious metals. His astonishment at these proofs of ingenuity and
civilization, so much higher than any thing he had ever seen in the
country, was heightened by the intelligence which he collected from
some of these Indians. Two of them had come from Tumbez, a Peruvian
port, some degrees to the south; and they gave him to understand that
in their neighborhood the fields were covered with large flocks of the
animals from which the wool was obtained, and that gold and silver were
almost as common as wood in the palaces of their monarch.

Later, when the Spaniards reached the coast of Peru, the natives
indicated that the place of greatest wealth, as well as the seat of
political power, was the capital city of Cuzco high up in the
Andes. Accordingly, Pizarro made this the goal of his second

expedition. Reporting the Spaniards' arrival at Cuzco in 1533, Prescott says (pp. 501, 504):

The capital of the Incas, though falling short of the *El Dorado* which had engaged their credulous fancies, astonished the Spaniards by the beauty of its edifices, the length and regularity of its streets, and the good order and appearance of comfort, even luxury, visible in its numerous population. It far surpassed all they had yet seen in the New World ...

The most important building was the fortress, planted on a solid rock that rose boldly above the city. It was built of hewn stone, so finely wrought that it was impossible to detect the line of junction between the blocks; and the approaches to it were defended by three semicircular parapets, composed of such heavy masses of rock that it bore resemblance to the kind of work known to architects as the Cyclopean [159].

The straight-line distance from Tumbes at the northern tip of present-day Peru to Cuzco in the south-central highlands is some 900 miles. (By contrast, the comparable distance between Veracruz and Mexico City is only some 200 miles.) Also, the approach to Cuzco on foot from the north coast involves extremely rough traveling by circuitous routes through high mountains. This trip undoubtedly gave Pizarro and his followers a healthy respect for the size of the empire they were invading. Yet when the first Spaniards reached Cuzco they had traversed scarcely half the distance to the southern extremity. At its heyday, about 1527, the northern limit of the empire reached approximately the present location of the boundary between Colombia and Ecuador. Already some thirty-five years before this the southern extremity had been fixed at the Maule River half way down the present Chilean coast. Between these two points the coastline is roughly 2,900 miles in length. On the other hand, the spread of the empire inland was limited by the rain forests east of the Andes more than by anything else. For this reason the greatest width of the empire, in what is now Bolivia and Argentina, was probably still somewhat less than four hundred miles.

No reliable figures on population size are available for the Inca empire, because the statistics assembled by the native administrators were nearly all lost at the time of the Spanish conquest. As already noted (pp. 33–44), modern estimates of the pre-conquest population of this area (designated 'Andean civilization') have a range identical to that for the Mexican civilization.

As far as is known, the homeland of the Inca tribe was the region of Cuzco. The almost explosive spread of this tribe's influence in the century preceding the arrival of the Spaniards was amazingly similar to that of the Aztecs of Mexico and seems to have come about, as in the latter case, through ambitious and capable leadership. One way the leaders controlled the many tribes they conquered was through insistence on the use of the conqueror's own language – Quechua. This language was used so widely by the time the Spaniards arrived that they in turn were able to turn it to their advantage through quickly gaining knowledge thereby of Incan defensive strategy.

In this all too brief account of the discovery and conquest of Mexico and Peru I have used incidental details in the historical record to convey the impression that the cultural level achieved by the peoples of these areas was well above that of their neighbors. I have more to say on this subject, but first I want to mention that the distinction between higher and lower cultures at the beginning of the post-Columbian period anticipates an important archeological generalization, to be dealt with later, that identifies a prehistoric area of cultural progressiveness (not strictly limited to the Aztec and Inca Empires of 1492) as 'Nuclear America' (cf. figs. 19 and 20). This implies that there was also a 'non-Nuclear America' in ancient times embracing the less progressive cultures. Therefore, it is but a simple extension of this archeological generalization to speak of the cultures of the post-Columbian peoples as either 'higher' or 'lower'. I take full responsibility, however, for the further simplification of the generalization; namely, the extension of the designation 'lower' to cultures of intermediate level located around and between the Aztec and Inca Empires.

Since gold was a good lead into the foregoing account of the discovery and conquest of Mexico and Peru, it may as well serve as the starting point of a brief summary of the higher cultures. The attraction that Aztec and Inca gold held for the Spaniards was almost entirely in terms of bullion. Few, if any, of the explorers cared that most of the gold they acquired was in the form of intricately contrived ornaments of high artistic merit. How much of the gold was still in artistic form when it arrived in Europe is unknown, but certainly only a few such pieces have survived from that period. Today, pieces derived archeologically from Mexico and Peru, as well as from intermediate areas (Ecuador, Columbia, Panama, Costa Rica), have values as art objects far above those of equal weights of bullion. Moreover, pieces in the distinctive art styles of the different areas where produced are valued equally.

The artistic expression of the Aztecs and Incas extended beyond metalworking to designing textiles, shaping and decorating pottery, ornamenting walls with realistic or abstract designs, and sculpturing stone and plaster. Of these, textile designing and wall decorating reached their highest levels in Peru and Mexico, respectively, although in Mexico wall decorating had passed its peak by Aztec times. The levels reached in ceramics and sculpture are not as clearly differentiated in the two areas. In general, however, the level of artistic endeavor in Mexico and Peru, involving as it did the effective use of so many media, was not matched elsewhere in the hemisphere.

In Mexico, but not in Peru (nor elsewhere in the hemisphere), developments in art had led to a form of ideographic writing – picture writing. A few accordion-folded paper 'books', known as 'codices', constitute the major part of the surviving records of this sort. Unfortunately, they are not very informative about Aztec institutions, largely because the writing system was incapable of rendering general statements or abstract ideas. The Mexicans also had well-developed numerical and calendrical systems, which they recorded. Although the Peruvians kept records on knotted-string devices (*quipus*), the nature of these records, especially as to whether they included numerical and calendrical data, is undetermined.

As the story of the conquest of both civilizations has made clear, Mexican and Peruvian cities and military arrangements were spectacular and represent roughly equal stages in the development of impressive engineering and social-planning skills. Peru, however, seems to have been ahead of Mexico in the development of irrigation systems for agricultural purposes and in the construction of road systems for communication purposes. Again, in all this there is nothing elsewhere in the hemisphere approaching comparability, either in size or complexity.

Except for the intensity of food-crop cultivation, as demanded by their large populations, Mexico and Peru may not have advanced much in agricultural pursuits beyond those in some other parts of the hemisphere. Yet the need to raise crops at very high altitudes in the Andes gave the Peruvians an advantage over all the other New World peoples in the total number of plants cultivated, including some known nowhere else. Among the mammals indigenous to the highlands of the west coast of South America is the llama, a handsome member of the camel family. Domesticated from early times in the middle Andean region, the llama carried light burdens, yielded wool for weaving, meat for food and hides for sandals.

None of the remarkable accomplishments included in this incomplete listing explains why the geographically widely-separated Aztecs and Incas, of all the human groups in the hemisphere, became the leaders on so many cultural fronts. I mentioned earlier that much of the credit for this has been assigned to unusual political leadership. In addition, organized religion undoubtedly played a large part. This is nowhere better illustrated than in the public acceptance of a revoltingly cruel religious practice of the Aztecs: human sacrifice. It has a place in this book because of its bearing on population density.

## Human sacrifice

S. F. Cook of the University of California in Berkeley has stated that human sacrifice seems to have been carried to excess in ancient Mexico simply because human blood was deemed pleasing to the gods and therefore 'the more blood the greater their pleasure and the greater the benefits to be derived therefrom' [39]. Yet he had the suspicion 'that this was merely the rationalization of a far deeper tendency or drive. Certainly had it been socially undesirable to perform these acts of sacrifice, very cogent reasons would have been found for not doing so' (p. 84). Stated as a question, was this custom a manifestation of a social urge to provide a serious check on population increase? The answer lies in the existing density of population and to what extent this was causing a precarious situation as regards the margin of subsistence. Unfortunately, without a more reliable estimate of population size than now exists, the answer is not forthcoming.

Regardless of the full implications of the custom, its amazing scale should not be overlooked. According to surviving accounts, the scale of the sacrifices at the time the Spaniards arrived was the result of acceleration over a couple of hundred years. Originally it may have been limited to infants and children but, as the demand grew, the custom was extended to slaves and then predominantly to criminals and prisoners of war. Cook (p. 82) speculates that in this way 'war and religion became inextricably involved with each other on the material level and were simultaneously rationalized into a spiritual unit'. As an example of the numbers of war captives sacrificed on special occasions, the dedication of a new temple at Tenochtitlán in 1487 may be cited. According to the sixteenth-century historian Diego Durán [52], sacrifices were made simultaneously from four advancing lines of captives. From Durán's description of the lines, Cook estimates that each was about two miles long. Altogether the lines could have contained upwards of 15,000 individuals. Five men seized each victim and threw him back downwards on the sacrificial stone. Immediately the priest, armed with a knife, ripped open the chest from side to side, snatched or tore out the heart, offered it to the shrine, smeared its blood on the idol, and dropped the heart into a dish. In the meantime the five assistants had tossed the body down the steps. All of this took no more than two or three minutes. On the occasion being described the slaughter was kept going continuously day and night for four days. Durán placed the number of victims at 80,400, but the generally accepted figure is nearer 20,000.

Large-scale sacrifices of this sort on special occasions, along with those on a much smaller scale demanded regularly by the religion, undoubtedly took a high toll of the population of central Mexico. Supporting evidence comes from a count of the skulls stored at the great temple in Tenochtitlán. Andres de Tapia, who was sent by Cortés to examine the temple and who made the count, reported 136,000 skulls carefully stacked up, and still others in the form of two towers made of 'lime and skulls of the dead, without any other stone' [39]. In a town near Tenochtitlán Bernal Díaz [98] observed a temple plaza 'with piles of human skulls so regularly arranged that they could be counted. I estimated more than a hundred thousand. In another place there were so many thigh bones that they were impossible to count, as well as a large number of skulls strung from one place to another, with three priests in charge of them (p. 95). Such numbers are impressive, but tell nothing, of course, about the annual increments.

The counts of whole skulls fail also to tell about the numbers of infants and children sacrificed. Indeed, this age category was probably not even included in the skull counts, for the reason that until the skull is fully developed, the component bones are not sufficiently linked together to remain intact after the loss of the soft parts. Also, surviving reports refer to sacrifices of children on certain occasions having been accomplished by drowning. Whatever the method used, something of the situation may be gleaned from a statement by Bernardino de Sahagún, a sixteenth-century historian: 'According to the reports of some people, they collected the children they sacrificed in the first month, buying them from their mothers, and then killed them at all subsequent festivals until the rainy season came in full force' [39, p. 85]. Here, as in most other statements on the subject, a specific number of young victims is not given. In spite of this, Cook believes that the total for a year might have been around 2,000. Less conservative estimates made shortly after the conquest go as high as 20,000.

There is more than a suggestion in all this that the custom in Mexico had evolved to the point where justice and worship had become confused. In other words, what may have started simply as a gift to supernatural beings to secure their favor or minimize their hostility had changed into child sacrifice with an overlay in the form of retributive sacrifice directed against criminals and war captives. Judging by what is known of the custom in other parts of the world – and few races and religions can show a history free from human sacrifice – the stage of the custom which the Aztecs had reached is in itself indicative of their relatively high culture. Had they remained undiscovered for another century or so, perhaps, like the Spaniards, they might have reached the next stage – that of symbolic sacrifice – and been viewed by historians as much less sanguinary.

Granting at least that through the custom of mass human sacrifices the Aztecs may have retarded the rate of population growth in central Mexico, we have seen that more effective measures generated by the conquest – pestilence, cultural disruption and famine – took over even as the formal sacrifices were being stopped. As a result, for the next thirty years or so, as we have also seen, the Mexican population declined sharply.

As for Peru, where no such restraining custom is known to have operated against the population, much the same story was repeated in early post-conquest times, except that the sharp decline in population there seems to have been of shorter duration, perhaps only about fifteen years (cf. Table 2, p. 34).

### Group contact and interbreeding

As both populations began their slow climb upwards from their numerical nadirs of the mid-seventeenth century, a new demographic situation had already appeared. The population in each area had now to be reckoned, not in terms of the Indian racial stock alone, but in terms of Indians, Spaniards and mestizos or cholos (names for Indian–Spanish mixtures in Mexico and Peru, respectively). Of course, armies of conquest always take their toll of the native women, and there was no exception to this rule in Mexico and Peru. But in addition, the Spaniards followed up their conquests in both places with large-scale settlement, which included initially relatively few European women. Many of the early male settlers, therefore, had native wives and/or mistresses. The rapid proliferation of a mixed-breed class was the natural result.

The diffusion of genes from one racial group into another in the circumstances outlined is somewhat like the spread of wild fire. As the fire grows in intensity, sparks dart in all directions, hastening and extending the spread. In the same way, human beings who have acquired new genes not only pass them along in their own neighborhoods through the usual marital arrangements, but, being among the most mobile of mammals, they carry these genes over long distances and add them to the gene pools of other neighborhoods. Taking twenty-five years as the average period of time between the birth of one generation and that of the next, so far more than eighteen generations have engaged in this mixing process. Probably as a result few, if any, Mexican and Peruvian Indians have escaped some genetic change.

As a rule, most racial mixture has occurred in places where the different races have had the longest and most intimate contact. Cities are pre-eminent in this regard. And at the other extreme, rural areas, especially those difficult of access, are more likely to have retained populations in a state of racial purity more or less approaching that of prehistoric times. These facts have not escaped the attention of the physical anthropologists and as a consequence the groups that have been studied for comparative purposes are those judged to be the least changed.

Lending support to the anthropologist's judgments on this score is the finding, already noted, that the 'pure' Indians of Central and South America tend to be 100% blood group O. The gene $O$ is present, therefore, in almost every individual tested. This fact, taken together with the fact that various blood group studies of Spaniards in Spain show only 39·5% in this category (gene $O$ frequency 62·9%), indicates an original frequency spread of 37·1% for this gene between the two races. The size of this spread makes it possible to estimate from the frequency of gene $O$ alone the extent of mixture existing today in samples of different populations.

The formula used for this purpose, according to Matson, is as follows:

$$\frac{q_x - Q}{q - Q} \times 100,$$

where $Q$ and $q$ are the frequencies of gene $O$ in the base populations and $q_x$ is the frequency of this gene in the hybrid population [124]. When the present populations of Mexico City and Lima are analyzed by this means, they show White admixtures ranging from 20 to 64%, depending on the selection of the samples. This finding does not take into account, of course, the admixture with Negroes and other foreign racial groups.

### Physical anthropology in Mexico

The year 1859 is usually recognized as the founding date of physical anthropology as an organized science. On 19 May of that year Paul Broca and eighteen associates held the first meeting of the Anthropological Society of Paris. The Society, still in existence and still publishing, undertook from the beginning to establish standards of observation and measurement and to promote expeditions to study native peoples in all parts of the world. Many years would pass before physical anthropology in the New World would reach this stage of organization. It is understandable, therefore, that French anthropologists were among the first to collect information on the Indians of Mexico and Peru. The first French scientific expedition to Mexico in which the new science of anthropology was represented was authorized by Emperor Napoleon III in 1865. As it turned out, however, any measurements that may have been obtained in this way on the living Indians were never made available.

Thus, the first successful effort to study the Indians of central and southern Mexico – the part of Mexico of immediate concern here – was that by Frederick Starr, a professor of the University of Chicago, in 1898–1901 [190]. Working three months in the field in each of those four years, Starr planned to measure a hundred males and twenty-five females in each of twenty-three widely scattered tribes. He fell short of his goal (2,875 persons) by only forty-eight. Figure 12 gives the location of these tribes, and Table 3

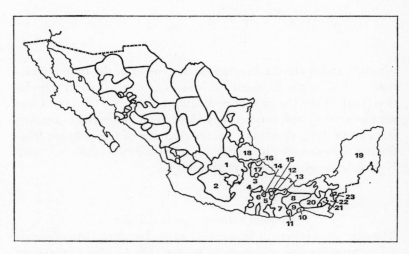

Fig. 12 Starr's tribal map of Mexico used to show the locations of the 23 groups which he studied between 1898 and 1901. For key to numbers see table 3. From Starr [190]

summarizes selected body and head proportions of the males. It is apparent from the latter that on the average the great majority are under 160 cm in height, have a sitting height more than 52% of stature, and a head width more than 80% of head length; in other

TABLE 3

Selected dimensions of Mexican Indians: Males*

| Key to numbers in figure 12 | Stature (cm) | Sitting height (cm) | Sitting-height index | Head length (mm) | Head breadth (mm) | Cephalic index |
|---|---|---|---|---|---|---|
| 1. Otomis | 158·0 | 82·0 | 51·9 | 189·7 | 147·2 | 77·6 |
| 2. Tarascans | 160·0 | 83·3 | 52·1 | 184·3 | 146·5 | 79·5 |
| 3. Tlaxcalans | 160·3 | 84·6 | 52·8 | 185·2 | 149·1 | 80·5 |
| 4. Aztecs | 159·0 | 82·6 | 51·9 | 185·7 | 146·5 | 78·9 |
| 5. Mixtecs | 156·1 | 81·6 | 52·3 | 182·5 | 149·4 | 81·9 |
| 6. Triquis † | 155·1 | 80·2 | 52·1 | 183·6 | 147·5 | 80·3 |
| 7. Zapotecs (Mitla) | 158·6 | 83·0 | 52·3 | 183·5 | 148·7 | 81·0 |
| 8. Mixes | 157·4 | 82·2 | 52·2 | 184·5 | 150·7 | 81·7 |
| 9. Zapotecs (Tehuantepec) † | 160·5 | 83·0 | 51·7 | 185·3 | 150·2 | 81·1 |
| 10. Juaves | 159·9 | 83·1 | 52·5 | 181·3 | 153·1 | 84·4 |
| 11. Chontals ‡ | 159·8 | 82·5 | 51·6 | 180·3 | 149·9 | 83·1 |
| 12. Cuicatecs | 156·2 | 82·3 | 52·7 | 181·5 | 147·6 | 81·3 |
| 13. Chinantecs | 157·6 | 84·8 | 53·8 | 181·4 | 151·9 | 83·7 |
| 14. Chochos | 156·2 | 82·4 | 52·8 | 187·6 | 151·0 | 80·5 |
| 15. Mazatecs | 155·1 | 81·5 | 52·5 | 181·5 | 150·9 | 83·1 |
| 16. Tepehuas | 156·0 | 82·8 | 53·1 | 180·0 | 151·2 | 84·0 |
| 17. Totonacs | 157·3 | 83·8 | 53·3 | 179·2 | 153·8 | 85·8 |
| 18. Huaxtecs | 157·0 | 83·1 | 52·9 | 177·8 | 150·1 | 84·4 |
| 19. Mayas | 155·2 | 80·4 | 51·8 | 181·8 | 154·1 | 84·8 |
| 20. Zoques | 160·0 | 84·2 | 52·6 | 182·3 | 146·2 | 80·2 |
| 21. Tzotzils | 155·9 | 83·0 | 53·2 | 188·1 | 144·6 | 76·9 |
| 22. Tzendals | 155·7 | 83·0 | 53·3 | 187·7 | 144·1 | 76·8 |
| 23. Chols | 155·8 | 81·8 | 52·5 | 182·5 | 147·5 | 80·8 |

* From Starr [190]. Except where noted, samples number 100
† Sample of 99
‡ Sample of 80

words, they are small people with relatively long trunks and fairly broad heads.*

Subsequent observers of some of the same groups measured by Starr have reported somewhat different average dimensions and

* Since the cephalic index will be referred to from time to time in the descriptions of the living Indians, the following classification will be useful for reference purposes [195]:

| | |
|---|---|
| Extra longheaded (hyperdolichocephalic) | 65·0–70·4 |
| Longheaded (dolichocephalic) | 70·5–75·9 |
| Intermediate (mesocephalic) | 76·0–81·4 |
| Broadheaded (brachycephalic) | 81·5–86·9 |
| Extra broadheaded (hyperbrachycephalic) | 87·0–92·4 |

for this reason are inclined to reject Starr's findings. But who can say whether the composition of these populations has not changed since the turn of the century, or that the later observers were not less precise in their measuring than Starr? Examination of the total output of work along this line, summarized in volume 9 of the *Handbook of Middle American Indians* [215], shows considerable within-group variation. In such cases it is almost impossible to say which are the most reliable figures.

### Physical anthropology in Peru

The first French expedition to study the survivors of the Inca empire was more successful than the earlier one that undertook a like mission to Mexico. This was mainly because it occurred later, in 1903, and the science of anthropometry was correspondingly better developed. By this time Alphonse Bertillon, who had applied anthropometric techniques to the study of criminals, was able to supply the expedition with a well-developed recording system and a compact set of measuring instruments. Officially known as the *Mission Scientifique Française dans l'Amérique du Sud sous la Direction de MM. G. de Créqui Montfort et E. Sénéchal de la Grange*, the measurements were made by Julien Guillaume, one of Bertillon's trained associates, and the report was written by Arthur Chervin [34].

The population studied by this French expedition was that of the highlands of Bolivia stretching southeastward from Lake Titicaca, and therefore representative of the Aymara-speaking peoples of the southern part of the original Inca Empire (fig. 13). To increase the representation, I will compare Chervin's findings with those reported (1916) by H.B.Ferris of Yale University Medical School for the Quechua population around Cuzco, some two hundred miles northwest of Lake Titicaca [56]. Just as in Chervin's case, Ferris reported measurements that were taken by someone else, namely, Luther T. Nelson, surgeon for the Peruvian Expedition of 1912 under the auspices of Yale University and the National Geographic Society. The Quechua around Cuzco provided the language that became the *lingua franca* of the Inca empire and that is still widely spoken in Peru and Bolivia. Indeed, Chervin divided his subjects into Aymara and Quechua, although Quechua was not the original language of any of the peoples of

Fig. 13 The central part of the Inca Empire about 1530 to show the location of the Aymara- and Quechua-speaking groups. After Rowe [177]

Bolivia. For this reason his division is ignored in Table 4, which summarizes the same set of body and head proportions as given for the Mexicans.

Comparison of Tables 3 and 4 shows that the Aymara and Quechua are at the upper range of Mexican stature and in the middle range of Mexican head shape. On the other hand, the relative sitting heights of the Aymara and Quechua differ considerably, the Quechua being within the Mexican range, but the Aymara being above this range. Just as in Starr's case, however,

TABLE 4

Selected dimensions of Bolivian and Peruvian Indians: Males

| Tribe (no.) | Stature (cm) | Sitting height (cm) | Sitting-height index | Head length (mm) | Head breadth (mm) | Cephalic index |
|---|---|---|---|---|---|---|
| Aymara (172) * | 160·2 | 86·6 | 54·0 | 183·0 | 148·8 | 81·4 |
| Quechua (121)† | 158·5 | 83·6 | 52·7 | 186·6 | 149·2 | 80·1 |

\* Chervin [34]
† Ferris [56]

it is not easy to decide whether Chervin's and Ferris' figures are reliable. Yet Georges Rouma, a Belgian physical anthropologist who made several expeditions to the highlands of Bolivia beginning in 1911, found the Aymara to have almost the same dimensions as those reported by Chervin [175].

## The effects of altitude

One of the limitations of the traditional system of body measurements developed in the last century is its inflexibility. Although the eye might detect a physical peculiarity in the group under study, the specified measurements are seldom entirely suitable for its analysis. This comes out clearly in the early anthropometric work in Peru. Throughout the nineteenth century, observers had noted that the Indians of the highlands of Bolivia and Peru had tremendous chests, which they correctly attributed to the effect of living at this high altitude. A lowlander has only to visit these highlands to appreciate the peculiar stresses to which he is subjected by the altitude and to become quickly aware that the people native to the region are well adjusted to these stresses. Yet the early twentieth-century anthropometrists made no special provision for measuring the chest. Chervin, it is true, reports chest circumference at nipple level, and Rouma reports chest circumference at this and two other levels, but both fail to compare their figures with those for any other group [34, 175]. And Ferris does not give a single chest dimension [56].

The anthropologists' neglect of such an important bodily adjustment was not rectified until the physiologists became interested in the problem in the 1920s and '30s. The first clear analysis of a large native population born and raised at altitudes ranging from 10,000 to 15,000 feet, was that by Alberto Hurtado of the University of San Marcos in Lima [96]. His study, made in Morococha, Peru, extends to 950 males between the ages of four and seventy-five years. Four of his graphs (reproduced here as fig. 14) show that the enlargement of the chest for more efficient utilization of rarefied air is present already in childhood and increases steadily until full growth is reached. Going hand in hand with these thoracic changes are numerous others, of course, and especially some involving the circulatory system that enable the blood cells to carry an extra load of oxygen to the vital organs.

The prehistoric Incas, like the modern Andean peoples, must have made the same sort of adjustments. Their ability, not only to adjust to one of the most extreme environments of the hemisphere, but to go on from there and found a high civilization, is a measure of the plasticity of human beings. Yet one would like to know whether these empire builders and their present descendants have been exposed to the selective pressures of high altitude continuously enough and for a sufficiently long time for the resulting physical and physiological changes to have become a part of their inheritance pattern. In other words, is the complex adjustment to altitude such that it is now transmitted from parents to offspring, or does each offspring start anew in developing his own adjustment? In answer to this question I would have to say that, so far as the evidence goes at present, the adjustment has not been proved to be transmitted; in other words, it is not a true adaptation. If this is the correct answer, the failure of these altered physical traits to reach the heritable stage probably signifies that man is a relatively latecomer to the highlands, just as he seems to be in the entire Western Hemisphere.

### The effects of change of environment

Other studies of the Indians of Mexico and Peru have revealed an aspect of human plasticity somewhat different from that caused by

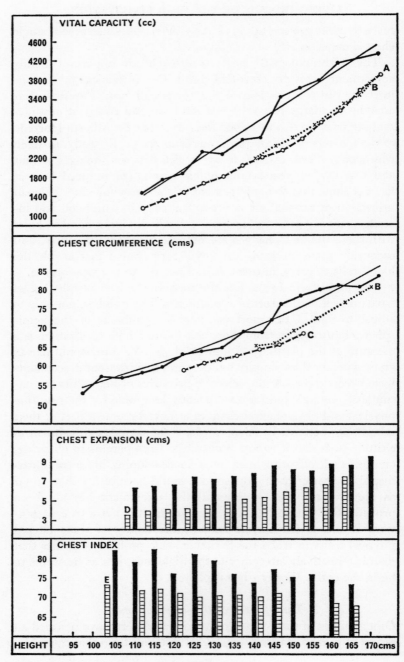

Fig. 14—*See caption on opposite page*

the stress of high altitude. The main environmental culprit in this instance is poor nutrition. Taking the studies of Mexicans first, since they were the earliest reported, it is interesting to note that the research opportunity was created by the migratory labor movement between Mexico and the United States. Opportunities for seasonal work in the central, southwestern and western parts of the United States have long attracted lower-class, rural Mexicans who are mainly of Indian descent. These Mexican Indians – often still teenagers when they move north – stay in the United States for varying lengths of time, many returning eventually to their homeland, but others remaining to become American citizens. The first anthropologist to measure any part of this population was Marcus Goldstein, during his brief sojourn at the University of Texas in Austin in the early 1940s [64]. Starting with a sample of 176 Mexican families, mainly from San Antonio, Goldstein decided that his data were meaningless until he knew how they compared with like data on the populations in Mexico from which the migrants had come. Where migration is concerned, the 'stay-at-homes' are usually designated 'sedentes'. Thus, the quest for comparative data on the sedentes took him to the Mexican States of Guanajuata, Nuevo Leon and Coahuila. The result was that he discovered the migrants to be larger in general than the sedentes. As indicated, he attributed the increase in size to the more favorable nutritional opportunities available to the migrants in the United States.

In the later 1940s Gabriel Lasker of Wayne State University Medical School followed up Goldstein's lead by studying more intensively one Mexican Indian tribe, namely, the Tarascans

---

Fig. 14 Chest characteristics of Indian natives during childhood and in relation to body height. Solid dotted lines and black columns represent the averages obtained, while the uninterrupted solid lines are mathematically fitted curves. After Hurtado [96]

A. Stewart, C.A. [194] – American children
B. Mumford and Young [136] – English children
C. Cometto [38] – Argentinian children
D. Bowditch [22] – American children
E. Hrdlička [78] – American children

[115]. Although the Tarascans were not strictly a part of the Aztec Empire, for the present purpose this does not matter, because it is largely an accident of history that the Tarascans offer better prospects for this type of study than any of the tribes originally under the empire. But in any case, Lasker selected Paracho, a town of some three thousand persons, in the State of Michoacan as the site for the study, and set forth the research model as follows (p. 243):

To make the most useful comparisons between migrants and non-migrants, it seemed desirable to deal with individuals from a single community and from the same families. By comparing sedentes in such a community with several classes of returned emigrants, one could eliminate some of the variables which may have affected similar comparisons in previous studies. A small community [such as Paracho] where climate, diet, and other conditions of life contrast with those which the migrants meet in the United States would be suitable.

Lasker's findings amplify those of Goldstein, particularly as regards stature (Table 5). Commenting on this table, Lasker continues:

. . . the most interesting of the statistical findings is that the males who went to the United States youngest and stayed longest – those who were less than seventeen when they went for the first time and who have stayed for two years or more – are the tallest of the migrants and significantly taller than the sedentes. They are larger than the stay-at-homes also in respect to all the other twenty-five measurements. Those who have migrated to the United States for the first time between seventeen and twenty-seven years of age and who have stayed two years or more also are significantly taller than the sedentes. These individuals, that is those who have migrated at an age near the end of the growth period, are intermediate in respect to virtually all dimensions between the sedentes and those who left home at a younger age. Those individuals who have first migrated at the age of twenty-seven or over closely resemble the sedentes in stature and other measurements [115].

Unlike Goldstein, who was inclined to attribute the bodily changes to improved nutrition alone, Lasker concludes that 'The question still to be answered is, just what environmental factors are specifically responsible for the enhanced growth.'

At this point it is illuminating to return to the north central highlands of Peru where an imaginative nutritional investigation was conducted by Marshall T. Newman in the 1950s and '60s while he was in the Division of Physical Anthropology of the Smith-sonian Institution. The selection of the particular locality, the 36,000-acre Hacienda Vicos, and its native population for study was rather fortuitous. Cornell University, represented by the late Alan Holmberg of its Anthropology Department, was planning to

### TABLE 5

Stature of adults in Paracho, Michoacan, Mexico, in relation to age at first migration to the United States and total duration of residence in the United States
(from Lasker [115], Table 1)

| Age at first migration | Duration of stay in the United States (years) | Number | Mean stature (mm) | Standard error of the mean |
|---|---|---|---|---|
| *Males* | | | | |
| Never (Sedentes) | 0 | 109 | 1,618·0 | ±5·6 |
| Less than 17 | 2 or more (mean = 16·0) | 29 | 1,642·7 | ±11·2 |
| 17–27 | 2 or more (mean = 8·3) | 65 | 1,635·6 | ±6·4 |
| 27 or more | 2 or more (mean = 6·9) | 13 | 1,610·2 | ±15·8 |
| 27 or more | 1 | 43 | 1,615·1 | ±8·8 |
| 15–27 | 1 | 30 | 1,633·1 | ±8·9 |
| *Females* | | | | |
| Never (Sedentes) | 0 | 155 | 1,512·3 | ±3·8 |
| Various * | 2 or more (mean = 7·7) | 22 | 1,532·9 | ±8·7 |

* Less than 17, 11; 17–27, 6; 27 or more, 3; born in the United States, 2.

take over Vicos, largely because of the latter's run-down state, and to attempt a social experiment directed towards improving the lot of the inhabitants – Quechua-speaking Indians. Although the improvements to be introduced after the acquisition of the property were to be of different sorts, they were to have the overall effect of raising the standard of living. In Newman's opinion it was most important, therefore, to record the physical status of the in-habitants before the improvements were introduced. Only by having a base line would it be possible to judge accurately the biological effectiveness of the changed Indian life-way.

Cornell never carried out its plan, unfortunately, but Newman was able to establish base lines for several aspects of the physique. Indeed, his base lines turned out to have a serendipitous quality in that, rather unexpectedly, they revealed the truly low subsistence level of the Vicos Indians [144, 146]. Two dietary surveys conducted in favorable months of good crop years found the average per-person caloric intake to be only 70% of the recommended level (adjusted INCAP, 1953). The protein, calcium and vitamin levels were even further below the recommended levels. As a result, the Indian boys showed no increase in bone mineralization from seven to seventeen years of age, whereas White boys in the United States show 50% increase in this growth period. The skeletal ages of the Vicos boys, as seen in X-rays, averaged two years nine months behind North American standards. Also, of course, both stature and weight were well below the highland means at all ages. Thus, adult male stature at Vicos, instead of being around 159 cm (the mean reported by Hurtado at Morococha), was only 154·6 cm. All of this moved Newman to conclude that such a pattern of slow growth and small body mass might be an advantageous adjustment to a terribly difficult total environment.

In spite of his fears that supplemental feedings of the Vicos school children might seriously disturb the delicate balance between physical size and available nutrition, Newman arranged to have large protein-rich lunches provided and vitamins administered at the Vicos school for four school years [145]. This was in addition to improvements in the community's food economy, which, incidentally, complicated the evaluation of the effect of the food supplements at school. Indeed, only the vitamins were shown clearly to have brought about definite improvement in physique. This is explained by the fact that not all of the children received vitamins; some received placebos. The vitamins seem to have produced some elevation in stature, but mainly they speeded up osteogenesis. Although suggestive of the important role of nutrition in shaping physique, it is still not clear what would be the result if such a program were continued for an extended period of time under closer supervision and with tighter controls.

*Descendants of the Aztecs and Incas*

To conclude this necessarily sketchy account of the surviving peoples of the New World's highest civilizations, their present situations from the standpoint of a physical anthropologist may be summarized. The modern nations which were created from the Aztec and Inca empires – mainly Mexico, Guatemala, Peru, Bolivia and Ecuador – still have populations predominantly of Indian racial origin. In general, the Indian element forms the lower social stratum and perpetuates customs that date back to pre-Columbian times. The upper social stratum tends to be the descendants of the European conquerors, still holding themselves aloof, but now in many cases admixed with Indian genes. The intermediate stratum of mestizos or cholos is the largest in size and obviously still growing at the expense of the other two. Present census figures distort the racial picture because of the use of inadequate definitions of race. Simply as a practical measure, Latin American census-takers usually identify Indians on the sole basis of whether they speak an Indian language. And, of course, they simply lump together all the others regardless of degree of admixture. This means that the Indians are far more evident to an outsider than the population statistics indicate.

Although the present lot of the descendants of the Aztecs and Incas is far from ideal, there are signs here and there, particularly in Mexico, that the capabilities underlying the ancient civilizations are still present and need only the right encouragement to reassert themselves.

# 6

# Living Indians encountered by the explorers: the lower cultures

The high civilizations of the Aztecs and Incas, to which the early Spanish explorers found their way so quickly and directly by running down clues about the sources of gold, naturally raised great expectations of equally spectacular finds elsewhere in the hemisphere. These expectations were not to be realized. Complete disillusionment on this score, although a long time in coming, involved eventually the explorers of other European nations besides those of Spain and sometimes intensive rivalry between them. But whether these Europeans were seeking gold, other natural resources, a Northwest Passage to Asia and the Indies or favorable places to colonize, gradually they explored and opened up the rest of the hemisphere. In the process they 'disturbed' (i.e., either slaughtered, enslaved, pushed aside or tolerated) the Indians in accordance with their natural inclinations and the policies promulgated at home. That the Indians of the lower cultures, as compared with the Aztecs and Incas, offered less opposition to the disturbance, was in keeping with the simple nature of their cultures and the usually thinner densities of their populations.

An explanation has already been given (page 77) of the dichotomy in Indian cultures – 'higher' vs. 'lower' – used throughout this book. Also in that connection, the nature of the higher cultures was outlined. Here, then, a few summary statements about the nature of the lower cultures should give the reader an understanding of the distinction being made that will suffice for the present purpose. It should be noted, however, that in only a few respects is this distinction based on absolute differences or, in other words, on the presence or absence of individual cultural traits. Rather, it reflects much the same situation existing today, both in the Old and New Worlds, as regards the so-called 'progressive' and 'backward' countries, namely, a wide range in the 'quality' of the total culture from one place to another.

One of the causes of the variation exhibited by the American lower cultures was environment; another was isolation. As peoples were subjected to more and more severe environmental pressures, and were situated further and further from the reach of influences from the higher cultures, they tended to be proportionately slower in making cultural progress. Thus, at the remote tip of South America, where it is too cold to cultivate food crops, the Fuegians were barely able to exist at a lowly stone-age level. Yet, by contrast, one of the groups peripheral to the Aztec Empire – the Pueblos of the relatively arid southwestern part of the United States – was living in large unadorned communal structures made of stone, weaving attractive textiles, fabricating good-quality pottery, and cultivating several food plants. Between these extremes – again according to climate – the dwellings varied from simple brush shelters to fairly intricate wooden structures; clothing was either almost entirely absent or consisted principally of dressed skins, sometimes sewn together; pottery was mostly utilitarian; and dependence on agriculture was determined largely by the availability of wild food plants.

In all of the mentioned aspects of the lower cultures, the levels of achievement nowhere reached those of the higher cultures. In addition, there was only limited metal working, except in the areas intermediate between Peru and Mexico. Outside the intermediate areas artistic expression was confined mainly to simple decorations on pottery, molded or carved figurines and woven and painted geometrical designs. Although alliances existed between groups, they lacked the organizational capacity to marshal armed forces for warfare or working forces for community projects on scales anywhere near those of the groups in the areas of higher culture.

The peoples of the West Indies – those first designated by Columbus as 'Indians' – had a culture that fits into the category 'lower'. They had migrated through these islands from South America, as already described, bringing with them elements of a simple culture suitable for the easy life of the near-tropics. Unfortunately for them, the Spaniards liked the beautiful islands too, and decided that here was the place to establish bases and ports for further exploration.

Moreover, on some of the larger islands the Spaniards were soon to find gold in sufficient quantity to mine and they would need the Indians to work the mines. Although naturally the Indians resented being taken over, their means of defense were no match for Spanish power. It was also the Spaniards' nature to over-react in retaliation to any Indian resistance.

### Enslavement of the Indians of the West Indies

The oppression of the island Indians seems to have begun after Columbus returned to Spain on his first voyage. He had left a colony on Hispaniola, the island of the Greater Antilles now politically divided between Haiti and the Dominican Republic. As so often happened in cases of early isolated colonies, this one fell into dissension. As a result, the colonists scattered over the island, causing so much trouble for the Indians that one of the chiefs exterminated the whole lot. Whether or not Columbus' discovery of the colony's fate on his second voyage led to retribution is not clear, but this is the time that he sent the first Indians to Spain as slaves. His excuse was that this was the best way to convert them to Christianity and at the same time teach them the Spanish language in order to prepare them to serve later as interpreters. The excuse did not fool Queen Isabella, who was insistent on the Indians being treated humanely. She failed, however, to take a strong stand in this instance and as a result pressure mounted for her approval of slave trading as a means of defraying the expense of colonization. Only her continued resistance held the trade in check.

In view of the royal opposition to the shipment of slaves to Spain, Columbus substituted a tribute, in the form of gold or cotton, laid upon the entire population of Hispaniola, including the Indians. The amount was so excessive, however, that he was forced in 1496 to allow the Indians to render their tribute in the form of labor. This was the beginning of an indirect slavery system, known as the *encomienda*, which was an extension of the feudalism of Europe. Under the *encomienda* system the Indians became vassals of Spaniards who supposedly protected and Christianized them and in return were entitled to their labor.

The Spaniards' need for labor, especially for work in the mines, was not satisfied by the *encomienda* system and hence the latter gave way to a new system called *repartimientos*. Essentially this consisted of labor levies placed upon Indian villages for men to work for the public interest. The Indian workers were paid modest cash wages from which the crown's tribute and the church's tithe were deducted. Although designed theoretically for the benefit of the Indians, the new system was badly abused. The Indians were overworked and ill-fed; many of them starved to death and others committed suicide. In addition, European diseases, smallpox in particular, took their toll. By 1535 only five hundred natives were left on Hispaniola. To replace them the colonists imported Negroes, along with Indians from other parts of the Caribbean.

According to Rouse (p. 518):

Between 1540 and 1550, when the gold of the islands had been exhausted and most of the colonists had turned to richer fields in Mexico and Peru, the system of *repartimientos* was abolished, but the damage had been done. When Sir Francis Drake visited Hispaniola in 1585, he reported that not a single Indian was left alive.

. . . The fate of the Indians was the same in Puerto Rico and Jamaica, which the Spaniards settled in 1508 and 1509 after the conquest of Hispaniola had been completed. In the Bahamas, too, the Indian population was destroyed before 1600, as the result of slave raids undertaken by the colonists of Hispaniola to replenish the diminishing supply of Indians on that island.

In Cuba, on the other hand, the situation was different. Partly because this island was the last in the Greater Antilles to be conquered and partly because of its great size, the natives there succeeded in surviving the system of *repartimientos*. When it was abolished in 1550, there were still over two thousand Indians in Cuba, as compared with some seven hundred Spaniards [176].

It would take too much space and be too repetitious of the already stated sequence of events to tell the sad story of the disappearance of the Indians from each of the other islands. The point is that any Indians who survived the early colonial period rapidly became absorbed in the ever rising flood of European immigrants and African slaves. Thus, almost the only recognizable

Indians in the whole of the West Indies today are a few reservation Caribs on the island of Dominica. In the early 1930s the anthropologist Douglas Taylor put their number at about four hundred, 'of whom less than a quarter are entirely free from Negro blood' [225]. He described them as 'a small though sturdy people, the men averaging around 5 feet 3 inches [160 cm] and the women about 5 feet [152·4 cm]'. This is the extent of the scientific observations on a people estimated conservatively to number at the time of discovery somewhere between 200,000 and 3,000,000–4,000,000 (see Table 1, p. 33).

### Explorations in the rest of the New World

The existence of other Indians with lower cultures besides those in the West Indies rapidly became evident to the Spaniards as they pushed their explorations around the Caribbean. Columbus found them on the north coast of South America on his third voyage, and others soon took up the task of exploring this coast in more depth. Yet the Spaniards could not push on to the adjacent east coast of South America because of the Treaty of Tordesillas (1494), which demarcated the interests of Spain and Portugal by a line running from pole to pole 370 leagues west of the Cape Verde Islands. Unknown to either country at the time they signed the treaty was the fact that this line intersects South America from the mouth of the Amazon River to Santos, the modern port city in the southern part of Brazil. This was one of two accidents which allowed the Portuguese to get a foothold in South America. The other accident occurred in 1500 when the Portuguese navigator Pedro Álvares Cabral was attempting to sail around Africa and sought to avoid the calms off the Gulf of Guinea by taking a south-westward course. His excessive precaution carried him to the coast of Brazil. Thereupon Portugal claimed the new-found land.

To simplify the presentation of living Indians of lower culture from this point on I will leave the account of what happened in South America here until I have dealt with North America. If further reason is needed, it is sufficient to note that most of the scientific activities in South America since the colonial period have lagged behind those in North America.

# North America

North of the Caribbean, Spanish encounters with Indians of lower culture began with Juan Ponce de León's 1513 discovery of Florida, which he mistook at first for another island. Fifteen years later the expedition of Pánfile de Narváez visited the Gulf Coast of North America, from which only four survivors (not including Narváez) emerged in northwestern Mexico some eight years later after a harrowing cross-continental trek. Fernando de Soto got further inland from the Gulf coast in 1539–40, but he too lost his life in the process of probing into the unknown.

### The southwestern United States

The unexpected arrival in northwestern Mexico of the four survivors of the ill-fated Narváez expedition aroused the Spaniards in that part of the continent to consider overland exploration northward. Cabeza de Vaca, the best known of the survivors, told of having seen permanent settlements, the inhabitants of which wore cotton garments and possessed turquoises. Just where these settlements were located he could not be sure, but he thought they were north of Mexico. His reference to turquoise conjured up images in the minds of his listeners of other mineral resources in the same region. Hopefully, gold could be found there, even though Cabeza de Vaca had not seen any. But could his account be trusted? The Viceroy in Mexico City needed confirmation before mounting a full expedition, so he arranged to have a representative of the Church, Fray Marcos de Niza, make a reconnaissance, in in company with another of the Narváez expedition survivors, a Negro called Estevánico.

Fray Niza and his party set out from Culiacán in northwestern Mexico in March of 1539. In September they returned with news of the existence of a country to the north called 'Cibola' where there were seven wondrous cities. Estevánico, who had preceded the monk as they neared Cibola, had visited one of the cities and had been killed there, probably because of liberties he took with the Indian women. After receiving news of this disaster Fray Marcos had dared to look at the city only from a distance and then turned and headed back to Mexico. But even so, he likened its size to that of the Mexico City of his day.

Fray Marcos' findings were enough to convince the Viceroy that a full-scale expedition should be sent northward. The result was the famous Coronado expedition of 1540–2 which subdued the major *pueblos* of the present States of New Mexico and Arizona, reached the Grand Canyon and penetrated the Great Plains as far as the Indian 'province' of Quivira in the present State of Kansas – all without finding any gold.

Once these and other exploring expeditions had determined that gold in worthwhile quantities did not exist in practically any of the areas visited north of the Caribbean and Mexico, the competing nations turned to establishing colonies in these areas. Spain took as her area of settlement much of the southern part of what is now the United States. Britain belatedly claimed most of the Atlantic coast of North America between Florida and the St Lawrence River, at which point the French had already gained a foothold. The only other colonizing activities were those of the Dutch and Swedes, on the Hudson and Delaware Rivers, respectively.

In contrast to the often cruel treatment which the Indians of all stages of culture received at the hands of the Spaniards during the early years of their colonizing effort, the British, French, Dutch and Swedes were able to avoid or limit this by adopting a policy of token payments to the Indians for the desired lands. Often the Indians, all of whom were of lower culture, were not actually occupying the lands and were glad to get something novel in exchange. This is not to say that savage fighting did not take place occasionally between the Indians and the north European colonists, but rarely on the large scale or for the same reason reported for the Spanish colonies. The result was that, by and large, throughout the British and French colonies in North America the Indians yielded ground to the advancing colonists and moved inland instead of resorting to warfare in defense of their territories. Thus, unlike the Spaniards, who ended up living intimately with the Indian remnants, the British, French, Dutch and Swedes separated themselves completely from the Indians.

There is little point here in detailing the many political, social and technological developments, beginning with the seventeenth century, that led to almost all of North America north of Mexico finally coming under British influence. In the present context, however, a little more should be said about the developing relationships between the Indians and Whites which led increasingly to confinement of the Indians on reservations.

In retrospect one can see the process getting under way in the late seventeenth and eighteenth centuries as the coastal Indians were forced to turn over more and more of their lands to the Whites and finally were left with no alternative but to appeal to friendly tribes further inland for refuge. To control the resentment caused by such tribal encroachments and displacements, the colonists negotiated treaties with the larger and more powerful tribes whereby, in exchange for their lands, some sort of payment was made and certain well-defined parts of the lands were allocated or reserved for Indian use. In this way title to the lands passed to the governing bodies negotiating the treaties. Following the American Revolution the new national government confirmed most of the earlier treaties and continued in one way or another the process of acquiring Indian lands and of resettling the original occupants. In Canada the governments generally followed a similar course.

A new period of reservation history began in the United States in 1809 when the Cherokees, then living in the southeastern part, requested permission of President Jefferson to move west of the Mississippi River. Soon other Southeastern tribes – particularly the Chickasaws, Choctaws, Creeks and Seminoles – joined the movement. As a result, in 1834 the Congress set aside much of what is now the State of Oklahoma as 'Indian Territory', specific parts of which were allotted in due course to individual tribes. Since then the allotments have undergone constant rearrangement, with some tribes relinquishing their claims and others being moved in. Eventually, although the Territory became a State in 1907, more displaced tribes are still represented there than in any other area of equal size.

The most violent stage of the process of bringing the Indians under government control followed the American Civil War of 1860–5. During these remaining years of the nineteenth century the tribes of the Great Plains west of the Mississippi River came under increasing pressure from settlers and buffalo hunters. These tribes were largely nomadic and depended on the meat of the buffalo for food and on buffalo hides for clothing and shelter. Also, these tribes in the course of time had acquired horses from the Spanish settlements to the south and firearms from the French traders to the north and were thus able to give a good account of themselves when they felt molested. The 'Indian Wars' that finally broke out late in the century were won by the US Army, but at a great cost in lives on both sides. The wars revealed both sides in their most brutal, and yet also in their most picturesque and heroic, aspects. Partly as a result of the Indians' last magnificent defiance of the government's efforts to curtail their freedom, the fierce nomads of the Plains created an image which now stands as a generally recognized symbol of the North American Indian [54].

Today there are some 240 Federal Indian-reservation areas in the United States, principally located in twenty-four States west of the Mississippi River. There are also some reservations under State jurisdiction in the East. The health service program extends also to Aleuts, Eskimos and Indians in Alaska and is now administered by the Public Health Service of the Department of Health, Education and Welfare. Otherwise the reservations are the responsibility of the Bureau of Indian Affairs of the Department of the Interior. The equivalent areas in Canada, called reserves, are under the jurisdiction of the Indian Affairs Service.

### The Chicago 'Fair' and its stimulus to anthropology

It is noteworthy that, although the foregoing events cover a long period of time, it was only at their culmination at the end of the nineteenth century that the physiques of the North American Indians of lower culture were studied scientifically and in large numbers. The delay was for the same reason as that given in connection with the Indians of higher culture, namely the late development of the science of physical anthropology. That such studies could be made easily and quickly at the end of the nineteenth century was due, of course, to the concentration of the Indians on reservations.

Not inappropriately, the occasion that led to the first intensive Indian studies in North America was the four hundredth anniversary of the discovery of America, as memorialized in the Chicago World's Columbian Exposition of 1893. One of the notable features of the 'Fair', rarely matched by any other celebration of this kind before or since, was the effort made to increase knowledge through research programs. This was particularly true of the Department of Ethnology, headed by Frederick Ward Putnam, one of the greatest anthropological promoters of all time. Years later, Alfred L. Kroeber of the University of California put the Fair and Putnam's program into perspective thus (p. 715):

As in its whole spiritual effect on American life, so the influence of this exposition upon American anthropology, under the guidance of Professor Putnam, was so profound as to have served ever since as a point from which one dates. Collections were assembled from all parts of the world and housed in a building which for the first time bore over its portal the name of the science. The studies prosecuted enlisted young men whose careers were determined for all time [110].

The reference to 'enlisted young men' goes to the heart of Putnam's program in anthropometry. He himself was not one to go into the field and do the work; he was the man of vision who developed the plans and picked the people who could carry them out successfully. His key lieutenants in this instance were experienced people selected to head each of the sub-disciplines of anthropology. Of these, the only one of interest in the present connection is Franz Boas, who was charged with securing the measurements of as many living North American Indians as possible during the two- or three-year duration of the program. In turn, Boas, who was thirty-four years old in 1892, picked and trained a corps of younger men to assist him in his work.

### Franz Boas and the German tradition

The selection of Boas for this role is interesting from the standpoint of the history of physical anthropology. In describing the anthropometric work on the Indians of higher culture, I mentioned the beginnings in France of physical anthropology as an organized science, and the subsequent work of French physical anthropologists in Mexico and Peru. If the French are credited with taking the initiative in this field, the Germans were not far behind. Yet the development of physical anthropology in Germany during the nineteenth century took a somewhat different course from that in France, in part because of the distinctive German scientific tradition, and in part because of the antagonisms resulting from the Franco-Prussian War of 1870. Since Boas moved permanently to the United States from Germany in 1887, whatever methodological leanings he may have acquired were naturally those of his homeland. Following the Chicago 'Fair' he would head an anthropological faction in America representing the German school, whereas another European immigrant just beginning to take an interest in anthropology, Aleš Hrdlička, would represent the French school. Hrdlička is mentioned in this connection because he became the other main contributor to the anthropometry of the living North American Indians who will be brought into this picture.

To continue with Boas, it is noteworthy that, as is true of so many of the early physical anthropologists, his formal training was in quite a different area – physics and geography – from that of his ultimate specialization. He completed his doctorate at the University of Kiel in 1881 – his dissertation dealt with the recognition of the color of water – and two years later he joined a geographical expedition to Baffin Land. There he came in contact with the Eskimos and they converted him to ethnography. A little later in Berlin he had the opportunity of studying a touring party of Bella Coola Indians from northwestern North America and became fascinated with their language, a tribal connection which he pursued through much of his later life. The interest in physical anthropology developed still later as a result of his studies of the culture of the Northwest Coast tribes.

When picked for the Chicago 'Fair' post, Boas' experience included not only extensive field work among living Indians and Eskimos, but about four years as a lecturer at the newly-founded Clark University in Worcester, Massachusetts. While at Clark he had had the honor of producing the first graduate in America with a PhD degree in anthropology. This teaching experience may have given him the contact with young men that enabled him to staff his anthropometric project. The uncertainty on this score is due to the fact that his 'enlisted young men' have never been fully identified by name, much less by background. This is surprising, but even more so is the fact that the anthropometric results themselves have never been reported in full. To date only the measurements on the Shoshonean tribes and the Sioux have been reported in detail, by Boas and Sullivan respectively [15, 223]. It is a shame that so much important material, already 400 years late when obtained, still remains neglected.

Boas put the total number of Indians and Eskimos measured at about 17,000 [13]. This includes at least 3,900 adult males, or perhaps as many as 5,500 of both sexes, free (or relatively free) from admixture. The remainder are mixed-bloods and children. In the only summary report on this work giving any detailed figures, sixty-two tribal units are listed [14].

Some of the data on stature and cephalic index, the only findings fully reported by Boas, are given in Table 6. The omitted tribal units lack either the measurement or the index. As the series numbers indicate, Boas' original arrangement [13] has been retained. The tribes were considered as geographical groups and some were subdivided according to their location at the time of the survey. For instance the Ojibway (Chippewa) of Canada were divided into an eastern and a western section. On the other hand groups of small tribes inhabiting the same region and showing no differences in type were combined.

The last column in the table attempts to interpret the arrangement in the more understandable, although still general, geographical terms of figure 15.

Clearly, as compared with the data for the Mexican and Peruvian Indians (Tables 3 and 4), the North American Indians of three-quarters of a century ago were from three to fifteen cm taller on the average and in many cases were broader headed (maximum average cephalic index 85·1). The higher statures in this zone of temperate climate conform with Bergmann's rule discussed earlier (page 49).

Unlike most physical anthropologists since his time, Boas was not averse to measuring the individuals of mixed ancestry along with those of 'pure' ancestry. He knew in advance, of course, that most of the tribes would prove to be racially admixed, and perhaps for this reason he decided to see if the results of admixture could be more exactly defined. At any rate, he subsequently placed considerable emphasis on this aspect of his findings and pointed out some biological laws – somewhat advanced for their time – regarding the inheritance of stature, face breadth and hair and eye characters.

On the basis of statistics of stature, he classified Indians into three groups: tall tribes, measuring more than 170 cm; tribes of middle stature, 166 to 170 cm; and short tribes, less than 166 cm. In comparing the statures of the tall tribes with those of half-breeds

TABLE 6

Stature and cephalic index of North American Indians,
by tribes
(from Boas [14])

| Series no. | Tribe | Stature | No. of male subjects | Cephalic index | No. of subjects, both sexes | Geographical area* |
|---|---|---|---|---|---|---|
| 1 | Micmac⎫ | 171·7 | (79) | 79·8 | (220) | N.E. US |
| 2 | Abnaki⎭ | | | | | |
| 4 | E. Ojibwa | 172·3 | (143) | 82·2 | (157) | Canada |
| 5 | W. Ojibwa | 171·2 | (198) | 80·2 | (244) | Canada |
| 6 | Ottawa⎫ | 169·9 | (98) | 81·4 | (113) | N.E. US |
| 7 | Menomonee⎭ | | | | | |
| 8 | Delaware | 171·5 | (43) | 79·8 | (126) | S.C. US† |
| 9 | Cree | 168·5 | (57) | 79·8 | (81) | Canada |
| 10 | Blackfoot | 171·5 | (49) | 79·8 | (146) | N.W. US |
| 11 | Cheyenne | 174·7 | (36) | 80·3 | (57) | ?‡ |
| 12 | Arapaho | 172·8 | (61) | 78·6 | (60) | ?‡ |
| 13–14 | Iroquois | 172·7 | (94) | 79·3 | (351) | N.E. US |
| 15a | E. Cherokee | 167·7 | (104)⎫ | 81·7 | (211) | ⎧S.E. US |
| 15b | W. Cherokee | 171·2 | (76)⎭ | | | ⎩S.C. US |
| 16 | Sioux | 172·6 | (612) | 79·8 | (580) | N.C. US |
| 17 | Omaha⎫ | 173·3 | (82) | ⎧81·8 | (225) | N.C. US |
| 18 | Winnebago⎭ | | | ⎩85·1 | (160) | N.C. US |
| 20 | Crow | 173·2 | (213) | 80·6 | (200) | N.W. US |
| 24 | Pawnee | 171·3 | (41) | 80·0 | (84) | S.C. US |
| 25 | Arikara | 169·0 | (46) | 81·5 | (174) | N.C. US |
| 26 | Choctaw | 170·0 | (260) | 81·9 | (10) | S.C. US§ |
| 27 | Chickasaw | 167·9 | (59) | 79·9 | (84) | S.C. US§ |
| 28 | Creek | 173·5 | (53) | 81·6 | (20) | S.C. US§ |
| 29 | Apache⎫ | 168·6 | (147) | 84·2 | (77) | S.W. US |
| 30 | Navajo⎭ | | | | | |
| 31 | Zuni⎫ | 162·9 | (104) | ⎧83·3 | (106) | S.W. US |
| 32 | Hopi⎭ | | | ⎩84·9 | (193) | S.W. US |
| 34 | Commanche | 167·8 | (74) | 84·6 | (29) | S.C. US |
| 35 | Kiowa | 170·9 | (58) | 82·0 | (40) | S.C. US |
| 37 | Ute | 166·1 | (121) | 79·5 | (123) | S.W. US |
| 39 | Kutenai | 169·0 | (46) | 79·9 | (84) | N.W. US |
| 46 | Hupa | 166·1 | (32) | 80·2 | (22) | S.W. US |
| 51 | Sahaptin | 169·7 | (71) | 84·7 | (267) | N.W. US |
| 57 | Shuswap | 167·3 | (114) | 84·9 | (72) | N.W. US |
| 61 | W. Eskimo | 165·8 | (34) | 79·2 | (114) | Alaska |

* See fig. 15 for explanation of abbreviations
† Moved here from N.E. US
‡ No information as to which branch of tribe was measured
§ Moved here from S.E. US

of the same tribes, the latter were found to be taller than the full-blooded Indians. Boas concluded that the cause was the effects of intermixture, since the social surroundings were so much alike that they could not account for the differences in stature.

In his comparisons of face breadth, he found that of the Indian to measure one centimeter more on average than that of the American White. The face breadth of half-breeds always stood between the two, but was nearer to that of Indians than to Whites.

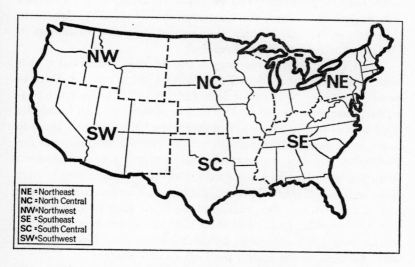

Fig. 15 Sketch map of the United States to locate the tribes measured by Boas [14]

He also compared measurements of children at yearly intervals beginning with the fourth year, and proved that the differences noted for adults existed just as markedly among children. The faces grew in such a way that the relationship between the three groups always remained the same.

Finally, Boas found that the same facts applied with regard to hair and eye color. Light hair was very rare among half-breeds, who nearly always had the typical dark, coarse hair of Indians; the color of the eyes also was almost invariably dark. The conclusion was that the half-breed resembles his Indian parent more than his white parent [13].

## Aleš Hrdlička and the French tradition

Like Boas, Hrdlička had not planned on a career in anthropology. Instead, he had qualified in medicine at the Eclectic and Homeopathic Medical Colleges in New York City in 1892–4. Soon, however, he became involved in studies on the populations of the New York State Hospitals and saw the need for anthropological training. The result was that he went to Paris in 1896 for four months' work with Leon Manouvrier, one of Boas' students. When Hrdlička returned to New York, this new interest led him to the American Museum of Natural History, then one of the principal centers in America for anthropological research.

The Curator of Anthropology at the American Museum at that time was none other than F.W.Putnam, who had set Boas to work measuring North American Indians in 1891. Ever the promoter, Putnam arranged for Hrdlička to accompany Carl Lumholtz on his 1898 trip to Mexico, and thereafter (from 1899 to 1902) to serve as physical anthropologist on the Hyde Expeditions of the American Museum to northern Mexico and the southwestern United States. Hrdlička made a sixth trip to the Southwest in 1903 after he joined the Smithsonian Institution. The fact that Hrdlička never went back to the practice of medicine after he had set foot among American Indians in their natural environments suggests an obvious further parallel to the experience of Boas with the Eskimos (and of Rivet with the Indians of Ecuador).

A large part of the results of Hrdlička's work among the Indians is contained in a monograph published by the Bureau of American Ethnology in 1908 [80]. According to my analysis, he examined 1,510 adult males from thirty-eight tribal groups, and 556 adult females from twenty-four tribal groups, scattered all the way from central Mexico to Colorado and Oklahoma. In addition, he examined 331 boys and 371 girls belonging to the Apache and Pima tribes. Not surprisingly, in view of Hrdlička's training, the orientation of the initially reported subject matter is predominantly medical, so much so, in fact, that stature is the only adult measurement included for any of the tribes except the Apache and Pima.

Some thirty years later (1935), Hrdlička published a second report in which he supplied the adult anthropometric data withheld from the earlier report [90]. The connection between the two reports is easily missed, since the second one is entitled simply 'The Pueblos'. Anyway, the belated completion of this project supplies additions to Boas' data on North American tribes and a connection with Starr's data for the tribes of central Mexico. But owing to the fact that the data on each tribe are not reported in equal fullness, the form of Table 7 is a compromise between the one

TABLE 7

Stature, sitting height and cephalic index of North American Indians (by order of stature): Males
(From Hrdlička [90], tables 17, 23, 66)

| Tribe (no.) | Stature (cm) | Height Sitting (cm) | Sitting-height index | Cephalic index | Geographical area |
|---|---|---|---|---|---|
| Otomi* (50–60)† | 158·5 | 82·6 | 52·1 | 78·1 | C. Mexico |
| Tepecano (25–23) | 160·2 | — | — | 82·8 | W.C. Mexico |
| Aztec* (51–46) | 160·8 | 83·9 | 52·2 | 79·1 | W.C. Mexico |
| Mazahua (41) | 160·9 | — | — | 77·1 | C. Mexico |
| Tarasco* (50–48) | 163·1 | 85·2 | 52·2 | 77·4 | W.C. Mexico |
| Pueblos (183–306) | 163·7 | 85·8 | 52·4 | 80·0 | Ariz.–New Mexico |
| Huichol (24–30) | 163·8 | 84·3 | 51·4 | 81·3 | W.C. Mexico |
| Tarahumare (23–22) | 164·2 | 87·0 | 53·0 | 75·9 | North Mexico |
| Nahua (50–49) | 164·3 | — | — | 80·0 | W.C. Mexico |
| Cora (51–50) | 165·0 | 86·2 | 52·2 | 81·0 | W.C. Mexico |
| Tepehuane (40) | 165·3 | — | — | 79·7 | N.W. Mexico |
| Southern Ute (50) | 166·9 | 88·8 | 53·2 | 79·2 | Colorado |
| Opata (30–31) | 167·0 | — | — | 79·3 | N.W. Mexico |
| Mayo (53–50) | 167·3 | — | — | 80·2 | N.W. Mexico |
| Walapai (35–34) | 168·5 | 89·5 | 53·1 | 83·3 | Arizona |
| Apache (212–144) | 169·1 | 90·0 | 53·2 | 84·5 | Ariz., N.M., and Col. |
| Yaqui (50–47) | 169·6 | — | — | 78·3 | N.W. Mexico |
| Navaho (90–28) | 169·9 | 90·5 | 53·3 | 83·7 | Ariz.–New Mexico |
| Papago (50) | 170·9 | 90·6 | 52·9 | 78·5 | Arizona |
| Mohave (45) | 171·6 | 90·8 | 52·9 | 84·4 | Arizona |
| Pima (53–52) | 171·8 | 90·4 | 52·6 | 76·4 | Arizona |
| Yuma (29–14) | 173·1 | 90·6 | 52·3 | 84·7 | Ariz.–California |
| Maricopa (40–38) | 174·9 | 91·2 | 52·1 | 81·5 | Arizona |

* Also measured by Starr [190] (See Table 3)
† Where two numbers are given, the second relates only to the cephalic index

relating to Boas (Table 6) and the one relating to Starr (Table 3). Also, Hrdlička's data are arranged by stature in Table 7 in order to render more apparent the south-to-north increase in size that he witnessed (he began his work in Mexico and finished in the American Southwest).

Four Southwestern groups were measured by both Boas and Hrdlička. This duplication permits comparison of their figures for stature (Table 8). The first thing to note is that Hrdlička is more

TABLE 8

Comparison of statures as measured by Hrdlička and Boas

| Hrdlička's tribal designation* | Stature (cm) | No. of male subjects | Boas' tribal designation† | Stature (cm) | No. of male subjects |
|---|---|---|---|---|---|
| *Apache* | | | | | |
| Jicarilla | 171·4 | (40) | *Apache* | | |
| White River | 171·1 | (52) | | | |
| San Carlos | 169·6 | (43) | | 168·6 | (147) |
| Mescalero | 167·5 | (25) | | | |
| *Navaho* | 169·9 | (90) | *Navajo* | | |
| | | | | | |
| *Pueblos* | | | | | |
| Isleta | 168·3 | (30) | | | |
| San Juan | 166·0 | (29) | | | |
| Santo Domingo | 165·3 | (40) | | | |
| Acoma | 165·0 | (14) | | | |
| Taos | 164·1 | (38) | *Taos* | 167·6 | (27) |
| Hopi | 164·0 | (105) | *Moqui* | | |
| Laguna | 163·7 | (65) | | 162·9 | (104) |
| Zuni | 163·5 | (60) | *Zuni* | | |
| Jemez | 162·7 | (40) | | | |
| Sia | 162·4 | (7) | | | |
| Hano | 161·9 | (19) | | | |
| | | | | | |
| *Ute* (southern) | 166·8 | (50) | *Ute* | 166·1 | (121) |

\* Hrdlička [80], pages 132–3; Hrdlička [90], page 269
† Boas [14], pages 369–70

specific as to the sources of his samples. Because he distinguished between the subdivisions of the Apache and Pueblos, it is possible to see that considerable intratribal variation in size existed. Generally, however, Hrdlička's statures are slightly higher than those of Boas. Whether or not this is due simply to sampling highly variable populations or to a difference in measuring techniques is difficult to say from such limited evidence.

## Genetic studies on the Navaho

Change has come slowly to the Indians of the Southwest. This is still the place where most of the scientific observations on living Indians are being carried out. Only today the traditional anthropometric observations, made mainly for comparative purposes, tend to be superseded by a variety of observations – medical, anatomical, serological, dental, etc. – made mainly for genetic analysis. One especially noteworthy study of the latter sort is known as the Ramah Navaho Project from the fact that it concentrated on the members of the Navaho tribe in the vicinity of the town of Ramah in western New Mexico. Clyde Kluckhohn and others of Harvard University had been making culture and personality studies on the Navaho for some years [109] when in 1948 they were joined by James N. Spuhler for the purpose of coordinating some rather novel physical observations with geneological data. Spuhler, a graduate of Harvard then teaching at Ohio State University, had been trained in physical anthropology and genetics. By coincidence, 1948 was the year when the American Society of Human Genetics was founded.

The then somewhat unusual observations made by Spuhler, of which the following are examples (only eight have been reported), indicate how far removed this new phase of Indian studies is from traditional physical anthropology [188, 189]: 'secretor factor' (the saliva of some individuals is nearly devoid of the ABO antigenic substances); 'PTC taste reaction' (PTC is the abbreviation for p-ethoxyphenylthiocarbamide, a chemical which not everyone can taste); 'phlebograms of the anterior thorax' (there are two distinct patterns of superficial veins over the upper chest); 'occipital hair whorl' (the head hair diverges from a point behind the crown in either a clockwise or counterclockwise direction); and 'number of vallate papillae' (circular structures which range in number from three to fourteen and form a V on the upper back surface of the tongue). Analysis of all eight characters in the Navaho has helped elucidate the mode of inheritance in each case. But comparison of any one of these characters between different groups of American Indians is virtually impossible because of the lack of the same sort of information for most other groups besides the Navaho. Judging from like data from other parts of the world, however, Spuhler could say [188, p. 183] that the comparison 'substantiates the general anthropological conclusion that American Indians are more closely related to the mongoloid division of mankind than to the negroids or caucasoids'.

# South America

At this point I will leave the North American Indians of lower culture and return to the course of exploration of South America. This radical shift in the story, which is necessary to introduce the South American Indians of lower culture, involves turning backwards chronologically to the sixteenth century and turning downwards geographically to the southern shores of the Caribbean.

After the earliest Spaniards had followed these shores to Darien and either turned northward to Mexico or crossed over the isthmus to the Pacific, the Spaniards that followed (being cut off by treaty from the Portuguese territories to the east) had to settle for other places, but chiefly the southern shores themselves. The most important activities here centered in what are now the countries of Colombia and Venezuela. In Colombia, the coastal settlement of Santa Marta was founded in 1525; in Venezuela, another coastal settlement, known as Coro, was founded in 1527.

Following the settlement of Coro, the Spanish emperor Charles V in 1529 took the unusual step of leasing this settlement, along with a large part of Venezuela, to the house of Welser & Co. of Augsburg, Germany. The Welsers were merchant princes who in their heyday rivaled the Medici of Florence in power. From 1529 to 1546, when the arrangement came to a tragic end, several Germans led the Spaniards in exploring the region between the Caribbean coast and the Amazon River.

### The legend of El Dorado
From the beginning the settlers of Santa Marta and Coro heard from the Indians of lower culture in their vicinity about a chieftain somewhere in the mountains in the interior who powdered his whole body with gold dust on ceremonial occasions, so abundant

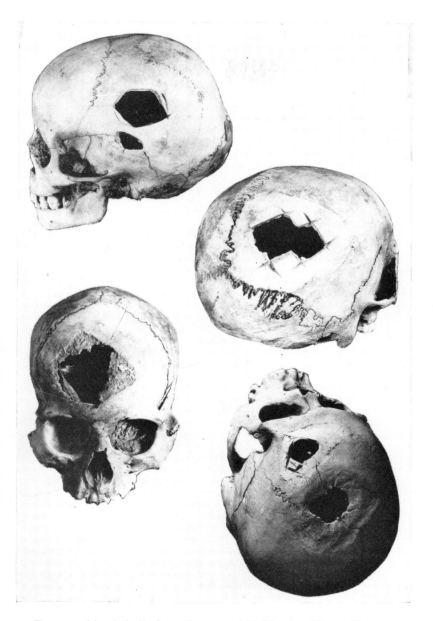

**17** Four trephined skulls from the central highlands of Peru. *Upper left:* child about six years of age with right-angled lines of bone infection beginning above and behind the wound. *Upper right:* young adult male with post-operative infection at the same stage. Note that the lines of infection border a bleached area where removal of the scalp exposed the bone. Note also the tic-tac-toe ('noughts and crosses') pattern of bone cutting. *Lower left:* adult male with advanced bone infection. *Lower right:* adult male with a healed opening and a fresh opening (note lines of infection). After Stewart [208].

18 A trephined skull from Cuzco, Peru, in the British Museum (Natural History) holds the record for the number of healed openings – seven. (*Courtesy of the Trustees of the British Museum (Natural History)*))

was gold in his country. This story of the gilded man – *el hombre dorado*, or, more briefly, *el dorado*, 'the gilded' – was to provide the incentive for the exploration of northern South America during the remainder of the sixteenth century. And ultimately, of course, the expression 'El Dorado' would be used metaphorically to denote a place where wealth could be gained rapidly.

The story of El Dorado seems to have reached the Caribbean coast by way of the Magdalena River, an important trade route from the interior mountains to the Caribbean just west of Santa Marta. Incidentally and rather surprisingly, salt was an important commodity in this trade because of the ease with which it could be carried downstream. Not known to the Spaniards at the time was the fact that the Magdalena River does not flow straight northward, but that most of its course – to about one hundred miles from the coast – is northeastward; in other words, its sources are nearer to the Pacific Ocean and the northern limit of the Inca empire than to the center of the continent. Not far from these sources the river passes just to the west of a high plateau surrounded by mountains, much like the Valley of Mexico. This plateau, known to the Indians as 'Bacotá', was the homeland of the Muisca tribe whose chief at one time had been the legendary El Dorado. Today the name of the plateau is preserved in the name of Colombia's capital city, Santa Fé de Bogotá. This exhausts the Muisca tribe's claim to fame; in spite of its gold, it was just another tribe of lower culture.

The geographical and ethnological facts underlying the El Dorado story emerged over a period of about nine years as three groups of Spaniards, one with a German leader, pursued the source of this story by different routes. Exploration in northern South America during the second quarter of the sixteenth century was not limited to three groups of Spaniards, but the three selected for brief description here were the most significant and probably had the greatest effect upon the Indian population.

The first of the three groups set out from Coro in 1529 under the leadership of Ambrosius Dalfinger, the Governor of Venezuela. Although the expedition reached the foothills of the mountains the next year, the reduction in numbers due to hardships along the way and battles with the Indians forced it to retreat. Almost immediately another expedition set out from Coro under the leadership of Nicolaus Federmann, but it too was unsuccessful.

And finally, in 1535, both Federmann and Georg von Speyer, the new Governor, led expeditions southward. Of these, only the one led by Federmann succeeded in reaching Bogotá, to find the gold already in the hands of other Spaniards, as will be explained later.

In 1536 Santa Marta launched its first and only expedition under the dual leadership of Pedro Fernández de Lugo and Gonzalo Jiménes de Quesada, Governor and Governor's lieutenant respectively. As it turned out, Governor Lugo, who was to ascend the Magdalena River in a flotilla of brigantines, soon lost most of the vessels in a storm and died before more could be constructed.

The disaster left the thirty-seven-year-old Quesada in full command. In the role of leader he seems to have had the fullest confidence and cooperation of his men. Hence, in spite of immense hardships and considerable loss of life, the group was still an effective fighting force when it succeeded in reaching the highlands during the following year. Once there, Quesada cultivated the good will of the highland Indians and resorted to fighting only when necessary. In this way he was probably able to locate and seize more gold than otherwise would have been the case. Actually, however, the amount of gold obtained by Quesada in this home-land of El Dorado – the last such hoard in the New World – was much less than that of the Inca emperor's ransom.

With the gold in hand, Quesada was confronted next with the necessity of securing the conquered country. To this end he laid the foundations of the present city of Santa Fé de Bogotá in 1538. Almost immediately, however, he received reports of Spanish forces advancing from the east and south. The force from the east was the one mentioned earlier as coming from Coro and being led by Federmann. The southern force proved to be under the leadership of one of Pizarro's lieutenants, Sebastián de Benalcázar, who had founded Santiago de Quito in 1534. He had heard the legend of El Dorado as far south as Quito and had been drawn northward thereby. Although it looked for a while as if the three forces would clash, they avoided this by agreeing to submit their claims to the Crown for arbitration. The outcome is beyond our present interest.

In outlining these involved expeditions in northwestern South America, the antagonism aroused in the Indians by the invaders and the consequent disruption in Indian life have been barely hinted at. Apparently the expedition of 1529 led by Dalfinger found the fertile valleys populated by Indians of lower culture and was able to live off their stored provisions and ripening crops. Dalfinger, according to Bandelier [9],

... was a valiant soldier, who permitted no obstacle interposed by tropical nature, or resistance offered by the natives, to keep him back. He was, moreover, a rough, heartless warrior of a kind of which the European armies of the time supplied many examples. Gold and slaves were his object, and in pursuit of them he plundered the inhabited country, and then devastated it in so terrible a manner that even the Spanish historians relate his deeds with revulsion [9].

The result was that subsequent expeditions along the same river routes found the valleys largely deserted, food scarce and the remaining Indians hostile.

Speaking of the highland tribe that gave rise to the El Dorado legend, Bandelier also says:

The Muysca, plundered and plagued by the whites amongst them, and warred upon on their borders by the Panches and Musos living around them, who were not subjected to the Spaniards till some time afterward, went down almost irresistibly to extinction. Their vigor was broken, and they had no hope of consideration from their rulers.

### South America's Atlantic coast

Returning to the Caribbean and moving eastward we reach the Atlantic Ocean at the present eastern limit of Venezuela. From here to the present northern limit of Brazil the coastal region is known as Guiana, possibly because some of the Guayana Indians were living there at the time of the conquest. This portion of the coast did not attract early Spanish settlement. Perhaps this was due to uncertainty regarding the exact location of the line, defined by treaty as already noted, separating the areas of Spanish and Portuguese interests. Anyway, Spain's failure to lay claim to this coast, and Portugal's slowness in following up her claim to Brazil, encouraged the British, Dutch and French to colonize here, just as they were doing along the Atlantic coast of North America. These efforts at settlement, however, were sporadic and the national holdings changed back and forth until late in the eighteenth century. While all this was going on along the coast, the local Indians, who were of lower culture like their neighbors on the islands and south shores of the Caribbean, largely melted back into the interior.

In Brazil the Portuguese did not establish an organized government until 1532. Their first settlement was on the island of São Vicente along the southern part of this section of the coast. Of the several settlements on this island in the period from 1532 to 1546 the one that flourished and still exists is Santos. It became the seaport of the great city of São Paulo some fifty miles inland, which in turn is the capital of the State of the same name. Although other settlements were established by the Portuguese along the coast to the north within the next few years, notably at Pernambuco (now Recife) and Bahia (which served as the capital for two hundred years), the early developments in southern Brazil are of primary interest so far as the Indians are concerned.

São Paulo was originally one of fifteen hereditary captaincies into which the whole country was divided. Each captaincy extended fifty leagues along the coast and an indefinite distance inland. Largely because of the presence along this part of the coast of a high tableland (the city of São Paulo is situated on its edge) the climate here is agreeable, a factor which undoubtedly contributed to the immediate success of the colony. Finding the soil fertile and water plentiful, the settlers began establishing large plantations for raising sugar cane and other crops. But labor was needed for the plantations to succeed and the local Indians of lower culture represented the only available source. Consequently, it is understandable that the Portuguese settlers, having the same European feudal background as their Spanish neighbors, introduced the *encomienda* system, which, as we have seen, amounted to enslaving the Indians.

Fortunately, the oppression of the Indians by the plantation owners of São Paulo lasted only until 1574. At that time the Jesuits, who were as influential in this Portuguese colony as in some of the Spanish colonies, successfully appealed to the Crown for control over the Indians that they converted. By this arrangement the Jesuits were able to assemble the converted Indians into villages or *aldeas* much like later missions that were formed in the Amazon valley and in far away California. The denial of Indian labor in Brazil led in due course to the introduction of Negro slaves.

Brazilian exploration and settlement beyond this point, made more complex by reason of the vastness of the country and its ecological diversity, cannot be considered here. It is enough to show, by means of the initial settlement, that the Indians fared much the same under Portuguese as under Spanish rule. Furthermore, the nature of the country gave the Indians room for maneuvering.

South of Portuguese Brazil, in what is now Argentina, Paraguay and Uruguay, Spain emerges again as a colonial power. Here the 138-mile-wide mouth of a river estuary first attracted the attention of voyagers from that country. Juan Díaz de Solís explored the lower part of the river (it was known for awhile as the Rio Solís) in 1516 and established Spain's territorial claim to the area. He was followed some ten years later by Sebastian Cabot (the son of the more famous navigator John Cabot) whose main claim to fame in this part of the world was his discovery of crude silver ornaments in use among the Indians living upstream. When these ornaments were seen in Spain, they aroused hopes of finding mineral wealth in the interior of the country and led to the Spanish word for silver (*plata*) being used from then on as the name of the river system. Actually, the Indians everywhere along the system were of lower culture and their few silver possessions had reached them in trade, probably from what is now Bolivia.

The hopes aroused by the silver ornaments, coupled with the reports of Pizarro's discoveries of Peru's vast wealth, stimulated the first attempts at settlement along the Plata River. The south side of the estuary seemed at first to offer the best place for settlement. However, unlike most of the Indians encountered elsewhere by the Spaniards in their colonizing efforts, those around the estuary were not agriculturalists and had no stored supplies. Instead, they lived in scattered bands, eking out a precarious living by hunting small birds and animals. This explains why the first Buenos Aires, founded here by Pedro de Mendoza in 1536, failed to flourish and had to be abandoned five years later. For once the Spaniards found the Indians unreliable as a source of food supplies when ships from home failed to arrive on time.

Already by 1537 Mendoza had become so discouraged by conditions at Buenos Aires that he had headed for home. One of the officers to whom he turned over the venture, Domingo Martínez de Irala, promptly went up the Paraguay River, one of the Plata's main branches, to a point 900 miles from the coast where he found Indians engaged in primitive agriculture. Realizing that in this situation a settlement might flourish, he founded Asunción, which became the first permanent city in the Plata basin.

The success of Asunción had considerable effect upon the local Indians beyond the resulting rapid reduction in their numbers and loss of their lands. In the first place, Irala encouraged his men to marry Indian women and to begin developing a mixed-breed population. In the second place, the plantation owners, like their Portuguese neighbors to the north, instituted the *encomienda* system, which placed the Indians in bondage for the rest of the century. And in the third place, the domesticated animals brought in from Europe – horses, cattle, sheep and goats – were allowed to go unattended and to multiply in the wild state. In only a few years these animals multiplied to such an extent that they spread southward across the rivers of the Plata basin into the pampas to transform the economic possibilities of that part of the country, from the standpoint of both the Spaniards and the Indians.

Considering the fortuitous basis of Portugal's claim to Brazil and the limitations of knowledge about the whole interior of the continent (who would have guessed that the Plata River system drained Southern Brazil?) it is not surprising that Spanish settlement soon ran foul of Portuguese land claims. The dispute over boundaries kept the area unsettled for years and delayed until 1610 the Jesuits' successful efforts at Asunción to terminate the *encomiendas*. Once freed from this type of bondage, the Indians here, as in São Paulo, still had little alternative except to adjust to, and join with, the Spaniards, or retreat into the interior. Both courses seem to have been resorted to in the early days even though the interior was occupied by other Indians who offered resistance to encroachment by any group. As a consequence this part of South America, and particularly Brazil, is divided into zones of Indian–White admixtures (the Brazilians often call them *mamelucos*) and pure-blood Indians, the latter being mainly in the most inaccessible parts.

Unlike North America, where the necessity arose mainly in the nineteenth century to move the Indians to, and confine them on, reservations, South America did not reach a comparable stage until this century, and then only in Brazil where the largest population of 'wild' Indians exists. The delay in this instance was a consequence of the generally slower pace of technological development in the southern continent. It had been unnecessary, if not unfeasible, until this century for the Brazilians to extend telegraph and railroad lines through previously little-disturbed Indian territories. Also, not until this century did the demands for forest products, especially rubber, lead to intrusions of large numbers of forest workers into the Indian territories. Activities of these and other sorts by the Neo-Brazilians – misunderstood, naturally, by the Indians – produced violent reaction on the part of the Indians. Under the growing pressures the Indians, disadvantaged by their simple forest culture, lack of firearms and vulnerability to the diseases of civilization, lost ground and succumbed in great numbers. Although the contest is still going on, it is now less violent and less disastrous for the Indians than might have been expected on the basis of the North American precedent.

Brazil's recent remarkably successful handling of its 'wild' Indians is due almost entirely to the leadership of one man, Candido Mariano da Silva Rondon (1865–1958). Through his early experiences on the Indian frontier as a military officer, Rondon developed a humanitarian philosophy regarding the Indians which is expressed in his motto: 'To die is necessary, to kill never.' In 1910 this motto became the guiding principle of the '*Serviço de Protecção aos Indios*', which he helped found and of which he became the first and long-time head. By the time of his death he had been honored for his compassionate accomplishment by innumerable distinguished institutions and many governments. His own government had given him the military rank of Marshal.

As its full name indicates, the *Serviço* stresses protection for the Indians while they continue in, or are in transition from, their traditional ways of life, rather than immediate assimilation into the national way of life. For this purpose over a hundred Indian 'Posts' are maintained [153]. These fall into four graded categories: (1) 'Posts of Attraction', where initial contacts are made; (2) 'Posts of Assistance, Nationalization and Education', where, in addition to giving basic help, some information is imparted about the nation of which the Indians are a part; (3) 'Posts of Instruction and Health', where Indians already partly assimilated can further their education and protect their health; and (4) 'Posts of First Class', where opportunities for higher education are offered, along with vocational training, to prepare the advancing Indians for participation in the national life. Owing to this protective arrangement, Brazil, more than any other country in the hemisphere, may succeed longer in maintaining large numbers of Indians in a relatively aboriginal state.

### Physical anthropology recorded by explorers

Many parts of South America occupied by Indians of lower culture remained attractive to explorers through the nineteenth century. This means that as physical anthropology developed into a more widely practiced science, some of the exploring expeditions to the remote parts included physical measurements of the Indians in their schedules of observations. The French, for instance, set a good example in 1882–3, during the so-called *Mission Scientifique du Cap Horn,* when Paul Hyades and Joseph Deniker added substantially to the records of the physiques of the southernmost Indians, the Alacaluf of Tierra del Fuego and the Yaghan of the Chilean southern archipelago [97]. A little later (1887–9) the second German expedition to explore the Xingu River, led by Karl von den Steinen, gave Paul Ehrenreich the opportunity to make the first physical records of a number of tribes deep in the interior of Brazil [53]. Karl Ranke followed him on the third Xingu expedition [162]. Although in these and all other early instances only small numbers of Indians were studied (as late as 1908 Lehmann-Nitsche's summary of the available data totaled less than 450 individuals [118]), the recording had begun early enough to ensure that a high percentage of the subjects measured were free from racial admixture. Thus, whereas in North America the Indians of lower culture were first measured in large numbers *after* they had already become racially admixed, in South America the Indians of lower culture were first measured in small numbers *before* they had become racially admixed. Additional measurements from more recent times can be found in volume 6 of the *Handbook of South American Indians* [193].

A few of the early measurements assembled over sixty years ago by Robert Lehmann-Nitsche of the Museum of La Plata in Argentina are shown in Table 9. The geographical areas where the groups or tribes were living when the measurements were made are indicated on the right side of the table. Figure 16 helps in the

## TABLE 9

Selected dimensions of South American Indians. Males
(From Lehmann-Nitsche, pages 71–2 [118])

| Group and tribe (no.) | Stature (cm) | Head length (mm) | Head breadth (mm) | Cephalic index | Geographical index (see figure 16) |
|---|---|---|---|---|---|
| *Carib:* | | | | | |
| Bakaïri (10)[1] | 160·8 | 186·5 | 147·0 | 78·8 | U. Xingu R., Brazil |
| Nahukwa (15)[1] | 162·1 | 188·0 | 151·1 | 80·4 | U. Xingu R., Brazil |
| Nahukwa (65)[2] | 161·8 | 185·2 | 147·3 | 79·5 | U. Xingu R., Brazil |
| *Arawak:* | | | | | |
| Mehinacú (6)[1] | 164·1 | 185·5 | 144·3 | 77·8 | U. Xingu R., Brazil |
| Paressí (9)[1] | 160·5 | 188·1 | 145·9 | 77·6 | Plateaus, Matto Grosso |
| Paumari (3)[1] | 164·3 | 181·0 | 152·0 | 84·0 | U. Purus R., Brazil |
| Ipuriná (2–9)[1] | 158·7 | 178·3 | 145·9 | 81·8 | U. Purus R., Brazil |
| Yamamadí (4)[1] | 159·8 | 178·0 | 146·0 | 82·0 | U. Purus R., Brazil |
| *Trumaí* (8)[1] | 159·2 | 179·0 | 145·4 | 81·2 | U. Xingu R., Brazil |
| *Trumaí* (14)[2] | 159·5 | 182·0 | 149·0 | 81·9 | U. Xingu R., Brazil |
| *Bororo* (20)[1] | 173·7 | 190·3 | 154·5 | 81·1 | S. Lourenço R., Brazil |
| *Carajá* (12)[1] | 168·9 | 191·2 | 142·8 | 74·7 | U. Araguaia R., Brazil |
| *Ge:* | | | | | |
| Cayapó (5)[1] | 167·6 | 173·2 | 145·6 | 84·1 | U. Araguaia R., Brazil |
| *Tupí-Guaraní:* | | | | | |
| Auetö (14)[1] | 159·9 | 187·1 | 148·4 | 79·3 | U. Xingu R., Brazil |
| Auetö (24)[2] | 158·1 | 185·6 | 148·8 | 80·2 | U. Xingu R., Brazil |
| Camayurá (14)[1] | 164·1 | 184·8 | 146·6 | 79·3 | U. Xingu R., Brazil |
| Guaraní (6)[3] | 153·0 | 187·0 | 151·8 | 81·2 | Itararé R., S. Paulo |
| Cainguá (2)[4] | 154·5 | 177·5 | 144·0 | 81·1 | S.W. Paraguay |
| Chiriguano (4)[5] | 160·2 | 187·8 | 152·5 | 81·2 | N. Argentina |
| Chiriguano (40)[6] | 163·4 | 184·2 | 147·7 | 80·1 | S.E. Bolivia |
| *Guaicurú:* | | | | | |
| Takshik (2)[7] | 163·3 | 186·5 | 147·0 | 78·8 | N.E. Argentina |
| Toba (20)[6] | 169·8 | 188·1 | 148·4 | 78·9 | N.E. Argentina |
| *Matuco-Macán:* | | | | | |
| Chorotí (20)[6] | 161·7 | 186·8 | 145·0 | 77·6 | N.E. Argentina |
| Mataco (30)[6] | 163·8 | 188·3 | 147·1 | 78·1 | N.E. Argentina |
| *Araucano* (5–4)[8] | 161·7 | 189·5 | 156·0 | 82·3 | C. Chile (?) |
| *Araucano* (2)[5] | 162·0 | 194·0 | 153·5 | 79·1 | W. Argentina |
| *Chon:* | | | | | |
| Tehuelche (3)[9] | 179·3 | 188·0 | 166·0 | 88·3 | Patagonia, Arg. |
| Tehuelche (3)[5] | 168·9 | 184·0 | 162·7 | 88·4 | Patagonia, Arg. |
| Ona (20)[10] | 173·6 | — | — | — | Tierra del Fuego |
| *Alacaluf* (11–8)[11] | 157·4 | — | — | 77·5 | S. Chilean islands |
| *Yahgan* (67–26)[11] | 157·7 | 189·0 | 153·0 | 81·0 | S. Chilean islands |

[1] Ehrenreich [53]
[2] Ranke [162]
[3] Krone [112]
[4] La Hitte et ten Kate [113]
[5] Ten Kate [227]
[6] Lehmann-Nitsche [118]
[7] Lehmann-Nitsche [117]
[8] Manouvrier [122]
[9] Janka, [237]
[10] Lehmann-Nitsche (previously unpublished)
[11] Hyades et Deniker [97]

Fig. 16 Map of South America to locate tribes and groups listed in Table 9

further identification of the named areas. In interpreting the measurements it is necessary to remark again on the small size of the samples. Except in random samples of twenty or more individuals, there is a good chance of the averages being biased by the presence of individuals of unusually large or unusually small size. Nevertheless, the range of the total listed averages is sufficiently narrow to give one confidence in according significance to the generally lower statures here as compared with those given in Tables 6 and 7 for North American Indians of lower culture. So much of South America is in the tropical climatic zone where, according to Newman, human size is at its smallest, that the finding of low stature here is not surprising [143].

The presence of more long-headedness (cephalic index below eighty) in South America than in North America is not so readily explained. On the other hand, the extreme broad-headedness of the Tehuelche (cephalic index over eighty-eight) may reflect some artificial deformity due to a cradling practice.

### Genetic studies in the interior

Aside from these points of general interest, Table 9 emphasizes the fact that the most extensive early anthropometric work on the South American Indians of lower culture was that of Paul Ehrenreich in Brazil. By coincidence one of the areas where Ehrenreich worked – the eastern part of the Mato Grosso of Brazil – is the locale of a recent (1962–4) investigation by an international and interdisciplinary team headed by James V. Neel of the Department of Human Genetics, University of Michigan Medical School. The purpose of the investigation is best stated in the words of the first report:

For perhaps 99 per cent of its biological history, the human species has lived in small aggregates whose livelihood came primarily from hunting and gathering. The time factor in evolution being what it is, there can be little doubt that many – most – of the genetic attributes of civilized man have been determined by the selective pressures and breeding structures of these primitive communities. If we would understand modern man, we must study such of these primitive groups as still remain [and] in a way in which they have rarely if ever been investigated to date. So rapidly are the remaining primitive communities disappearing, the matter of these investigations has an urgency not common in scientific problems [140, p. 53].

The tribe selected for study was the little-known Ge-speaking Shavante (Xavante), located mainly on the Rio das Mortes (a tributary of the Rio Araguaia), but also to the northwest of the headwaters of this river on the headwaters of the Rio Teles Pires (the Rio Xingu also arises near here). This tribe was selected because it is 'at that critical point in its relations with the outside world when it is approachable but yet culturally intact' [140, p. 53]. The Indian Protective Service established its first 'Post of Attraction' in Shavante territory in the early 1940s. Hostility on the part of the Indians was great at first and was not really overcome until some ten years had passed. Such a reaction is understandable in view of the fact that, following a long history of fighting the encroaching settlers somewhere to the east, the tribe had moved to this remote area in the nineteenth century. The tribe's acceptance of the scientists in the early 1960s is evidence of the further extent of the pacification program and of the continuing effective work of the Indian Protective Service.

Since we have been reviewing the anthropometry of the Brazilian Indians, it is interesting to note the way in which the present-day Shavante fit into the established picture for the peoples related to them. The late Friedrich Keiter of the University of Hamburg took the new measurements [140, 147]. A sample of his results is compared in Table 10 with Ehrenreich's sixty-five-

TABLE 10

Selected dimensions of Brazilian Indians. Males

| Tribe (no.) | Stature (cm) | Head length (mm) | Head breadth (mm) | Cephalic index |
|---|---|---|---|---|
| Shavante (24) * | 168·1 | 194·9 | 149·0 | 76·4 |
| Shavante (42) † | 170·2 | 200·0 | 148·9 | 74·5 |
| Carajá (12) ‡ | 168·9 | 191·2 | 142·8 | 74·7 |
| Cayapó (5) ‡ | 167·6 | 173·2 | 145·6 | 84·1 |

\* Neel et al. [140], Table 1, page 65
† Niswander et al. [147], Table 1, page 492
‡ Ehrenreich [53]

year-old figures for the Carajá and Cayapó of the same river system [53]. The only real difference here has to do with the head shape of the Cayapó, which is relatively much broader than that of any of the others. However, the sample in this instance is too small to be reliable.

Several other findings from the Shavante study are of interest here. One that came as a surprise to the observers relates to the genetic differentiation of human groups. Some of the Shavante villages had undergone fission just before they were studied, with the smaller splinter groups going off on their own or to other villages. Pedigrees from the splinter and parent villages suggest that such fissions among the Shavante are along kinship lines, leading to a highly non-random sampling of the gene pool. Theoretically, if for some reason one of these splinter groups would lose contact altogether with the tribe, it might end up with physical characteristics quite different from those of the parent group. Geneticists who have been accustomed to thinking of a splinter group as having a random representation of the genes in the parent group's gene pool (the 'founder effect') will now need in these circumstances to give more attention to social organization (the 'lineal effect').

Life expectancy among the Shavante, as among most other groups in a comparable stage of culture, is low. They keep no track of their ages, but it was possible to make a reliable judgment that less than 20% of the living were thirty-one years of age or older. As against the relative absence of elderly individuals in this population, there is the paradox of the apparently excellent health noted among the young. 'The young Xavante is a superb physical specimen,' the investigators note [139]. 'Health is more than freedom from disease,' they go on to say, and they add (p. 566)

An American [White?] population is healthy but fails to project the sense of feral vitality and physical resilience of the Xavante. There are differences of the more objective criteria we attempt to use – specifically, the [well-toned] musculature, the keen vision, the lack of dental caries, the slow pulses, and low blood pressures – but these tell only a fraction of the story. Under these circumstances, the relative absence of individuals over 40 years of age is one of the most troublesome observations to emerge from this study.

Actually, when blood samples from this population were studied by immunologists, antibodies to a wide variety of agents of disease were demonstrated, but none for treponemal infections [141]. The investigators add (p. 488): '[the latter] finding is supported by our failure to observe clinical signs of syphilis, yaws, or pinta'. Viewed in the perspective of the hemisphere's human history already presented, many of the demonstrated diseases may date from post-Columbian times, and if so, indicate their ability to spread beyond the apparent limits of civilization and to become endemic in sparsely settled areas. However, other types of endemic diseases, demonstrated by the presence of parasites in the feces of the Shavante, must be much older, judging from the evidence presented about the presence of these parasites in America in pre-Columbian times. Among the parasites recovered were: *Ascaris lumbricoides*, *Entamoeba histolytica*, *Giardia lamblia*, *Trichuris trichiura*, and *Strongyloides stercoralis* [142].

These few highlights from the mid-twentieth century Shavante studies indicate that a new period of Indian investigation is opening in the southern continent comparable to that described for North America. The stimulus, quite obviously, has come from the relatively newly-organized field of human genetics. As soon as Neel proved that such studies are now feasible and yield unexpected new knowledge, other investigators naturally started planning similar programs. Naturally, too, one of the first to follow in Neel's footsteps was one of his students, Napoleon Chagnon. He elected to study the Makiritare (Yecuana) and Yanamama (Waica) residing around the headwaters of the Orinoco River in southern Venezuela and the adjacent part of Brazil [31, 138]. Unfortunately, anthropometry was not included in this second effort and, so far as it is possible to tell from the preliminary reports, Chagnon is following Neel's example of omitting the characters observed by Spuhler on the Navaho.

## Physiological adaptation to cold

The Indians studied by Neel and his associates in Brazil and Venezuela still go about wholly, or almost, naked much of the time. Any clothing that is worn by them now is the result of contact with white men. Living as they do in a hot equatorial climate, the problem of coping with body chilling during sleep at night is a minor one. But the same is not true of the canoe-using coastal Indians at the southern end of the continent – the Ona, Yaghan and Alacaluf – where the mean annual temperature is close to 43° F. and where light snowfalls occur in the coldest season. Coon [40] believes that this climate is like that which may have prevailed in Western Europe during glaciated episodes of the Pleistocene.

The classic account of the original primitive state of these southernmost Indians is that recorded by Charles Darwin on a

stop in their area in December of 1832 during his voyage on the
H.M.S. *Beagle* [44, p. 212]:

While going one day on shore near Wollaston Island, we pulled alongside a canoe with six Fuegians. These were the most abject and miserable creatures I anywhere beheld. On the east coast the natives . . . have
guanaco cloaks, and on the west, they possess seal-skins. Amongst these
central tribes the men generally have an otter-skin, or some small scrap
about as large as a pocket-handerkerchief, which is barely sufficient to
cover their backs as low down as their loins. It is laced across the breast
by strings, and according as the wind blows, it is shifted from side to
side. But these Fuegians in the canoe were quite naked, and even one
full-grown woman was absolutely so. It was raining heavily, and the
fresh water, together with the spray, trickled down her body. In another
harbour not far distant, a woman, who was suckling a recently-born
child, came one day alongside the vessel, and remained there out of mere
curiosity, whilst the sleet fell and thawed on her naked bosom, and on
the skin of her naked baby!

Only recently have the physiologists become interested enough
in cold adaptation among peoples of lower culture to extend their
scientific observations to them. A leader in this field is P.F.
Scholander, Director of the Scripps Physiological Research Laboratory in California. It is owing to him and a group of associates that we know the nature of the adaptation in one group of
Indians in southernmost South America – the Alakaluf [66]. In
this group the adaptation is the type called 'metabolic acclimatiza-
tion'.

Because the amount and pattern of fat deposition on the bodies
of the Alakaluf are much as in Whites, the loss of body heat is
nearly at the same rate in both groups. Yet when Whites are
stripped naked in this climate they quickly succumb to uncontrol-
lable shivering, a form of involuntary exercise which helps the body
generate heat. To understand why the Alakaluf do not shiver much
one must take into account the fact that they consume a lot of fat
and other high-caloric food – in response, it is thought, to a high
basal metabolism. Whatever the relationship between the food-
intake and the high metabolism, the latter constitutes an adaptation
which is lacking in Europeans and probably other groups accustomed to milder climates. By means of their high basal metabolism
the Alakaluf are able to maintain a balance between internal heat

production and the loss of heat from their naked bodies during sleep and thus to endure conditions which few persons of other races could tolerate [40].

The adaptation of the Alakaluf to the cold is rather special. In the other cold place in the southern continent, the high Andes, the inhabitants are still benefiting from the high culture of their Inca ancestors and are wearing finely-made wool clothing. They supplement this when unclothed during sleep, however, by an unusual physiological adaptation, called 'hypothermic climatization'. This consists of balancing the not-unusual basal metabolism reached during sleep with an extraordinary loss of heat from the core of the body. There is no evidence here or in Tierra del Fuego, however, that cold adaptation of the physiological sort is inherited rather than acquired.

# 7

# Eskimos and Aleuts
# encountered by explorers

The climate of the southern tip of the hemisphere and of the Andean highlands is not really cold at all as compared with that of the inhabited parts of the American Arctic and sub-Arctic. The Arctic, in fact, is so cold much of the time that humans cannot survive there without the warmest clothing. It is appropriate at this point, therefore, to turn our attention to the northernmost part of the hemisphere and its inhabitants and to consider them in much the same way as in the previous two chapters. The main reason the Far North was not covered earlier is that most authorities regard the major human groups in this region – Eskimos and closely related Aleuts – as physically distinct from all the Indians.

In addition to being physically distinct from the Indians, the Eskimos and Aleuts have developed cultural specializations quite different from those of the Indians. This is because it is from the sea, more than from the land, that they obtain almost everything they need to support life. By catching sea birds, fish, seals, walruses and whales, they obtain meat for food, oil for light and heat, skin (including fur and feathers) for clothing, boat coverings, bags, thongs, sinews, etc., as well as bones and ivory for implements. In this nearly treeless part of the world the sea even provides a small amount of wood – driftwood from inland. Since the Eskimos and Aleuts are so dependent on the sea, they are primarily coastal dwellers.

# Eskimos

Earlier I mentioned having spent the summer of 1927 among the Eskimos of Nunivak Island in Bering Sea. On that occasion the crew of the ship on which I traveled northward from Seattle included some Eskimos – the first living Eskimos I had ever seen. At one point during the trip I saw these Eskimos in company with some Chinese employed in the Alaskan fish canneries. Since both the Eskimos and the Chinese were wearing Western-style clothes, all cultural distinctions were lost; but if anything this emphasized their strikingly similar facial features. The Chinese, I was taught, represent the extreme type of Mongoloid that evolved in Asia after the ancestors of the American Indians left that continent. If this is so, the similarity in appearance between the American Eskimos and the Chinese means that the two did not part company until long after the Indians' forebears had left Asia. Thus, the timing of the migrations, rather than the climate, accounts for most of the physical differences between the Eskimos and Indians.

## The Eskimo language

My trip to Nunivak Island made me aware of another remarkable thing about the Eskimos: although they have an enormous geographical distribution across the Arctic from Siberia eastward to Greenland, their language is unusually limited in its diversification. (By contrast there were more than a score of small Indian linguistic families within the area of the present State of California). This fact had been strikingly demonstrated three years before my visit to Nunivak when Knud Rasmussen arrived at Nome, Alaska, at the conclusion of what was called officially 'The Fifth Thule Expedition – Danish Ethnographical Expedition to Arctic North America, 1921–24' [163]. Eskimos from various places around Bering Sea, including Nunivak Island, were in Nome at that time. But to Rasmussen's surprise he was able to communicate only with those from north of Norton Sound. In the case of the Nunivak Islanders he needed an interpreter and turned for help to Paul Ivanoff, a mixed-blood Eskimo from St Michael in Norton Sound, who was a trader on the island. As a trader crossing the linguistic boundary Ivanoff had to be able to communicate on both sides. The amazing thing about this episode is that Rasmussen, a Greenland-born speaker of Eskimoan, had traveled from Greenland westward all the way across Arctic America to this point – further, of course, than the 3,000 mile great-circle distance – without encountering any difficulty in talking with the Eskimos he met.

About the same time the Canadian anthropologist Diamond Jenness, who had collected vocabularies on both sides of Bering Strait and southward, noted that '. . . the dialects of the Siberian coast and of the Yukon and Koskokwim deltas diverged more widely from those spoken north of Norton Sound than the latter from the dialects of far-distant Greenland and Labrador' [103, p. 174]. Subsequently, this linguistic division was subjected to lexicostatistic dating by Morris Swadesh [224]. Comparison of Yukon and Greenland vocabularies by a complicated statistical technique, known as 'glottochronology', yielded a figure of a thousand years as the time of separation of the eastern and western branches of the Eskimo proper. In the same way the separation between Eskimoan and Aleut was set at three thousand years ago. All of which strengthens the long-held opinion that the Eskimos and Aleuts reached North America in relatively recent times.

A word of explanation about glottochronology is in order. This dating procedure assumes that every human group, regardless of cultural and environmental differences, has a basic vocabulary for the ordinary and recurrent things and situations of life. It assumes also that the constituents of the basic vocabulary undergo replacement at a fairly constant rate over long periods of time. The rate of replacement in certain European languages serves for the dating of preliterate languages. In the latter cases, however, the only recorded vocabularies representing a time difference sufficient for dating purposes are those of groups judged to be closely related, as in the examples cited (Eastern versus Western Eskimoan; Eskimoan proper versus Aleut). From the differences in the basic vocabularies of these groups the dates of their separations can be calculated. The accuracy of the results is often uncertain, but in the case of the Eskimos and Aleuts appears to agree with the archeological evidence.

### The eastern branch of the Eskimos

Although it is natural today to look to Alaska and other areas around the northwestern entrance to the American *cul-de-sac* for solutions to Eskimo problems, one should remember that the earliest contacts between Eskimos and Europeans occurred on the far-off coasts of what are now Greenland and eastern Canada. A time difference of some eight centuries separated the first contact there and that in Alaska. The mythical-seeming voyages of the Norsemen, and probably also the British, to Iceland, Greenland and the nearby coast of North America at various times before the famous first voyage of Columbus have already been mentioned. These voyages and the resulting settlements on Greenland were Medieval Europe's most daring colonial adventures. Yet before the end of the fifteenth century all of the settlements had disappeared, owing probably to the failure of supplies from the homeland, excessive inbreeding and the ravages of the climate. That the Eskimos had anything to do with the disappearance of these settlements has not been verified.

European interest in this part of the world revived after Columbus' discovery raised the possibility of reaching Asia by a Northwest Passage. Thereupon voyages of exploration in that direction, for the most part under English auspices, were undertaken in fairly rapid succession by such well-known navigators as John Cabot (1497, 1498), Martin Frobisher (1576, 1577, 1578), John Davis (1585, 1587), Henry Hudson (1610–11), and William Baffin (1615, 1616). Although a Northwest Passage remained undiscovered until the present century, the remarkable achievements of these men have been recognized by the naming of appropriate geographical features after them. In this connection, it is interesting to note that Baffin Bay commemorates the fact that Baffin reached a northern point that no one would pass for nearly 250 years.

Explorations in the area of the Western Eskimos can be passed over here, because they were carried out so much later (see under Aleuts, p. 141).

As for the contacts with the Eskimos and northern Indians made by the early explorers, generally these do not feature prominently in the records. Probably this is because the native population was sparse, the coasts appeared inhospitable and settlement was rarely the purpose of the voyages. Anyway, of these early explorers Frobisher alone seems to have brought back living Eskimos to England [11]. On his first voyage five members of his crew disappeared when they went ashore in Frobisher Bay and are thought to have been killed by the Eskimos. Soon thereafter, in retaliation, Frobisher seized an Eskimo who came near the ship in a kayak. Although the captive died shortly after the expedition returned to England, a colored drawing of him by Lucas de Heere, a Flemish painter then residing in England, is preserved in a manuscript kept in the University Library of Ghent (reproduced by Birket-Smith) [11]. Unfortunately, were it not for the cultural elements in the picture, the individual portrayed could not be identified as an Eskimo.

Early portraits of two other Eskimos, a man and a woman, are preserved among the John White drawings in the British Museum. Evidence indicates that these represent the natives brought back by Frobisher on his second voyage to the same region. Again the man lived but a short time. Whether White made the pictures from life after the expedition's return, or was a member of the expedition, is unknown. Certain defects in the costumes to which Birket-Smith has drawn attention, and the non-Eskimo faces, suggest that the artist had only limited knowledge of his subjects.

### Anthropometric knowledge of the Eskimos

After the geography of northeastern North America was worked out to the point of eliminating the possibility of an accessible Northwest Passage, and search of the coasts had excluded accessible mineral resources, about the only voyagers to this part of the world for many years were whalers. As a result, scientific knowledge of the Eskimos was slow to accumulate. In the field of physical anthropology the same pattern holds here as already noted for the rest of the hemisphere; and not until 1877, eighteen years after the founding of the Anthropological Society of Paris, were the first scientific measurements of living Eskimos obtained. By coincidence, the study was made in the Society's home town – Paris.

This was the period when Carl Hagenbeck of Hamburg, Germany, was catering to the growing interest in zoos and their needs by sending out animal-collecting expeditions. As a side line, he hit upon the ingenious idea of having the captured animals accompanied by some of the native people from the same country for the purpose of separate anthropological exhibition. Upon arrival at a zoo, the costumed natives would set up housekeeping according to their custom at home, even to the extent of making a house as nearly as possible in their accustomed style. Thus it was that in the fall of 1877 six Eskimos from Disko Bay on the west coast of Greenland, three men, one woman and two children, were on exhibit at the *Jardin d'Acclimatation* in Paris and a Commission was appointed by the Anthropological Society to study them [21]. The Commission included two famous physical anthropologists, Paul Broca and Leon Manouvrier, but its report does not indicate who took the measurements.

The following spring the same Eskimos were exhibited at the *Zoologische Garten* in Berlin and were studied by Rudolf Virchow, the famous physical anthropologist of the anthropological society in that city [231]. Table 11 shows how some of the measurements

TABLE 11

Measurements of the same Greenland Eskimos taken independently in Paris and Berlin

| Measurements | Males | | | | | | Female | |
| --- | --- | --- | --- | --- | --- | --- | --- | --- |
| | Okabak (Age 36) | | Kojangi (Age 23) | | Gokkik (Age 41) | | Okabak (Age 23) | |
| Stature (cm) | 155·4* | 155·0† | 142·1* | 143·4† | 164·1* | 166·0† | 143·2* | 144·5† |
| Head length (mm) | 196 | 195 | 180 | 182 | 191 | 190 | 180 | 183 |
| Head breadth (mm) | 143 | 144 | 138 | 140 | 142 | 142 | 142 | 141·5 |
| Ceph. index | 73·0 | 73·8 | 76·7 | 76·9 | 74·3 | 74·7 | 78·9 | 77·3 |
| Nose height (mm) | 49 | 51 | 47 | 46 | 52 | 54 | 41 | 54 |
| Nose breadth (mm) | 35 | 33 | 36 | 32·5 | 35 | 34 | 28 | 32 |
| Nasal index | 71·4 | 64·7 | 76·6 | 70·6 | 67·3 | 63·0 | 68·3 | 59·2 |

* Bordier [21] (Meeting of 22 November 1877). The spellings of the names and the age estimates are from this source

† Virchow [231] (Meeting of 16 March 1878). In this record two of the names are spelled differently (Kujanji and Kokkik) and two of the age estimates are different (the female Okabak: 24, Kujanji: 28)

and indices from the two studies compare. The agreement is good for all measurements except those on the nose. Surprisingly, these differ in all cases. This may well reflect the variations in measuring techniques which characterized the French and German schools for many years.

Hagenbeck also was indirectly responsible for the first measuring of Labrador Eskimos in Europe. And again Rudolf Virchow was the physical anthropologist in Berlin who recorded their physical characteristics [232]. The group consisted of two families, one from the Moravian mission at Hebron (a couple with two children and a young adult male) and the other from Nachvak some fifty-five miles further north (a couple with a daughter). Some of this group later succumbed to smallpox in Paris.

Another group of Eskimos from the mission stations in Labrador toured Europe in 1899–1900, possibly under the management of the American showman P.T.Barnum. They, too, were prepared to demonstrate their way of life. When they appeared at Olympia, in London, W.L.H.Duckworth and B.L.Pain of Cambridge University measured the adults and adolescents (eleven males and ten females) [50]. Since the group totaled twenty-seven, six children must also have been included. The next year, when the group visited Geneva, its total was down to twenty-six and Eugène Pittard of the University of Geneva, who took the opportunity to measure fifteen (eight males and seven females), mentions that the adults and adolescents numbered 'around a score' [154].

Of the measurements taken on the two Labrador groups, I will note only the average male stature: 157·7 cm for the eleven measured by Duckworth and Pain, or 158·6 cm for the eight measured by Pittard plus the three measured by Virchow. These figures compare well with the 157·5 cm for twenty-six males from Labrador reported by Boas [14] and are somewhat below the 160·6 cm for 140 West Greenlanders reported by Søren Hansen [68]. More generally, this means that the Eskimos are in the same stature category as the Indians of the southern tip of the hemisphere, and numerous other groups in between (cf. Tables 3, 7 and 9).

It is noteworthy also that probably the first group of Eskimos to be exhibited and studied in the United States was brought to New York in 1896 from Smith Sound by Lieutenant Robert E. Peary (later given the rank of Rear-Admiral for his discovery of the North Pole). Peary found no Eskimos living further north than those around Smith Sound. By coincidence, the six that he brought to New York had a sex and age assortment similar to the West Greenland group that Hagenbeck earlier took to Europe: three men, one woman and two children. In New York the group was housed in the American Museum of Natural History and examined by Hrdlička [81]. Unfortunately, within less than nine months the three men and one of the children (a girl) had died of tuberculosis.

Some thirty-five years later Hrdlička noted the Alaskan Eskimos' similar great susceptibility to tuberculosis, but this time in their native habitat: 'Examination of both sexes and all ages along the [Kuskokwim] river indicated that tuberculosis in some form and stage was present in about one-third of the population' [89, p. 102]. More recent clinical surveys have confirmed this observation. By now, of course, contacts with Whites have been of ample duration everywhere to permit the spread of a disease that perpetuates itself when introduced into sedentary communities with low sanitary standards.

Getting back to the physical description of Eskimos, the first, and still the most extensive, anthropometric study is that of Vilhjalmur Stefansson, as reported by Carl Seltzer [180]. On two expeditions to the Arctic – one in 1906–7 and the other in 1908–12 – Stefansson

TABLE 12

Selected dimensions of Eskimos. Males *

| Group and no. (see fig. 17) | Stature (cm) | Sitting height (cm) | Sitting-height index | Cephalic index | Source |
|---|---|---|---|---|---|
| Angmassalik (24–26) | 162·4 | 86·8 | 53·3 | 76·5 | Poulsen [157] |
| Smith Sound (8) | 157·4 | 82·5 | 52·4 | 78·1 | Steensby [191] |
| Labrador (11) | 157·7 | 81·0 | 51·4 | 77·0 | Duckworth and Pain [50] |
| Southampton I. (35) | 162·0 | 85·2 | 52·6 | 77·2 | Tocher [228] |
| Mackenzie (10–48) | 169·0 | 91·2 | 53·3 | 74·8 | Seltzer [180] |
| Mackenzie-Koupagmiut (12) | 167·5 | 89·3 | 53·5 | 73·9 | Boas [16] |
| Nunatagmiut (21–64) | 169·1 | 86·4 | 51·5 | 81·4 | Seltzer [180] |
| Nunatagmiut (11) | 167·9 | 86·8 | 52·6 | 81·6 | Boas [16] |
| Barrow (22–62) | 164·6 | 88·2 | 53·7 | 78·6 | Seltzer [180] |
| St. Lawrence I. (63) | 163·3 | 88·4 | 54·1 | 79·7 | Hrdlička [87] |
| S.W. Alaska (61) | 162·4 | 89·0 | 54·9 | 80·7 | Hrdlička [87] |

* From Seltzer, Tables 7, 19, 21 and 23 [180]

measured 298 males and 194 females at six localities scattered along more than 1,500 miles of coast from Kotzebue Sound in Alaska on the west to Coronation Gulf and Victoria Island in the Northwest Territories of Canada on the east. In Table 12 there are assembled from this study certain selected data for nine groups located in figure 17. The main showing is the exceptional character of the

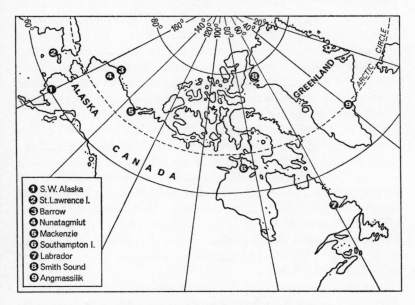

❶ S.W. Alaska
❷ St.Lawrence I.
❸ Barrow
❹ Nunatagmiut
❺ Mackenzie
❻ Southampton I.
❼ Labrador
❽ Smith Sound
❾ Angmassilik

Fig. 17 Map of Arctic America to locate the groups listed in Table 12

Nunatagmiut then inhabiting the region inland from Barrow. As Seltzer says (p. 347), 'They have the shortest heads, the broadest heads, the highest cephalic indices, the lowest cephalo-facial indices, and the lowest relative sitting heights of all the Eskimos considered . . .' They are also among the tallest. Otherwise, from a peak of stature in the central Arctic the groups to the east and west seem to drop down in size. Also, relative sitting height or the sitting-height index, which is the same thing, seems to increase in South-western Alaska.

The sitting-height index is the ratio between sitting height and stature; in other words, the percentage of stature represented by the combined trunk and head heights. Therefore, as the index increases the component of stature comprising the legs decreases in length. Also, as the legs decrease in relative length, so do the arms, since the ratio between the arm and leg lengths is fairly constant within a group. The Eskimos have, therefore, relatively short extremities and this is regarded as further evidence of the group's membership in the Mongoloid racial stock. According to a popular theory accounting for the origin of the Mongoloids, shortened extremities resulted from the selective pressure of an extremely cold environment over a long period of time [41]. It is thought that the Eskimos lack a prominent nose for the same reason. Short extremities and an unobtrusive nose are said to be less subject to frost-bite. Be this as it may, the Eskimos' physique does seem to afford them an environmental advantage.

On the physiological side, the Eskimos' adaptation to the cold is intermediate in some respects between that of the Alakaluf Indians already described and that of the Whites; in other words, it is not as impressive as the climate would lead one to expect. It will be remembered, however, that unlike the Alakaluf, who originally had nothing much in the way of clothing, the Eskimos had the most efficient clothing so far as defense against the cold is concerned. Perhaps this warm clothing, along with a rich protein and fat diet, made further physiological adaptation unnecessary – or caused it to be lost, if the Eskimos ever had it.

Not to be overlooked in this connection are the changes in the Eskimos' way of life which contacts with Whites have brought about. In particular their diet has undergone considerable change following the establishment of trading posts in their communities. This makes it easy for the Eskimos to substitute white-man's food for native food, with a resultant reduction in the nutritive value of their diet. Not only has the introduced food lowered the metabolic levels that help protect against cold, but it has adversely affected growth and development.

The clearest evidence of physical deterioration following this dietary change is in the teeth. In 1932, after having examined the mouths of 296 natives in nine population centers along the Alaskan coast, Henry B. Collins of the Smithsonian Institution came to the conclusion that caries had increased materially among the Eskimo since they came into contact with civilization and that change in diet was the main cause. As long as they had adhered to their native diet of sea mammals and fish, rich in essential elements and requiring hard usage of the teeth and jaws, dental decay and crowding of the teeth had been practically unknown. Deterioration begins when soft, manufactured foods are supplemented and increases in direct proportion to the extent that they are consumed [36, p. 460].

Changes in the Eskimos' original way of life have accelerated rapidly since the 1930s, and especially as a result of the many military installations for defense purposes constructed during and after World War II and the still more recent intensive exploitation of the Arctic's natural resources. Intensified racial contacts are always accompanied, of course, by racial admixture. Whereas earlier the whalers were the main source of foreign genes, now many new sources are present everywhere. Under these circumstances the Eskimos have become more mixed racially and their physical deterioration has increased.

# Aleuts

The Aleutian Islands, as already noted, were among the last of the major American coastal features to be discovered. The vastness of the New World and the slowness and other limitations of the early sailing vessels largely account for the fact that the northwestern part of North America – the part of the New World furthest from Europe – still had not been reached almost two and a half centuries after Columbus' first voyage. All maps up to 1758 based on actual records show nothing east of the Siberian coast in the area now known as Alaska (cf. plate 2).

The neglect of the northern Pacific by the navigators gave the Russians time to advance eastward across Asia and to reach the coast of Siberia in the vicinity of the Kamchatka peninsula around the beginning of the eighteenth century. The news of this accomplishment made Peter the Great realize the political importance of knowing the relationship of his eastern territories to America [63]. Accordingly, as early as 1718 he ordered two of his officers 'to go to Kamchatka and farther . . ., and determine whether Asia and America are united'. Nothing came of this first effort and hence it was not until 1724, when he assigned the same mission to Fleet-Captain Bering, that a real effort got under way.

The assignment was not an easy one, because it meant constructing seaworthy ships in far-away Kamchatka and voyaging into uncharted water in high latitudes. But Bering was equal to the challenge, not only because of his courage and organizational ability, but because he could command the help he needed, and because, before joining the Russian navy and while still a citizen of Denmark, he had gained navigational experience on two voyages to the East Indies.

The logistics of moving the necessary supplies, equipment and men from St Petersburg overland eastward through the vast stretches of European and Asiatic Russia – much of the way through territories still occupied by native tribes – was in itself formidable. This part of the expedition got under way in January, 1725, and concluded with Bering's arrival in Kamchatka in the early spring of 1728. The first vessel was completed on 10 July of that year and named the *St Gabriel*. Immediately Bering sailed her northward along the coast through the strait now called after him (but failed to see the American coast across the way) and into the Chukchi Sea, where finally on 15 August he turned back. Although Bering had established nothing more than the discontinuity of Asia and America, he still felt justified in returning to St Petersburg in person to give his report.

Much of the coast of northeastern Siberia explored by Bering, especially that occupied by the Chukchi near the strait, had not yet been taken over by the Russians. Therefore, Bering's report of this country led the Russians to advance in that direction in the years immediately following his arrival in St Petersburg. When they did so, they learned from the Chukchi about the rumored existence of a 'large country' to the east. But was it part of the American mainland or just an island? To settle this point, the local administrator was ordered to commandeer the *St Gabriel* in the spring of 1732 and to arrange for Michael Gvozdev to sail her eastward from East Cape in search of the reported 'large country'. When he did so in August, he reported sighting four 'islands' – possibly the Diomedes and part of the Alaskan coast. Although these sightings impressed very few and Gvozdev least of all, they now suggest that he was the first European to set eyes on the eastern side of Bering Strait.

## Bering and the Aleuts

In St Petersburg Bering found that the results of his voyage did not satisfy the questions asked by the authorities regarding the location and extent of the American shoreline. Also, Gvozdev's voyage raised more questions than it answered. All of this led to authorization being given Bering for a second expedition directed generally eastward from Kamchatka. The authorization also called for two new ships to be built and the recently founded Imperial Academy of Sciences to be represented on the voyage.

Again the logistics of getting everything and everybody to the Pacific and the ships built and under way was formidable – even more so than on the first expedition. Just how formidable is indicated by the long interval of time between the departure of the first detachments from St Petersburg (February, 1733) and the sailing of the ships (June, 1741): over eight years.

Continuing the tradition of naming the ships used on these expeditions after saints, the one commanded by Bering was called the *St Peter* and the other (with Alexei Chirikov as captain) the *St Paul*. On 19 June, sixteen days out from port, the ships lost sight of each other and did not regain contact during the rest of the voyage, although they pursued roughly parallel courses. On 15 July Chirikov discovered land – one of the small islands west of Prince of Wales Island in what is now southeastern Alaska; and on 16 July Bering saw in the distance Mt Elias, an 18,000-foot peak at the southwestern angle of the boundary between Alaska and Canada's Yukon Territory.

Chirikov sent fifteen members of the *St Paul*'s crew in the vessel's two boats to investigate his landfall. They did not return at the appointed time and in this situation Chirikov dared not take the ship into the shallow waters in search of them. Presumably the men were seized by the local natives, some of whom were seen at a distance in canoes.

Bering also sent members of the *St Peter*'s crew to investigate an island near his landfall, but only a single boatload. These men were fortunate, perhaps, to avoid capture, since they returned with evidence of recent human occupation. Thereupon both navigators, by previous agreement, followed the coast northward, and turned with it when they found it trending southwestward and eventually westward.

The reason for reporting Bering's voyages in so much detail up to this point, aside from focusing attention on their great general significance, is to provide a background for an episode involving the Aleuts. Since this episode involves only Bering and the *St Peter*, we need not follow Chirikov and the *St Paul* further.

Surprisingly, in view of what was known then about scurvy, Bering had not provided proper food and medicines and as a result more and more of his crew became incapacitated on account of this disease. He himself suffered from it and probably it contributed to his death later that fall on Bering Island just off Kamchatka. But even more worrying by 27 August, after head winds had delayed progress homeward, was the shortage of fresh water. Accordingly, the decision was made to go in search of water on the land judged to lie to the north. Two days later they sighted some islands – the Shumagin group, which are just south of the western end of the Alaska Peninsula (fig. 18). Although these islands were Aleut territory, they may not have been used for human habitation, except seasonally for fishing and hunting sea mammals. In any case, it was on one of these islands – probably Bird Island – that the first meeting between Aleuts and Europeans occurred.

Lieutenant Sven Waxel reported the episode in the following words [63, I, p. 274]:

... About noon on the 5th [of September] we heard a loud noise and saw two men, who sat in two *baidarkas* rowing towards our ship. When they came within fifty fathoms of us they stopped and called to us in their tongue, which our interpreters of the Chukchi and Koriak languages could not make out. Our interpreters hailed them in Koriak and in Chukchi, and it was evident that they could not understand, because they pointed to their ears, waved their hands to us, and motioned to the shore. After this, one of the two approached much closer to our ship but would not come alongside. At the order of the Captain Commander [Bering] we threw to him, tied on a board, several arshins of red (Chinese) silk, mirrors, iron pipes for smoking Chinese tobacco (called *shar*), and several small copper bells. He seemed to receive these gifts with pleasure, and in return he threw to us two thin sticks planed smooth, to one of which were tied birds' feathers and to the other a bird's claw with the feathers on, which feathers we identified as that of the hawk. When we had accepted the presents the Americans pulled

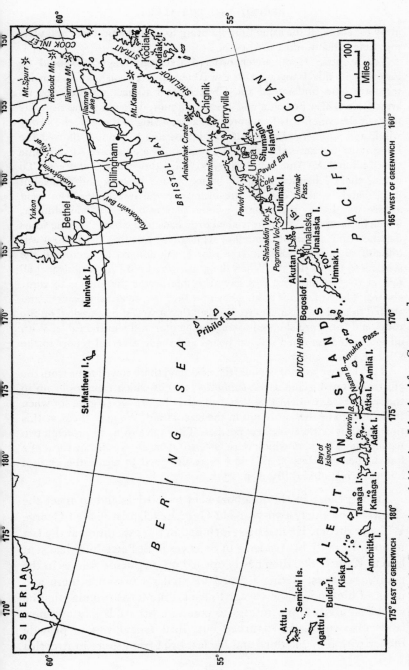

Fig. 18 The Alaska Peninsula and Aleutian Islands. After Capps [30]

away for shore, at the same time shouting to us in a loud voice and waving their hands toward the beach.

The Captain Commander ordered that the longboat should be lowered; in this I was sent to the Americans. I took with me an interpreter who understood the Chukchi and Koriak tongues, several armed men, also presents and Russian liquor. When I came near the place of the Americans I anchored because, owing to the surf, the strong wind, and submerged rocks, it was impossible to land. I allowed the interpreter and several men of my party to wade ashore. At the same time I offered the Americans presents, which they would not accept. To one of them I handed a cup of liquor, which he took and drank but immediately spat it out. In the meantime the interpreter who went ashore was led to their camp, where he was offered whale blubber, which he accepted. When he wished to go back to the boat the Americans detained him and would not allow it; just how fast they held him it was difficult to say. In order to free him I was obliged to command the soldiers to fire in the air. When the guns were fired [the Americans] all fell on the ground, and this gave the interpreter the chance to come aboard. The Americans made a dash for the boat, seized the painter, and started to haul the boat ashore. I feared that it would be smashed on the rocks and therefore shouted to cut the painter and slip the cable. With all my men I returned safe on board and made a verbal report to the Captain Commander . . .

. . . While we were at anchor [the next day] there rowed to us from the aforementioned island seven *baidarkas*, two of which came right up to the ship. It was evident that they had never before seen a gun, for when they came to us they were not in the least afraid. We gave them at this time an iron kettle and a few needles. They gave to us as presents two hats made of bark on which were fastened ivory images in the form of a human being. (Hats of this sort were designed to shade the eyes of hunters while at sea) [63, I, p. 274].

Among those in the longboat sent to Bird Island to meet the Aleuts was a thirty-two-year-old German scientist named George Wilhelm Steller. He had been included in the expedition at the last minute. In 1738 the Academy of Sciences in St Petersburg had sent him to Kamchatka, then newly opened up, to pursue studies in the natural sciences. Bering learned of Steller's presence there and induced him to join the voyage to America, on the promise that he would be given opportunities to continue his studies in any new lands discovered. As it turned out, Bird Island was to provide Steller with only his third and his last brief trip ashore in America

[63]. From his standpoint he had become involved in 'a six months' miserable sea voyage [productive of] few useful discoveries'. Yet despite the intruding natural resentment for the way he was treated, Steller's account of the voyage is far more interesting and informative from the anthropologist's standpoint than those of the ship's officers.

Included in Steller's report is a description of the Aleuts encountered on Bird Island – the first description of any members of this human group:

As far as the personal appearance of the islanders is concerned, of whom I counted on the beach nine, mostly young or middle-aged people, they are of medium stature, strong and stocky, yet fairly well proportioned, and with very fleshy arms and legs. The hair of the head is glossy black and hangs straight down all around the head. The face is brownish, a little flat and concave. The nose is also flattened, though not particularly broad or large. The eyes are as black as coals, the lips prominent and turned up. In addition they have short necks, broad shoulders, and their body is plump though not big-bellied.

. . . I observed also on all these Americans that they had a very scant beard, but most of them none at all, in which respect they . . . agree with the inhabitants of Kamchatka [63, II, pp. 96, 104].

As is evident in the foregoing quotations, neither Waxel nor Steller had any way of designating the inhabitants of Bird Island except by calling them Americans or natives. The word 'Aleut' was introduced after 1742 by the Russians and is of obscure origin. More properly these Americans should be referred to as *Unangan*, their own general name for themselves, but the name bestowed upon them is now too firmly established to be replaced.

The subsequent exploration of Alaska by the Russians and such famous navigators as Cook (1776–9) and George Vancouver (1791–4) filled in many geographical details but added nothing to the anthropological picture that needs to be considered here.

Hrdlička could not determine from the historical records the eastern limit of the territory occupied by the Aleuts and assumed it to be somewhere in the Alaska Peninsula, including the Shumagin Islands [93]. The total population of this territory is believed to have reached at least 16,000 and possibly as much as 25,000. Yet, since the latter part of the eighteenth century when counts of uncertain reliability began to be recorded, the total has rarely exceeded 2,500. Probably the decline set in soon after the first contacts with Whites and was due, as among most of the American peoples, first of all to the introduction of diseases to which immunity was lacking, and secondarily to the barbarity of the Whites.

### Anthropometric observations on the Aleuts

By 1860 when physical anthropology first became an organized science, the opportunity to study Aleuts free from foreign admixture must already have been lost. This assumption is based on the fact that they lived mostly on small islands favoring inbreeding, and on the fact that foreign genes spread faster as the population declines. Certainly Hrdlička saw only mixed bloods during his visits in 1936–8 [93], and this convinced him that the group of 138 measured by the wife of Waldemar Jochelson in 1909–10 [104] was also made up of mixed-bloods. Anyway, Mrs Jochelson's work, which is the only attempt at scientific anthropometry among the Aleuts during the first 169 years of their known history, yielded a mean cephalic index of eighty-four. She seems to have measured only the head.

Hrdlička's discouraging attitude towards the racial status of the Aleuts was not shared by one student member of his 1938 field party – William S. Laughlin, now at the University of Connecticut. Laughlin took his graduate work at Harvard University and in the process organized the Peabody Museum Aleutian Expedition of 1948. Besides serving as field director, he concentrated on measuring samples of the living population on three islands: Attu, one of the Near Islands at the western end of the Aleutian chain; Atka, one of the Andreanof Islands in the middle; and Umnak (Nikolski), one of the Fox islands near the eastern end (fig. 18).

The details are not readily accessible since the study is still in the form of a doctoral thesis [116]. Fortunately, however, the main conclusions have been summarized elsewhere [106]. On the basis of statistical differences in twenty to thirty measurements and indices, Laughlin suggested that it is possible to separate the Eastern from the Western Aleutian populations. The metric data indicate that the Aleut population is closer to Eskimo than to Indian populations, and that it is most closely related to a small series from the Bristol Bay area.

We will leave the Aleuts at this point since there is nothing more of general interest in the area of physical anthropology to report. Let me repeat again that it has been necessary here and in the preceding chapters on the living to present a 'broad-brush picture' and therefore to omit much detail. I hope, however, that the selected highlights make quite clear how poorly the native peoples have fared since their discovery and how imperfectly the scientific knowledge of their physiques has been studied in the last century. It so happens that this is as true of the last coastal residents to be discovered – the Aleuts – as of the first – the West Indian Arawak.

# 8

# The emerging archeological picture: The Paleo-Indian, Archaic and Formative periods

In the Introduction I likened the pre- and post-Columbian periods of American history to the submerged and exposed parts respectively of an iceberg. I wished to convey by this simile, as it relates to the native population, the idea that the submerged (pre-Columbian) part is larger and less accessible than the exposed (post-Columbian) part. Viewed in this way, the examination of the more accessible post-Columbian period and the eye-witness records of its living population have been completed. Turning to the less accessible pre-Columbian period and the chance records (skeletons mostly) of its ancient population, we will be looking for answers to questions suggested by all that has been related up to this point. What is the earliest type of man in the hemisphere? Is there evidence of successive waves of immigration? Was the original population altered by accretions other than those crossing Bering Strait? What is the evidence of cultural practices registered in the human remains?

The shift of attention from living populations to skeletal populations involves also a shift of dependence for cultural information from the field of ethnology to the field of archeology. According to one of the current historians of the latter field – Glyn Daniel of Cambridge University – archeology, like physical anthropology, had its modern beginning around the middle of the nineteenth century [43]. Daniel argues for the year 1866 being the beginning point, since it was then that the first meeting was held in Neuchâtel of what the next year was to be called the *Congrès International d'Anthropologie et d'Archaeologie Prehistorique*. In America, the year 1866 was the date of the founding of Harvard University's Peabody Museum of Archaeology and Ethnology. In any case, only during the past century has an impressive record of American prehistory been collected together and significant samples of the population from the several constituent periods been accumulated. In other words, the study of America's past is a relatively late development so far as the story of the native population is concerned.

### Cultural development in prehistoric times

For the present purpose the current record of American prehistory can best be illustrated by what is known about the course of cultural development. In 1960 Gordon Willey of Harvard University assembled the pertinent information in three charts, and I have heightened their dramatic effect by rearranging the three into two, one for each continent (figs. 19 and 20). Although no finds for the succeeding years are included, there is no reason to believe that the overall picture has changed essentially. The points to note particularly are, firstly, the earlier and more intense cultural progress which occurred in the area designated 'Nuclear America'; secondly, the similarity of the developmental patterns in the two continents when the separation between the two centers of Nuclear America is made just below Middle America; and thirdly, the time depth for which documentation is available.

The concept of Nuclear America as an area of accelerated cultural progress, which comes out so strikingly in each of Willey's charts, was given its first clear enunciation – albeit without the use of the name – by Herbert Spinden at the XIX International Congress of Americanists in Washington in 1915 [187]. His maps on the hemispheric distributions of the so-called 'Archaic' culture, pottery and agriculture show in each case essentially the same limits for a culturally most-advanced area centering around Mexico and Peru. For many years, however, the lack of a convenient name for the area in question limited the references to it. Thus, it was not

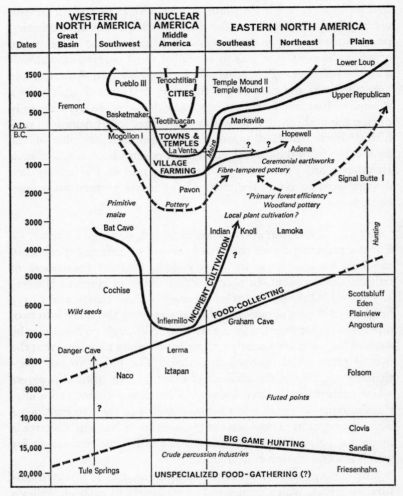

Fig. 19 Diagram showing 20,000 years of differential cultural development in the northern center of Nuclear America and in eastern and western North America. After Willey [239]

until the 29th meeting of the same Congress, held in New York in 1949, when both Wendell Bennett and Duncan Strong used the present designation in their papers, that the concept gained full currency [10, 221].

It is noteworthy in passing that Nuclear America is one of three

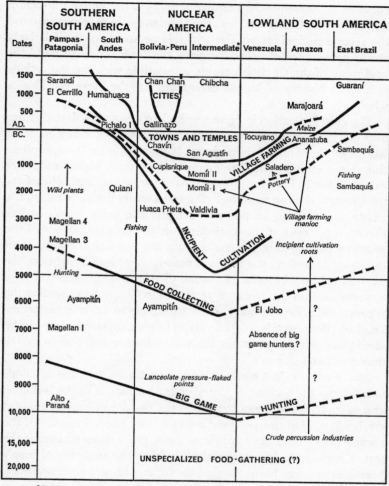

Fig. 20 Diagram showing 20,000 years of differential cultural development in the southern center of Nuclear America and in southern and lowland South America. After Willey [239]

such areas in the world – the other two are the Near East and China – where early high civilizations arose independently on foundations of comparable but different food-producing economies. The nuclear center in the Near East was the earliest, its stage of a complex urbanized society dating perhaps to the fourth millenium BC, and that in China was next, the same stage there coming around the second millenium BC. Seen in this perspective, the relatively recent appearance of urbanization in the New World (around the beginning of the Christian era) is compatible with the indications of a short history of human occupancy for the New World as a whole.

The clear indication in figures 19 and 20 of intermediate cultures between the highest and lowest at the AD 1500 level bears out what was briefly mentioned on page 77. It also confirms the complication that anything more than a simple dichotomy (higher and lower cultures) would have introduced into my organizational scheme for the chapters dealing with the living Indians. By the same token, the whole post-Columbian period – roughly 500 years – may be less than two per cent of the total duration of man's occupancy of the Western Hemisphere. In considering the pre-Columbian part of the story, therefore, the time element is more important than the cultural element in so far as human physique is concerned. I base this assertion on the evidence presented in Chapter 3 regarding the regional variations in body size attributable to environmental influences (Bergmann's rule). So far as known, no such effect can be attributed to culture within the much shorter interval in which major cultural changes have occurred.

Attention is called also to the differences in the time intervals listed under the heading of 'dates' on the left side of Willey's charts: 500 years at the top, 1,000 years in the middle and 5,000 years at the bottom. Had the 500-year interval been used throughout, the named sites would have appeared much more concentrated at the top. This is in keeping with the fact that the evidence of man's presence becomes harder to find the further back in time one goes, because population density has been rather steadily increasing, as has the amount of time the erosional processes have had to destroy the evidence. And if this is true of the cultural evidence upon which the charts are based, it is even truer of the skeletal evidence; the latter is much more dependent upon environmental factors for survival than most of the former. Not surprisingly, therefore, the sites named on these charts are not necessarily the ones which have yielded the most significant skeletal remains.

*Claimed finds of early man*

As a general rule, the rarer things are the more they are esteemed. In anthropology the rarest things are the finds, both cultural and physical, relating to the most ancient human beings. If the oldest find on record is, say, 20,000 years old, then anyone who finds something older than this is assured of good publicity, because of the fascination which the history of the human race holds for scientist and layman alike. On the other hand, the circumstances of each claim had better be well documented for otherwise they will surely be challenged.

# Lagoa Santa (Brazil)

The working of this rule in a few actual finds of putatively ancient American skeletal remains exposes the many vicissitudes and un-certainties besetting this subject. Take, for instance, the first find suggesting considerable antiquity, namely, that at Lagoa Santa (Brazil) in 1835–44 [82]. News of the find reached Europe and North America in a series of letters from the discoverer – Peter Wilhelm Lund, a Danish naturalist – or from local correspondents and was spread by publication in scientific journals, sometimes simultaneously in several. The essence of the news was that in the course of exploring more and more of the caves (ultimately over 800) in the Lagoa Santa region of the State of Minas Gerais, a little more than 200 miles north of Rio de Janeiro, Lund had found the bones of humans and extinct Pleistocene animals associated in a way suggestive of contemporaneity. Although he usually expressed his opinions cautiously, as was prudent in those pre-Darwin times, he ended up (1844) with the conclusion that 'a number of species seem to have disappeared from the ranks of the creation since the appearance of man in this hemisphere'; and that the people who occupied South America in 'remote antiquity' were of the same general type as those who inhabited the country at the time of its discovery by Europeans.

I have stated elsewhere [201] that the scientific world of Lund's day accepted his finds and unorthodox conclusions with a calmness that, in retrospect, belies the later controversies surrounding them. Throughout the remainder of the nineteenth century the antiquity of the Lagoa Santa remains came in for discussion mainly when the human bones were subjected to anthropometric study. While agreeing with Lund that the remains are of the modern form, the tendency of many authorities was to reserve judgment on the matter of antiquity in view of the lack of any means of exact dating.

In 1912, however, Hrdlička, who was waging a campaign to discredit all American claimants to considerable antiquity, denied Lund's conclusions simply on internal evidence and not on the basis of anything new [82]. Since Hrdlička's denial of antiquity in this case followed his review of the accumulated evidence from the whole hemisphere, the forcefulness of his arguments was impressive.

Reversal of this situation did not come until a quarter of a century later (1937) when an International Symposium on Early Man was held at the Academy of Natural Sciences in Philadelphia. Among those presenting new evidence of man's antiquity was a trio from Brazil – H. V. Walter, A. Cathoud and Anabal Mattos [233]. Their contribution, read by title and published in full in English, reports the finding in one of the Lagoa Santa caves (Confins) of a deliberately-buried human skeleton in a stratum containing bones of extinct Upper Pleistocene animals such as the mastodon and horse. The authors took care to point out that this need not necessarily imply that Confins man was of great age, since other studies in the region had shown that certain Pleistocene mammals still survived when man first appeared in the Rio das Velhas Valley.

A means of tackling the dating problem was provided in the 1950s through a revival of the fluorine test widely used in Europe in the nineteenth century. This is a method of relative dating in which the percentages of fluorine in human and associated animal bones are compared. Theoretically, the amount of fluorine taken up by buried bones from percolating ground water increases with time. Moreover, similarity of the amounts of fluorine in the two kinds of bones is believed to indicate contemporaneity. To find out what the test would tell about Walter's Confins Cave bones, I arranged in 1954 to have samples sent to Washington for testing [219]. The results showed fairly large and similar amounts of fluorine in all of the samples. On this basis the human bones appeared to be both ancient and contemporary with the animal bones.

At this point (1956) the Museu Nacional of Brazil and the University of South Dakota jointly sponsored a project under the direction of Wesley R. Hurt, Jr., an archeologist from the latter institution, to explore certain Lagoa Santa caves and rock shelters with modern techniques. In reporting the results of this work in 1960, Hurt states that

In none of the caves . . . was there any evidence whatsoever that man was contemporaneous with the extinct Pleistocene animals such as horse, cave bear, or ground sloth. In the Gruta de Lapa do Chapeu a tooth of a mammal tentatively identified as a camel was found in a bed containing sherds, clearly an example of secondary deposition. In the other caves and rock shelters the fossil bones lay below the strata containing human bones and midden deposits [95, p. 583].

And he went on to say: 'The fact that no evidence was found in the caves of Lagoa Santa of Pleistocene man by the 1956 project does not in itself prove that other caves in the region may not have been so occupied.'

This qualification turned out to be a wise precaution, because in 1962 the University of South Dakota reported $C_{14}$ dates for occupation levels of Rock Shelter No 6, excavated in 1956, that give the finds at this site an entirely different significance [2]. Levels 2 and 3, at 1–1·5 meters, had an average age of 9,311 ± 120 years (7349 BC); and Levels 6 and 7, at 2–2·5 meters, had an average age of 10,024 ± 127 years (8052 BC). The report pointed out that, although no bones of extinct animals were found in the human occupation deposits, on the basis of other finds in the Lagoa Santa area it seemed possible that these hunters of 10,000 years ago were acquainted with giant forms of cave bear and armadillos. They used projectiles tipped with square-stemmed points; and the presence of pitted hammerstones suggests that they cracked vegetable products such as small palm nuts with these implements.

Who can say whether this is the end of the story? Anyway, the interpretational vicissitudes of this first American early-man find, including the remaining uncertainty as to its true status, typify in many respects most of the other skeletal finds for which a considerable antiquity has been claimed. Today few of the multitude of human bones once believed to be old – and by old I mean dating back 10,000 years or more – are still taken as seriously as formerly.

Elimination on such a scale would favor the idea of man's relative recency in America, and especially South America, were it not for the more promising replacements and the newer dating techniques applicable to a wider variety of substances. Actually, since ancient human bones are seldom recovered, most of the effort today is being directed toward the dating of the more plentiful ancient cultural remains.

# Ayacucho Valley (Peru)

For example, recent reports from the southern center of Nuclear America suggest that caves in that region were occupied before those of Lagoa Santa [120, 121]. The locale of the new find is the high Ayacucho Valley in the south-central Peruvian Andes. While exploring caves there in 1969, R.S.MacNeish of the Robert S. Peabody Foundation for Archaeology in Andover, Massachusetts, found crude artifacts 'in direct association with bones of extinct animals, two of which have not been previously found in association with man' [121]. Fortunately, just prior to this discovery one of MacNeish's collaborators, Rainer Berger of the University of California at Los Angeles, had developed a new technique for $C_{14}$ determination utilizing the organic element of bone (collagen) as the source of the carbon to be tested. In the present case Berger used one of the extinct animal bones from the top of the artifact zone for testing purposes and obtained from it a collagen date of 12181 $\pm$ 180 BC. The investigators conclude their report with a pertinent question: 'If man was well south in the Andes of South America by at least 13000 BC, when did he first enter South America?'

The fact that the first and most recent reports of early man in America have come from Brazil and Peru should not be taken to mean that most of the attention has been focused on the southern continent. If anything, similar finds in North America have received wider attention, as will be shown presently. In the early days, however, South America had a large number of claimants to great antiquity, greater than for most of those in North America. This was owing especially to the energetic collecting of the Ameghino brothers in Argentina and to their consistent over-estimation of the ages of the geological strata containing the bones and/or artifacts. Only when Hrdlička, with the aid of the geologist Bailey Willis, successfully reduced the geological ages of these specimens from Pliocene (pre-Pleistocene) to Recent did it become clear that little remained of any consequence – other than at Lagoa Santa – elsewhere in the southern continent [82].

Hrdlička's campaign to discredit the putatively ancient human skeletal remains in South America had followed a similar campaign in North America [79]. Here, too, most of the finds proved to be vulnerable to his arguments. In a few instances, however, some of the circumstances resembled those in Lagoa Santa and again his arguments never entirely prevailed for much the same reasons. Also, subsequent developments have changed the picture considerably. A few examples will show the direction of the change.

## Natchez, Mississippi (US)

One of the first North American skeletal finds for which a likely claim of antiquity was advanced is a partial right hip bone or innominate uncovered at the base of a high cliff near Natchez, Mississippi, in a clayey deposit two feet below three associated skeletons of '*Megalonyx*' (an extinct sloth-like creature) [79]. In October of 1846 M.W. Dickesen of Natchez, who engaged in geological activities in the southeastern part of the United States, presented this human bone and the bones of the associated extinct animals (including also some identified as *Mastodon* and *Equus*) to the Philadelphia Academy of Natural Sciences. In announcing the gift, the Academy characterized the human bone as 'an ancient relic of our species' [79].

The Academy's characterization of the Natchez innominate reflects the publicity which earlier had attended the discovery, and which in March of 1846 had led the English geologist Sir Charles Lyell, while making his second tour of the United States, to visit the site and to inspect the collection of bones. Lyell later (1849) described the site and his impression of the find as follows:

I examined the perpendicular cliffs, which bound a part of this watercourse, where the loam, unsolidified as it is, retains its verticality, and found land-shells in great numbers at the depth of about thirty feet from the top. I was informed that the fossil remains of the mammoth (a name commonly applied in the United States to the mastodon) had been obtained, together with the bones of some other extinct mammalia, from below these shells in the undermined cliff. I could not ascertain, however, that the human pelvis had been actually dug out in the presence of a geologist, or any practiced observer, and its position un-equivocally ascertained. Like most of the other fossils, it was, I believe, picked up in the bed of the stream, which would simply imply that it had been washed out of the cliffs. But the evidence of the antiquity of the bone depends entirely on the part of the precipice from which it was derived. It was stained black, as if buried in a peaty or vegetable soil, and may have been dislodged from some old Indian grave near the top, in which case it may only have been five, ten, or twenty centuries old; whereas, if it was really found in situ at the base of the precipice, its age would more probably exceed 100,000 years [119, II, p. 151].

Lyell's skepticism and the generally-acknowledged modern character of the innominate were all that Hrdlička needed in 1907 to discredit the antiquity of the find. Although he did not place much stress on the modern character of the bone in this instance, usually he automatically charged a lack of antiquity to any human bone, particularly a skull, which was indistinguishable in his opinion from that of a present-day Indian. In effect, he argued that the antiquity of a skeletal find was proportional to its primitive appearance. Since he held that the Indians were of recent origin, skeletal finds indistinguishable from the remains of Indians, even though found in situations suggesting antiquity, could not be ancient. In 1949 I labeled this concept 'morphological dating' to distinguish it from geological dating as explained by Lyell above [201]. It is to be distinguished also from Oakley's 'chronometric dating' [148] which became important after the introduction of the $C_{14}$ and other isotopic tests for age.

The next development in the case of the Natchez innominate came in 1951 when I discovered by accident and called attention to a 'lost' reference to this specimen in the literature [203]. A 'lost' reference is one that has been overlooked and not cited for a long time. What had happened was that in 1895 Thomas Wilson, then Curator of Prehistoric Archeology in the National Museum in Washington, had reported the results of testing for fluorine a sample of the human bone against that of one of the associated sloth-like bones (now called *Mylodon*) [240]. Both samples proved to contain similar amounts of fluorine and enough to indicate a respectable antiquity. Although this report must have attracted some attention at the time of publication, no one who had not read it could detect its significance from the ambiguous title: 'On the presence of fluorine as a test for the fossilization of animal bones.' The record of this early Mississippian rests at this point.

## Melbourne, Florida (US)

Let us consider next a North American example of putatively early man from the first quarter of this century: the Melbourne (Florida) find. I have selected this find partly because of some curious twists in a history that is otherwise rather similar to the foregoing, and partly because of my own involvement with it.

In 1925, the year this find was made, I was serving as temporary assistant to Hrdlička in the National Museum in Washington and seeking ways to gain more insight into the field of anthropology. Accordingly, when I learned about the annual meeting of the American Anthropological Association, scheduled to be held at Yale University in New Haven, Connecticut, during the Christmas holidays, I made arrangements to attend. The highlight of that occasion for me was a session of the Paleontological Society – meeting simultaneously in New Haven – which was opened at the last moment to interested anthropologists. Apparently word had got around that J.W. Gidley, Assistant Curator in the Division of Fossil Vertebrates at the National Museum, was presenting a new early-man find from Florida and Hrdlička had requested that the session be opened to the anthropologists. Needless to say, the anthropologists appeared in full force, mainly, I suspect, in the hope of hearing a heated debate between Gidley and Hrdlička, neither of whom had any love for the other (Gidley published for private distribution a series of tracts, entitled 'Anthropological Scraps', savagely attacking Hrdlička's writings). The session went off quietly, however, and Hrdlička's invited discussion of Gidley's paper merely emphasized the division of opinion that existed over man's antiquity in America.

As for the find itself, Gidley described it generally as a geologic horizon or layer, primarily deposited and definitely of Pleistocene age, in which human bones were associated with fossil bones of the Pleistocene fauna. But he attached greatest importance to a crushed human skull which he had removed from this layer in its entirety by the paleontological technique of enclosure in plaster-of-Paris, and which he exhibited to the audience as if it were a roast on a platter – truly a *pièce de résistance*. To top off the show he stated as a possibility that the crushed state of the skull was due to its having been stepped on by one of the mastodons or mammoths whose bones had been found in association.

Gidley died in 1931. A few years later the Melbourne skull, still on its plaster platter, was transferred to the Division of Physical Anthropology and thereupon Hrdlička seized the opportunity to disprove its claim to antiquity. Since he was unable to tell from its crushed state whether or not it looked like a recent Indian skull, he assigned to the Division's laborer the task of removing the fragments from the platter and reassembling them into the original form. I was present when Hrdlička gave the directions for this procedure and heard him tell the laborer to make a ball of plasticine of head size for the support of the fragments as they were removed and fitted together. As it happened, the laborer made the ball round and thereon pieced together a skull reflecting this roundness.

Hrdlička was satisfied with the restored skull and never inspected it closely. His satisfaction was due to the support which the roundness lent to his view of the skull's lack of antiquity. In his studies of recent Indian crania he had discovered that those from Florida were roundheaded and he saw no reason, therefore, to regard the Melbourne specimen as any older than these recent Indians. The evidence – another example of morphological dating – was part of his contribution to the 1937 International Symposium on Early Man mentioned earlier [91].

In turn, Hrdlička died in 1943. As his successor, I now took charge of the Melbourne skull and investigated the restoration which he had supervised. In short, by removing the fragments from the ball of plasticine, fitting them together by their edges and letting the overall form of the restoration follow therefrom, I ended up with a longhead [198]. Consequently, the Melbourne skull can be regarded as different from the recent population and to this extent once more an acceptable candidate for the early-man category.

The next step, of course, was to test the Melbourne bones for fluorine. Robert Heizer and Sherburne Cook of the University of California in Berkeley took the initiative in this instance [71].

Their comment (p. 299) on the test results supports the indication of the second skull restoration:

The human sample is slightly lower than the mammoth and horse bone in fluorine [0·096% vs. 0·116% and 0·119%, respectively], and is intermediate between the horse and mammoth in carbon, nitrogen and water. The data, so far as they go, are quite constant and it thus appears that the human sample is of the same order of antiquity as those of the extinct mammals . . . [in other words] that man was present in Florida prior to the final extinction of some elements of the Pleistocene fauna.

Unfortunately, this is not the last word on the subject. Overlooked in interpreting the fluorine tests is the low elevation of the site relative to sea level – no part of the Melbourne area (located midway down the east coast of the peninsula) is more than 20 feet above the sea. This fact suggests that both the human and animal bones may have been affected, either directly or indirectly, by their proximity to sea water, which has a high fluorine content. The question arises, therefore, whether the water that bathed the bones in the ground carried enough fluorine to equalize the fluorine content of the bones regardless of their ages. The possibility that this may have been the case makes it seem doubtful that the results of the tests prove the contemporaneity of all the bones found in association.

## Laguna Beach, California (US)

The third and last early-man example which I will present brings the subject up to date for North America, much as does the Ayacucho (Peru) example for South America. Like the latter, the locale of the North American example is on the west coast, but near sea level rather than at high altitude, at Laguna Beach, California. The find was made in 1933 by W. Howard Wilson, then an amateur archeologist in his teens. Having heard reports of Indian skeletons being uncovered in grading operations for some new buildings, Wilson investigated the excavations and was rewarded by finding at a depth of five feet parts of a skull and an incomplete long bone said to be a tibia. In the course of the next ten years or so he showed these bones to a number of scientists in several California institutions and around 1953 permitted Dr J. J. Markey of Oceanside, California, to take them to Paris, Rome, Madrid, Brussels and

London for appraisal by some of the leading anthropologists of those cities. Everyone agreed that the skull, in spite of its modern form, looked old (an incrustation of calcite heightened this impression), but no one would hazard a guess as to its age.

Discouraged by the reports, Wilson put the bones aside and forgot about them until 1967 when L.S.B.Leakey, the discoverer of several ancient men in East Africa, came to California to lecture. Then someone remembered the earlier local find and arranged for Wilson to show the specimens to Leakey. The latter was much impressed and saw in these specimens support for his belief that Hrdlička to the contrary, man has been in America far longer than generally believed. Consequently, since Rainer Berger had already perfected his method of $C_{14}$-dating of bone collagen, as already mentioned, Leakey persuaded Wilson to allow Berger to take samples of the bones for testing.

Unlike most of the other early man finds discussed here, that from Laguna Beach had been redeposited and probably had been washed down from the nearby mountains. Recent extensive supplementary excavations in the area of the find failed to yield more human bones or any faunal remains, except shells which proved to be of younger age (those above the skull level were older than those below). This accounts for the fact that the age of the human bones had to be determined directly from the bones themselves. In this respect the tests constitute a 'first', at least in so far as the determined age is concerned, namely, $17,150 \pm 1470$ BC. Put in another way, this is the first time that such an early date for man's presence in America has been derived directly from evidence in the form of human bones.* I was privileged to announce this new date at the annual meeting of the American Association of Physical Anthropologists in Mexico City in 1969 [213].

### Newest dates

To understand the impact of such firm early dates as those for Ayacucho and Laguna Beach, it is necessary to take a fuller look at the cultural evidence. Slowly over the years archeologists have

---

* Since this was written a 100-gram sample of skull bone from the so-called Los Angeles Man has yielded a $C_{14}$ (collagen) date of $< 23,600$ years [10a]. The skull was found in 1936 in an excavation for another purpose at the same depth as, and only about 95 feet from, the remains of a mammoth. Failure to obtain a finite date is due to the smallness of the bone sample.

achieved sophistication in the interpretation of chipped stones. Earlier they were easily misled into thinking that American chipped stone artifacts resembling those of established early age in the Old World had to be equally old. Gradually, however, they became critical of the patterns of the artifact assemblages, their geological settings, and even the details of the chipping on the individual pieces. When good documentation was lacking for reported associations of chipped stone blades and bones of extinct animals, discerning archeologists generally withheld acceptance and at most regarded the associations as only a possibility. In this respect the situation closely resembled that for the human bones just discussed as of about 1953. In both areas of investigation conceptual progress was virtually at a standstill for lack of convincing evidence.

The first breakthrough came in 1927 when J.D. Figgins, working at a site near Folsom, New Mexico, for the Colorado Museum of Natural History in Denver, found stone points or blades of distinctive form associated with the bones of an extinct species of bison and induced some of the foremost authorities on the subject to view the specimens *in situ*. By convincing these authorities of the association he convinced almost everyone. The type of blade found at Folsom and now bearing this name is usually distinguished by a rather blunt end, concave beveled base, delicate side chipping, and 'fluting' – evidence of the removal of a flake from a third or more of the length of each side (plate 12). Who would have attributed antiquity to such a masterful example of the stone-chipper's art?

It soon became apparent that fluted blades and obviously related forms occur widely over the United States and in some concentration in the Southwest. And already in the early 1930s another breakthrough came when John L. Cotter, while working for the Academy of Natural Sciences of Philadelphia at a site near Clovis, New Mexico, found larger and cruder fluted blades associated with mammoth bones in a stratum beneath one containing typical Folsom points and extinct bison bones. He concluded from this that the Clovis mammoth hunters had preceded the Folsom bison hunters. Numerous subsequent finds of Clovis sites have verified this conclusion. Plates 12 and 13 show typical Folsom and Clovis points.

Dating of certain of the Clovis sites by $C_{14}$ during the 1950s and 1960s, the next and undoubtedly the most important breakthrough, revealed a surprising situation. As summarized in 1968 by Vance C. Haynes, Jr. [69], a geologist–archeologist at Southern Methodist University in Dallas, Texas, six Clovis sites with satisfactory dates (shown ringed in figure 21) 'meet the chi-square test for a single event at $11,240 \pm 140$ BP. If we double that statistical error there

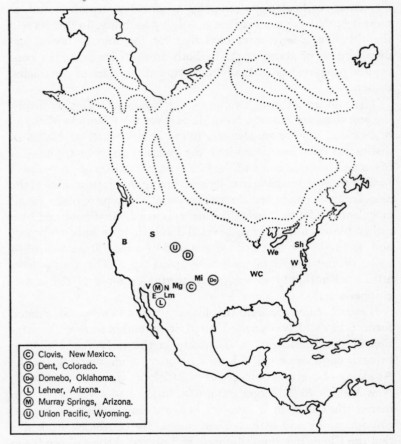

Ⓒ Clovis, New Mexico.
Ⓓ Dent, Colorado.
Ⓓₒ Domebo, Oklahoma.
Ⓛ Lehner, Arizona.
Ⓜ Murray Springs, Arizona.
Ⓤ Union Pacific, Wyoming.

Fig. 21 Dotted lines show the possible position of ice borders in North America about 12,000 BP. The ringed letters, identified in the corner, are Clovis sites that have been dated satisfactorily. After Haynes [69]

is 96 per cent probability that all of these sites were occupied between 10,960 to 11,520 years ago' (between 9550 and 8990 BC).

Haynes was well aware of other finds that might turn out to be older than the Clovis sites, but in 1968 when he was writing, none of these putatively older finds had been accepted. He felt justified, therefore, in repeating his hypothesis, first stated in 1964, to account for the Clovis situation. This was that after the end of the ice age, between 9500 and 9000 BC, mammoth hunters spread from Alaska into central North America, where they found abundant game and untapped resources. This caused something of a population explosion. The phenomenal dispersal of Clovis sites in less than 1,000 years, Haynes concludes, seems most compatible with a migration from the north in response to the removal of the ice block [69].

Getting back to the Ayacucho and Laguna Beach early dates, their impact is to lessen the doubts about a migration from Alaska into the American heartland having occurred before the one hypothesized by Haynes as giving rise explosively to the Clovis and later cultures. While recognizing this shifting attitude, Haynes, like a good debater, insists on every claimant to antiquity beyond 12,000 years – be it a human skeleton or an assemblage of artifacts clearly made by man – meeting two requirements for acceptance [70, p. 714]: (1) The 'evidence must lie *in situ* within undisturbed geological deposits in order to clearly demonstrate the primary association . . . with stratigraphy'; and (2) 'the minimum age of the site must be demonstrable by primary association with fossils of known age or with material suitable for reliable isotopic age dating'. He points out, for example, that *if* the Laguna Beach finds could be validated by stratigraphic documentation, the recent dating would make them the oldest human bones known from the New World.

Haynes' position in this matter does not differ from the traditional position of geologists as expressed in the quotation from Lyell given earlier; it differs from Hrdlička's in emphasizing geological dating (including isotopic dating) to the exclusion of morphological dating. Today anyone advocating it should not be accused of opposing an earlier arrival of man in the New World. Instead, he is simply acting like the apocryphal man from Missouri who always wants to see the proof. As Haynes sees the proof in the form of his requirements [70, p. 714], '[they] have been met repeatedly for the late Paleo-Indian period [11,800 to 7,000 years ago], but they have not yet been satisfactorily met for the middle Paleo-Indian period [28,000 to 11,800 years ago], and our knowledge of the early Paleo-Indian period [over 28,000 years ago] is still hypothetical'.

Haynes is the first to my knowledge to subdivide the time period during which the Paleo-Indians – those early New World hunters of animals now extinct – lived. With his knowledge of geology he finds convenience in subdivisions based on substages of the Wisconsin stage of the last glacial period (see fig. 1). Thus, his late Paleo-Indian period coincides with the Valderan substage and his early Paleo-Indian period coincides, probably in part, with the Altonian substage. So far as physical anthropology is concerned, this has no immediate utility, since so few of the putative Paleo-Indian skeletal remains now on record are dated or have an age exceeding 11,800 years.

Incidentally, the sudden disappearance of several varieties of large animals which had been common during the ice age is thought by some to be due to the hunting activities of the Paleo-Indians [123]. Because these animals had not been exposed before to, and were defenseless against, such wily predators, they rapidly dwindled in numbers. By not recognizing the need for conservation and by engaging in mass slaughter – especially by driving herds of buffalo over cliffs – the ancient hunters achieved an 'overkill' and thereby deprived themselves of a ready source of meat and hides. This in turn necessitated a cultural change.

### Paleo-Indians

The Paleo-Indians' physical characteristics are more obscure than their cultures. Besides the skeletal finds described above, at least two others with similarly shaky claims to antiquity need to be taken into account because of the anthropometric details they add. One of these, the Tepexpan skeleton from an old lake bed in the Valley of Mexico is possibly a representative of the mammoth hunters of that area [47]; the other, the Midland skull from the surface of a 'blow out' in west Texas, is believed to be the only representative of Folsom Man thus far found [238]. Both have been dated indirectly by $C_{14}$ at not less than 11,000 years BP. In addition, an unusually well-documented specimen was recently reported from northern

Colorado [1]. This is the Gordon Creek burial, directly dated from its collagen at 9,700 ± 250 years BP (7734 BC). Combining these three with the Confins (Lagoa Santa) and Melbourne specimens, we have five more or less complete skulls with the following cranial indices:*

| Name | Cranial index |
|------|---------------|
| Confins | 69·1 |
| Melbourne | 73·1 |
| Tepexpan | 79·9 |
| Midland | 68·8? |
| Gordon Creek | 75·0 |

The tendency here is to longheadedness, with the Tepexpan specimen being a notable exception.

If the high cranial index of Tepexpan Man increases the doubt about his antiquity (some maintain the skeleton was introduced into a Pleistocene layer in relatively recent times), this tendency is countered by the effect of other evidence. For instance, when the damaged ends of the long limb bones were reasonably reconstructed, they yielded lengths which correspond to a stature of 167 cm, according to a Trotter–Gleser Mexican formula [229]. This estimate is above the averages for late prehistoric and modern groups from the area and accords with evidence that the Indians of the warmer latitudes responded over long periods of time to environmental deficiencies by a lowering of stature (Bergmann's rule).

On the other hand, the Gordon Creek skeleton from over 1,500 miles to the north represents a much shorter individual – about 157 cm tall. Since this figure is well below the average stature of the present-day Pueblos, it is clear that generalizations from such meager data are hazardous.

At present, therefore, the only thing worth emphasizing about the skeletal remains attributed to the Paleo-Indians is the basic

---

* Note that the term 'cephalic index' applies only to the flesh-covered head. The tissues over the measuring points on the head are not everywhere of the same thickness and hence in the same individual the cephalic index is not the same as the cranial index. A classification of the cranial index comparable to that given in the footnote on page 85 is [195]:

| | |
|---|---|
| Extra longheaded (hyperdolichocranic) | 65·0–69·9 |
| Longheaded (dolichocranic) | 70·0–74·9 |
| Intermediate (mesocranic) | 75·9–79·9 |
| Broadheaded (brachycranic) | 80·0–84·9 |
| Extra broadheaded (hyperbrachycranic) | 85·0–89·9 |

similarity to those of the recent Indians. Nothing has been found thus far to indicate that the earliest Indians differed importantly from their descendants.

### Population increase in the Archaic period

The term 'Archaic' has been used for some years by American archeologists to denote an early level of culture (following the termination of the late Paleo-Indian period around 5000 BC, according to Haynes) in which hunting, fishing and gathering of wild vegetable foods were the dominant characteristics. The hunting was different from that undertaken by the Paleo-Indians, of course, because of the extinction of so many major elements of the earlier fauna. Otherwise the new period represents simply a slow cultural advance beyond the preceding one. Although the Archaic period varied in duration everywhere, depending on the assigned beginning date and on the date of the introduction of pottery locally (which signified the termination), for convenience here it will be limited to the 2,000 years between 5000 BC and 3000 BC. The selected terminal date recognizes the seeming importance of considering separately the next period – the Formative (3000 BC to around the beginning of the Christian era) – as developed by the late James A. Ford of the Florida State Museum in Gainesville [57].

The rare finds of Paleo-Indian skeletons in cultural and/or datable contexts contrast with the many skeletons found at one Archaic site in Kentucky and with the numerous skeletal parts found at another site of this period in New York State. The Kentucky site has a $C_{14}$ date of $5302 \pm 300$ BP – ca. 3350 BC [5]; the New York site has no radiometric date, but seems to be nearly as old. These sites have been selected for consideration here because of their yield of human skeletons; but they are important also, as will appear, because of their contribution to the development of the concept of the Archaic as a pre-pottery cultural stage.

Indian Knoll, the name of the Kentucky site, is located on the Green River, a westward-flowing tributary of the Ohio River. This location made it accessible earlier in this century to Clarence B. Moore of Philadelphia, a wealthy amateur archeologist who made a hobby of traveling by houseboat along the rivers of the southeastern part of the United States for the purpose of investigating

Indian sites reported by his agents. Moore spent most of a month during the summer of 1915 at Indian Knoll, which he found to be a shell midden (a deposit of refuse made up predominantly of shells). His excavations there yielded 298 burials with an associated assemblage of peculiar artifacts, but no pottery. Unlike most amateurs, Moore promptly analyzed, wrote up, and reported his findings. Thus, in 1916 the quarto-sized sixteenth volume of the *Journal of the Academy of Natural Sciences of Philadelphia* carried the well-illustrated story of the Indian Knoll excavations [129].

In 1916 probably anyone who noticed the absence of any mention of pottery in Moore's report was not surprised by this, because most of the shell middens then known were poor in artifacts. Also, the reader was diverted from any such consideration by the attention given in the report to the assemblage of peculiar artifacts from the burials. Among them were polished prismoidal stones of different kinds and colors with a centered hole drilled longitudinally. Previous finds of unusual artifacts of this sort had led to the belief that they had served some ceremonial purpose and largely on this account they were generally called 'banner stones'. Moore illustrated some of the fanciest of the Indian Knoll banner stones in color, an unusual luxury in that day. But his main contribution was an argument disposing of the popular belief as to their usage and instead identifying them as 'mesh-spacers' for the fabrication of nets. Since another frequently occurring class of artifacts in the burials consisted of pieces of antler with a hook carved at one end, he was able to strengthen his argument by identifying the latter as 'netting needles'. He identified a third class of artifacts from the burials – mostly antler cylinders drilled longitudinally – as cruder mesh-spacers. Seemingly unnoticed at the time was the fact that Moore failed to demonstrate the presence in the site of an unusual amount of fish bones in addition to the shells.

In 1939–40 William S. Webb, a physicist-turned-archeologist at the University of Kentucky, continued the excavation of Indian Knoll and in the process discovered 880 additional burials. Since the site was not fully excavated, there are probably more burials still undetected. But Webb's main contribution, just as in Moore's case, was a new explanation of the assemblage of peculiar artifacts accompanying the burials. He presented convincing evidence and arguments in his report to prove that, rather than these artifacts being net-makers' tools, they are surviving parts of atlatls (throwing sticks for propelling spears) [234]. The antler cylinder is the handle of the atlatl, the antler hook is the distal end (the butt end of the spear rested against the hook), and the so-called 'banner stone' is the weight that fitted on to the now-missing wooden shaft. According to this reconstruction, generally accepted now as the correct one, the Archaic Indians of Indian Knoll had no knowledge of the bow and arrow. Judging from cultural elements missing from the site, they also had no knowledge of pottery-making and agriculture. The physical type of these Archaic Indians will be dealt with following consideration of the New York site.

The first clearly defined and largest Archaic-period site in the Northeast came to light in 1925 – well before the era of $C_{14}$ dating – in the southern part of the Finger Lakes area of central New York [165]. It takes its name – Lamoka – from its location on a low terrace forming the east bank of a small marshy stream connecting Waneta and Lamoka lakes. The excavations, which began in 1925, were continued into 1928 by a group of trained archeologists from neighboring Rochester Museum of Arts and Sciences, with William A. Ritchie (later State Archeologist) taking full responsibility for the reporting. Although the material culture was found to be simple, the details of the deposits were not. Ritchie says, for example, (p. 85): 'The original surface was apparently uneven and had been abundantly pitted. Layers and heaps of accumulating debris grew up side by side, and as lodge sites and fire-beds were shifted, and new pits opened interrupting old deposits, a highly disorganized condition developed, by far the most pronounced ever seen by the writer.'

The artifacts recovered are mainly of stone, bone and antler. Perhaps the only ones that seem 'peculiar', to repeat the characterization used in referring to the Indian Knoll artifacts, are an array of incised antler pendants and pendant-like objects of uncertain usage. Pottery is absent, of course. Reviewing this situation in 1969, Ritchie notes that the Lamoka culture most closely resembles the Archaic cultures of the Southeast in the bone constituents, and at the same time differs from these cultures in many important respects, including the small use made of shellfish, the lack of the ground ax, atlatl weight, large stemmed points, etc. (page 78). Speculating about this, he adds: 'The Lamoka culture *per se* seems to have developed and concentrated in central New York, probably a few centuries prior to 2500 BC, in response to an ecosphere extremely well suited to the needs of a hunting and fishing culture' [166].

Turning now to the people themselves, the Lamoka site yielded skeletal parts of sixty-four individuals, including a few which had been intruded into the deposit at later times. Of the clearly Archaic-period skeletons, only five adults had skulls complete enough to provide a series of measurements (only general statements are available regarding the postcranial elements). On the other hand, Indian Knoll yielded skeletal parts of approximately 1,234 individuals, including 475 measurable adult skulls and 521 measurable adult postcranial skeletons [186]. The difference in sample size is due mainly to a difference in burial custom, but also in part to different preservation conditions at the two sites. Seemingly most, if not all, of the burials at Indian Knoll were in the site itself, whereas at Lamoka the main cemetery remains undiscovered elsewhere. The great concentration of shells at Indian Knoll probably provided the drainage and lowered acidity that assured the fine preservation of the skeletons interred therein. In any case, the large size, fine state of preservation and great age of the Indian Knoll sample make it unique, not only for the Americas, but for the world.

In thus characterizing the Indian Knoll skeletal population I have, of course, the benefit of hindsight. For nearly thirty-five years after Moore's initial work at the site the great age of this population went largely unsuspected. In particular, Hrdlička, who never paid much attention to archeological developments, was completely misled. He told Moore that 'None of the skulls is deformed and their type is that of the Algonquin . . . The location is in the region still generally ascribed to the Shawnee, but the remains evidently represent another tribe. This may have been the Miami, or one of the tribes from Illinois, or one of the Lenape' [129, p. 488]. Later, in his *Catalogue of Human Crania in the United States National Museum Collections*, he characterized the cranial series donated by Moore simply as 'pre-White' [86]. Understandably, therefore, the $C_{14}$ date given above came as a surprise to many anthropologists.

Some idea of the size and shape of the Archaic Indian's skull, as represented at the two sites selected for consideration, is given in Table 13. The assembled figures suggest that the moderate long-headedness of the Paleo-Indians continued into the Archaic-period Indians. On the other hand, the Archaic peoples may have been higher-headed than the Paleo-Indians (of those cited earlier only

TABLE 13

Selected dimensions of skulls from the Archaic period

| Site | No. | Maximum length (mm) | Maximum breadth (mm) | Bas.-breg. height (mm) | Cranial index | Mean-height index* |
|------|-----|---------------------|----------------------|------------------------|---------------|--------------------|
| | | | *Male* | | | |
| Indian Knoll† | 226–258 | 178·8 | 135·4 | 139·9 | 75·8 | 89·1 |
| Lamoka‡ | 1–3 | 179·0 | 131·0 | 146·0 | 73·2 | 91·5§ |
| | | | *Female* | | | |
| Indian Knoll† | 176–209 | 172·1 | 131·5 | 132·8 | 76·3 | 87·7 |
| Lamoka‡ | 1–2 | 181·0 | 130·0 | 141·0 | 71·9 | 89·2§ |

* This index represents the height of the skull as a percentage of the mean of the length and breadth: $(H \times 100) \div \left(\dfrac{L + B}{2}\right)$. The following classification (Stewart) [212] provides an interpretation:

| Lowheaded | 70–78 |
| Intermediate | 79–85 |
| Highheaded | 86–93 |

† Snow [186]
‡ Ritchie [165]
§ One specimen

Melbourne is known to be in the highheaded category). Incidentally, the main reason for introducing the mean-height index here is to prepare the reader for later regional differences in this character.

The average stature of the Indian Knoll males is close to 167 cm when the computation is made with a Trotter–Gleser Mongoloid formula [229]. This is almost identical with the figure given by Ritchie for the Lamoka males ('about five feet five or six inches' – 165–168 cm), although in this case the method of derivation is not stated. By reference to Table 6 (page 108) it will be seen that Boas reported average statures for living North American Indians mostly in excess of these figures.

A final point to note in connection with these Archaic-period skeletons is their relative freedom from disease. I have commented on this elsewhere [196, 217] and stressed its importance as evidence that syphilis does not appear to have been present in America in these early times.

## Cultural ferment and the Formative period

James Ford's definition [57] of the Formative period is 'the 3,000 years (or less in some regions) during which the elements of ceramics, ground stone tools, handmade figurines, and manioc and maize agriculture were being diffused and welded into the socio-economic life of the people living in the region extending from Peru to the eastern United States'. This gives a general idea of the cultural explosion that followed the Archaic period. The explosion led quickly to striking regional differentials in culture, among which Nuclear America stands out conspicuously, as already pointed out. Yet without some dynamic reconstruction of the preceding events such as Ford has offered, it is difficult to understand how this result was achieved in a relatively short time.

Ford's definition and reconstruction of the Formative period appear in volume 11 of the *Smithsonian Contributions to Anthropology* and were motivated largely by the contents of the first volume of the same series written by archeologists Meggers, Evans and Estrada [126]. They report the discovery on the coast of Ecuador of two unexpectedly sophisticated pottery complexes – given the names Valdivia and Machalilla – dating from the period 3000–1500 BC. Nowhere in South America have any clear antecedents of this unusual pottery been found so far. There is, in addition, no evidence of any group independently ever having developed the craft of pottery-making overnight, so to speak, and especially the craft of making well-tempered and fired pottery with decorations of an intricate nature, such as characterize the Valdivia and Machalilla wares. For this reason, and because the Ecuadorian specimens resemble in many respects Japanese pottery of the contemporary Jomon period, the authors argue for Japan as the place of origin of the craft in this instance and hypothesize a single accidental trans-Pacific boat-crossing as the means of its diffusion to South America.

Ford had a bolder idea [57]. He suspected that it might have been more in the nature of an exploring and colonizing expedition, as with later expeditions from Japan to Malaya and Polynesia. If more than just a few individuals were involved, it would account for the remarkable variety of the Valdivia ceramics. Further, the high selective fashion in which certain elements of the complex were spread to other parts of the Americas argues that specialization in the craft was well developed. He points out also that the Valdivia complex does not represent the entire range of pottery manufactured in southwestern Japan in 3000 BC, but that the products manufactured corresponded to the experience of the craftsmen from the mother country.

About 2000 BC a second group landed on the coast of Ecuador, bringing with them the Machililla culture. Their villages were built along the same stretch of coast already occupied by the Valdivia people; yet, in spite of their close proximity, the two ceramic traditions maintained their complete individuality for some 500 years (2000–1500 BC).

The mention of the spread of certain elements of the complex to other parts of the Americas is the part of Ford's historical reconstruction of main concern to us here. Only people with a tradition for colonizing, he believed, could have rapidly transplanted the new cultural elements from Ecuador to other places – first up the Pacific coast and across the isthmus to the north coast of Colombia, and then from somewhere near here (1) 'through the straits of Yucatán, around western Cuba, through the Florida straits, and northward to the mouth of the Savannah River [on the border between the present States of Georgia and South Carolina]' and (2) to central Mexico via either the Pacific or Gulf coast. The spread southward need not concern us here. Ford places the arrival of Formative (Valdivia) cultural elements in Georgia at about 2400 BC and notes (p. 185) that 'it was also at this early date, about 2300 BC, that the art of pottery-making arrived in the highlands of central Mexico'. In addition, he sees Formative (Machililla) cultural elements arriving on the Atlantic coast of Florida – only 150 miles south of the Savannah River – soon after 2000 BC.

The spread of pottery in the Americas by voyages and migrations between 3000 BC and 1500 BC highlights the Colonial phase of the Formative, according to Ford's reconstruction of events. Following the Colonial was the Theocratic phase, which Ford dates between 1500/1200 BC and 500 BC/AD 300, depending on the region. As the name implies, the second phase was characterized by the rapid spread of a religio-political system demanding public works and giving priestly groups a dominant share in government. Simultaneously, by chance perhaps, maize agriculture spread from its point of origin in Mexico to become an important factor in the subsequent population increase that sustained the Formative cultural florescence.

In contrast to the Colonial Formative, which Ford sees as a rather unexciting phase (although the concept of pottery-making was distributed to a number of widely separated places, only slowly was it picked up by neighboring peoples), the Theocratic Formative rapidly became, he implies, a wildly exciting phase. The origin of the shock wave, like that of maize, was Mexico, according to present evidence. Unlike maize, however, which had its origin in the plateau, the religio-political system seems to have appeared first in the coastal lowlands of Veracruz as a development of the Olmec civilization – the forerunner of the Maya and Aztec civilizations.

Tragically, Ford died before he formulated all of his ideas regarding the Theocratic Formative. Nevertheless, it is clear from the start he made in this direction, and particularly from his trait charts, that he saw Olmec influence, accompanied by maize, extending southward through Peru and northward to the eastern part of the United States. In both areas, as in Mexico, ceremonial structures are surviving prominent features of the landscape.

### Skeletal remains from the Formative period

It is too soon to tell whether the case that Ford made out for his historical reconstruction will meet with general acceptance or will need extensive modification. Be this as it may, in the absence of anything comparable, the scheme serves here nicely to bring order to the existing great mass of data from a relatively brief time period and to explain the obviously rapid cultural change taking place therein. Also, as Ford was well aware, the scheme goes far to explain the characteristics of the skeletal remains found in the cultural setting of the Formative period.

By good fortune, three of the sites on the Ecuadorian coast excavated by Meggers, Evans and Estrada – two from the Valdivia phase and one from the Machalilla phase – contained skeletal remains [126]. Although the bones were in poor condition, the fragmented skulls were saved. I had a hand in piecing them together in

1961, along with Juan Munizaga of the University of Chile in Santiago, who was working with me in Washington at that time. Subsequently, Munizaga prepared a report on the skulls for inclusion as an appendix to the report by Meggers, Evans and Estrada [137]. He was able to include in this report measurements on eleven undeformed adult skulls attributable to the Valdivia phase and a profile drawing of a single deformed adult skull attributable to the Machalilla phase. Two other skulls assigned to the Machalilla phase, both very incomplete, also showed signs of deformation. In all three cases the type of deformation is the same: fronto-vertico-occipital. Although the Valdivia skulls are not deformed, all but one are in the broad-headed (brachycranial) category. The exception is just under the borderline of broadheadedness. Moreover, I was able to verify in 1965 that most of these Valdivia skulls are in the high-headed category [212]. Evidently, therefore, these two small skull samples offer the earliest indication thus far in this hemisphere of (1) a clearly broad- and highheaded population; and (2) a population practicing artificial head deformation.

The occurrence of cranial deformation in skeletal collections datable to various parts of the Formative period is well established. Ford used this information in support of his argument that as the Formative culture spread it was accompanied by people with a distinctive head shape, even if achieved artificially. This led him to accept the widely-held view that a broad head is more readily deformed than a long head, and to disregard the view that a broad head in a population practicing deformation could represent incomplete achievement of the intended result and therefore be abnormal.

Two examples of skeletal finds at sites crucial to Ford's scheme will illustrate the care needed in interpreting evidence of this sort. The first comes from the Stalling's Island mound. This is the site on the Savannah River in the State of Georgia where Ford placed the first North American colony of the Formative-culture people. Perhaps it does not represent the original settlement, because it is located about 150 miles upstream from the mouth of the river. At any rate, the burials encountered during the excavation of the mound, as reported by William H. Claflin, Jr., in 1931, numbered eighty-four. Yet the only information as regards cranial form is contained in the following statement (p. 43):

Due to extreme decay, accurate cranial measurements of a sufficient number of skulls to draw any definite conclusion is impossible. However, it can be said in general that the Stalling's Island people were brachycephalic and did not as a rule practise cranial deformation. There are, however, several imperfect skulls that show partial deformation [35].

Unfortunately, no cranial indices are cited and the expression 'partial deformation' is not explained.

The second example of skeletal finds from the Formative period also comes from North America (the Ohio–Kentucky region), but differs from the first in two respects: it is from the Theocratic phase of the Formative (known locally as the Adena phase); and it is an assemblage from numerous sites. Most of the Adena sites that have been explored are burial mounds reflecting the elaborate ceremonial elements of the culture. Because twice as many males as females have been recovered from these mounds, a selected segment of the population may be represented. Be this as it may, Ford regards the population and culture as intruders into the Ohio–Kentucky region from the lower Mississippi Valley and as a late extension of an early Formative invasion, perhaps from Central America. He places the beginning of the Adena phase at about 800 BC and the end at about 200 BC, when it was replaced by the Hopewell phase.

The late Charles E. Snow provided an analysis of one of the best identified collections of Adena skeletons [235]. Of 100 skulls of all ages and both sexes he listed 92 per cent as deformed. In addition to having vertical occipital flattening, nearly a third have flattened areas on the sides of the forehead. The latter variant of frontal flattening has not been encountered outside of the Adena–Hopewell region. On the other hand, the small minority of measurable 'undeformed' skulls (those 'which show little or no deformation and are regarded as unaffected by the small deformation when present') amount only to sixteen (ten males and six females). They yield an average cranial index of 81·1 for the males and 84·6 for the females. Both figures are in the broad-headed range. Clearly, therefore, no difficulty would be encountered in distinguishing the skulls of the Adena people from those of the long-headed Indian Knoll Archaic people of the same region described earlier. They differed, too, in the matter of size: the stature of the Adena males averaged 170 cm as compared with 167 cm for the Indian Knoll males.

To give more details about individual skeletal collections from the Formative period would cloud, rather than clarify, the general picture. Essentially, there can be little doubt that forces set in motion at the beginning of this period from the vicinity of mid-America eventually penetrated to the heart of North America, causing cultural upheavals among the peoples of simpler culture along the way. That the same thing happened also in the southern hemisphere is now becoming evident, but will not be pursued here because details are not yet available. Since this book deals primarily with physical man, I have questioned only the idea that the distributors of the new culture in the Americas were a new breed of people. I find it difficult to believe that any Asiatics who might have crossed the Pacific 5,000 years ago could have established an element of their physical type – head shape – in the American population of the period so that it could be identified some 2,000 years later at a distance of some 4,000 miles from its point of entry.*

My criticism does not lessen the likelihood of trans-Pacific contacts having occurred, for the latter now rest on more substantial cultural evidence. Previously the main basis for this was the resemblances in art motifs of isolated specimens on both sides of the ocean. The art resemblances, together with fancied resemblances of some American crania to those of Old World peoples, called forth bizarre explanations. One such explanation, by H.S. Gladwin [62], offered in comic-book style to mollify anticipated objectors, had the survivors of Alexander's expedition to India make the long voyage to the New World, and accordingly set up the cultural resemblances in the latter area after 323 BC, the date of Alexander's death. In the light of the American chronology resulting from radiometric dating (figures 19 and 20), the weakness of the Gladwin hypothesis is all too apparent.

* After this was written Gordon Bowles (personal communication) called my attention to measurements on Jomon skulls in the Japanese literature [105, 149]. The figures give no evidence of the presence either of artificial cranial deformation or of normal brachycrany.

# 9

# Skeletal remains from the Recent period

During the final 2,000 years before the arrival of Columbus, a time which I will designate here simply as the Recent period, the pattern of change initiated in the Formative continued to expand, with the leading edge of the pattern ever more apparent in the nuclear areas, as figures 19 and 20 illustrate. Because of the recentness of this final prehistoric period, the amount of skeletal remains recovered is so large that a great deal of space would be required to deal with it in the same way as in the preceding chapter. As a compromise I will deal first with a different kind of problem, that of the Eskimos and Aleuts, and then take up a number of skeletal features of special interest because of their wide occurrence in the hemisphere.

### The Eskimo-Aleut problem

Alaska has attracted many archeologists on account of its location at the entrance to the great American *cul-de-sac*, as explained in Chapter 1. It was through this entrance, as has already been pointed out, that the original, and many subsequent immigrants passed in the course of the peopling of the hemisphere. Consequently, here is where the earliest immigrational evidence ought to exist and here indeed is where it has been intensively sought. Unfortunately, however, the finds to date have been disappointing and at the same time puzzling. The disappointment is due to the fact that the oldest discovered sites date back only about eight thousand years (the last transgression of the sea may have covered many of the earlier ones); the puzzlement is due to the recovery of fluted points in some of the only moderately-old sites. This combination of discoveries gives rise to the question, still not satisfactorily answered, as to whether the people who made the fluted points were ancestral to the later Eskimos and Aleuts, or descendants of Paleo-Indians who settled here instead of accompanying their fellows into the heart of the continent. Be this as it may, the origin of the Eskimos and Aleuts, together with their relatively late expansion and differentiation in the American Arctic, is usually treated as a separate problem from that of the Indians (cf. figs. 19 and 20). It is partly for this reason, and partly because the great bulk of the Eskimo-Aleut skeletal collections fall within the Recent period as defined above, that the subject is being discussed in this place.

Before taking up the question of the skeletal remains, a little more needs to be said about the present understanding of Eskimo and Aleut prehistory. First, that of the Eskimos. In addition to the fluted points mentioned above, some of the moderately-old sites in Alaska have yielded assemblages of small flint artifacts or 'microblades', together with the multifaceted ('polyhedral') cores from which they were struck. These have definite Asiatic affinities. However, most of the finds of microblades in the American Arctic have been in eastern Canada and around the periphery of Greenland. Here they constitute part of a cultural complex called 'Dorset', after a site at Cape Dorset on the southwest coast of Baffin Island. Archeologists have frequently found remains of the Dorset culture beneath the remains of a late prehistoric culture, more characteristically Eskimo, known as 'Thule' (it was first identified by the Fifth Thule Expedition of 1921-4). These two cultures appear to represent distinct migrational waves from Siberia via Alaska. After undergoing development in the eastern Arctic, a return movement of the Thule culture reached as far westward as northern Alaska.

Other Eskimo cultural traditions are known only from Alaska, and particularly the Bering Sea region, where their development may well have been affected by influences from eastern Asia. One of the earliest of these, appropriately called 'Old Bering Sea', was identified by Diamond Jenness in 1925 largely on the basis of unusually artistic decorations on ivory artifacts. A somewhat older culture (but still only about 1,500 years old), known from a site bearing the Eskimo name 'Iputak' and located at Point Hope northeast of Bering Strait, has yielded the oldest sizeable collection of Eskimo skeletons (about thirty-five measurable skulls of each sex).

Turning now to the Aleuts, the indications suggest that they are simply an extreme variant of the 'Bering Sea Mongoloids', to use W.S.Laughlin's phrase [116a]. Besides working with the Aleuts, as already mentioned, Laughlin has engaged also in Aleutian archeology. In the process he discovered (1938) and excavated (1952) a site on the little island of Anangula located off the western end of Umnak Island. As it happens, Umnak marks the southeastern terminus of the former land bridge from Siberia. For this reason Laughlin has argued that the division between the Aleuts and Eskimos proper derives from two distinct ancient routes across that bridge: one, used by the ancestors of the Aleuts, directed southeastward, and the other (further north), used by the ancestors of the Eskimos proper, directed eastward. Also, according to Laughlin, the area around the southeastern end of the land bridge, and subsequently the chain of islands extending westward therefrom, provided the ancestors of the Aleuts with 'a uniquely productive hunting station'. By remaining in this relatively isolated area for millennia they gradually increased their physical and cultural distinctiveness from the rest of the 'Bering Sea Mongoloids'.

Since for all practical purposes archeology can be said to have been initiated in the American Arctic by the Fifth Thule Expedition, not quite fifty years ago, it is understandable that the bulk of the Eskimo skeletal remains in museums are surface collections dating at most from the latter part of the last century. This means that there is limited evidence as yet on the changes in Eskimo physical type with time. By contrast, in the more accessible Aleutians careful archeological work was initiated still more recently, beginning perhaps with the American Museum's Stoll-McCracken Arctic Expedition of 1928. Because conditions for better preservation exist here, a good part of the collected remains go back to the period preceding the arrival of the Russians in the middle of the eighteenth century. Notable in this connection is the fact that, rather consistently, excavated Aleutian sites have yielded two distinct types of skulls always in the same stratigraphic relationship. The type that occupies the top position and evidently relates to the late Aleuts is decidedly lowerheaded (figure 26) and somewhat broader-headed than the type that occupies the bottom position. Laughlin refers to these two types as Neo-Aleut and Paleo-Aleut, respectively. In spite of a lack of gradation from one type to the other, he attributes the change to 'internal evolutionary processes'. In any case, the Paleo-Aleut type is not very different from that of the other 'Bering Sea Mongoloids', whereas the Neo-Aleut type is something else again. I will come back to this subject in a later section on lowheadedness in general.

In other respects it is sufficient here to note that the typical Eskimo skull exhibits a combination of features that makes it one of the most distinctive and easily recognized of all human types. Besides having a high, narrow vault, the typical Eskimo skull has a face that is broader across the cheek bones than across the vault, with relatively high orbits and a nose about as narrow as that of Europeans. The lower part of the face is unusually broad also, due to the lateral protrusion of the angles of the lower jaw. The combination gives the face a square, flat look. Two cranial details that are unique to the Eskimos are extremely narrow nasal bones and extremely thick tympanic bones – the structures that constitute part of the walls of the ear openings.

So much for the Eskimo-Aleut problem. Let us now turn our attention to the archeological Recent period as it involves skeletal finds throughout the hemisphere. The specific features to be dealt with are head flattening, tooth mutilation, skull surgery, head height and bone pathology.

### Distribution of the varieties of head flattening

The discussion of the Formative period brought out the fact that the custom of head flattening spread in a little over 2,000 years all the way from Ecuador, where it seems to have made its first appearance, to the Ohio–Kentucky region of North America. During the equally-long remaining part of the pre-Columbian era the custom spread still further and became more diversified in its details. As a result, skulls deformed in various ways have been found in three distinct areas north of Mexico and in four such areas south of the boundary between Mexico and the United States. The locations and extents of these seven areas are shown in figure 22.

Before considering the regional differences, something needs to

Fig. 22 Prehistoric skulls showing artificial shaping have been found in seven distinct areas of the Western Hemisphere: (1) northwest coast of North America; (2) southwestern United States; (3) eastern United States; (4) Middle America; (5) northern South America and the Antilles; (6) west coast of South America; (7) coast of Argentina

be said about the terminology developed for describing the altered head shapes. This inevitably involves the mechanisms of deformation. The simplest deformation appears only at the occiput of the skull and seems to have been unintentional, at least in its lesser manifestations (plate 16). Commonly referred to as 'cradle-board deformity', it resulted from the weight of the baby's head bending the soft bones of the occiput against the hard surface of the cradle. The amount of permanent flattening depended upon the extent to which the baby was able to move its head while fastened to the cradle (swaddled) and the length of time it was thus confined. In all cases, however, the plane of the flattened occiput is parallel to the axis of the body and hence vertical to the line of distant vision. From the latter circumstance the term 'vertico-occipital' is applied to this variety of deformation in much of the descriptive literature. In Latin America a frequent equivalent is 'tabular erect', a term introduced by the Argentine anthropologist José Imbelloni [99].

Much less commonly the flattening at the back of the skull is well above the prominence of the occiput (plate 16). This is called 'lambdoid flattening' after the name of the point (lambda) where the sutures between the parietal and occipital bones meet. In this instance, presumably, something rigid was held under tension against the upper back part of the head while the child was secured in the cradle. However, no such device has ever been observed in use or in the form of a relic. I find it difficult to decide, therefore, whether flattening of this sort was deliberate or accidental.

Flattening of the front part of the skull vault alone is seldom encountered, because it is not feasible to exert pressure on a baby's forehead without at the same time exerting counter-pressure on its occiput. The few observed cases of frontal flattening unaccompanied by evidence of counter-pressure have been attributed to the custom of carrying loads on the back by means of a supporting band (tumpline) across the forehead. This explanation applies only to very young children carrying loads in such a manner and then would represent unintentional deformation.

Evidence of the use of counter-pressure in altering the shape of a skull certainly signifies intentional deformation. In such cases the general descriptive term 'fronto-occipital' is widely used. But a further distinction is needed, because the plane of the occipital flattening may be either vertical or oblique (i.e., essentially parallel to the plane of the frontal flattening or just the opposite, namely, lambdoid). Accordingly the terms 'fronto-vertico-occipital', 'fronto-parallelo-occipital' and 'fronto-lambdoid' are current. For the first two of these varieties Imbelloni's terms 'tabular erect' and 'tabular oblique' again are generally applicable.

Counter-pressure was applied to the head in four main ways: (1) by use of a device, such as a band across the forehead, to force the back of the head against the cradle; (2) by use of small boards or tablets, one placed against the forehead and the other against the occiput, with the ends on each side tied tightly together; (3) by use of a board or tablet held against the forehead by a tight band passing from one end of the board around the back of the head to the other end; and (4) by use of a band wrapped tightly around the head so as to pass over the forehead and under the occiput. Note that only in the first method is the cradle an essential element. Variations of the several methods involve padding of the boards and bands in various ways, and possibly adding accessory bands.

In contrast to the bone flattening produced by the pressure of boards or tablets, the deformation produced by bands alone is best described as circular grooving. Not surprisingly, therefore, the term 'circular' is used to describe the skull deformation produced wholly by bands. Variants in which a combination of bands, pads and perhaps tablets may have been used are sometimes called 'pseudocircular.'

Returning now to geographical distribution, area no. 1 of figure 22 is located so far up on the Northwest Coast of North America that it is unlikely to have received influences from the Formative movement. Because of this the presence of the custom here can be accounted for only on the basis of independent invention or trans-Pacific contact. Supporting the latter is the historical record of drifting boats reaching this part of North America from the other side of the ocean [182]. Also, archeological evidence suggests that the custom first made its appearance here in late prehistoric time.

Boas was the first to record in detail the head-deforming customs in this area [12]. He recognized three main varieties: (1) a circular form (Koskimo) in the north not represented elsewhere in North America; (2) an extreme variety of fronto-parallelo-occipital flattening (Chinook) at the southern end of the area, particularly around the mouth of the Columbia River between the States of Oregon and Washington; and (3) a variant of fronto-lambdoid flattening (Cowichan) in the intermediate part of the area. The names Koskimo, Chinook and Cowichan refer to tribes practicing each particular kind of flattening intensively.

In 1804–6, long before Boas began his studies, Lewis and Clark led the first overland expedition across North America. Their route led northwestward up the Missouri River and then down the Columbia River to the Pacific coast. At the mouth of the latter river they met the chief of the Chinook tribe, Comcomly, who exhibited the tribal variety of head flattening. Washington Irving, sometimes called 'the father of American literature', tells about him in *Astoria* [101], a book written to promote John Jacob Astor's trading venture. In this connection Irving gives the following interesting account of the Chinook method of head flattening:

The process by which [head] deformity [among the Chinooks] is effected commences immediately after birth. The infant is laid in a wooden trough, by way of cradle. The end on which the head reposes is higher than the rest. A padding is placed on the forehead of the infant, with a piece of bark above it, and is pressed down by cords, which pass through holes on each side of the trough. As the tightening of the padding and the pressing of the head to the board is gradual, the process is said not to be attended with much pain. The appearance of the infant, however, while in this state of compression, is whimsically hideous, and 'its little black eyes', we are told, 'being forced out by the tightness of the bandages, resembles those of a mouse chocked in a trap' [I, pp. 66–7].

Irving goes on to make the point that among the Chinook possession of a deformed head was 'a sign of freedom' because their slaves – Indians from tribes not practicing head flattening – were not permitted to practice the custom on their own children. If Irving had had the opportunity of inspecting Comcomly's skull as I have had (plate 14), he might have added 'What price freedom!'

Area no. 2 in the southwestern United States was accessible from Mexico in prehistoric times and for this reason, not surprisingly, the predominant culture of the Southwest – that of the Pueblo Indians – gives evidence of influences from the south. Whether the Pueblos themselves reached this area from the south is debatable, but many see them as broadheaded intruders displacing earlier longheads (Basketmakers) [88, 185].

However the change came about, the head flattening practiced by the Pueblos was of only two simple varieties: vertico-occipital and lambdoid (plate 16). The lambdoid variety preponderated in the northern part of the area until about AD 1300; the vertical variety occurred almost exclusively in the southern part of the area until the arrival of the Spaniards. It is doubtful whether either form dates back as far as AD 1000.

The main thing that can be said about area no. 3, which includes most of the eastern United States, is that it has yielded a far greater number of varieties of deformed skulls than either of the two preceding areas. Considering that this is the part of North America north of Mexico where the Formative invasions are thought to have left their greatest impress, one cannot avoid the thought that the great differentiation of the custom of head flattening here supports such a reconstruction.

Leaving North America and going to Middle America (area no. 4), the information on head flattening, rather surprisingly, is poorly summarized. For example, volume 11 of the *Handbook of Middle American Indians* devotes only two and a half pages to the subject and does not include the geographical distribution [172]. However, from my own studies of the literature and of the available collections I see about the same range of varieties here as for the whole of North America [200, 205, 207, 214]. Neat geographical distributions are difficult to discern, except that in late prehistoric times the fronto-lambdoid variety was widespread and had largely replaced the fronto-occipital varieties (erect and oblique). So much variation is consistent with the high state of cultural development in this northern center of Nuclear America. As for the initiation of the custom here, the earliest evidence comes from a period corresponding to Ford's Theocratic phase of the Formative.

Area no. 5, centering as it does in the northernmost part of South America and including the Antilles, bears out in the skull forms what was said earlier about the origins of the islanders. The peoples who moved out into the islands, particularly in the later migratory stages, carried with them the custom of deforming the head in a single fashion. The result is one of the fronto-parallelo-occipital varieties in which the occiput is smoothly rounded by pressure of a band. An extreme example of this variety from Venezuela is shown in plate 15.

Other well-known varieties of head flattening are present in the mainland-portion of the area, but appear to have very restricted distributions. An example is the presence of the fronto-lambdoid variety at one site in the Panama Canal Zone [211]. Nothing reliable can be said about the age of the custom here.

Going down the west coast of South America to area no. 6, which includes the coast of Ecuador where the custom may have originated and corresponds to that of the Inca Empire at the beginning of the sixteenth century, I will note only that nearly all of the varieties of head flattening are represented, as again would be expected for an area of such high culture. The circular variety is sufficiently common in parts of Bolivia to have earned it the designation 'Aymara'.

The final area, no. 7, on the east coast of Argentina was probably not entirely isolated from no. 6. The most common variety here is fronto-occipital (vertical, oblique and pseudocircular). According to Imbelloni, the deformed skulls 'have been found . . . always in a cultural level above the layer of typically Pampean [longheads], who represent the truly ancient peoples of the patagonian region' [99, p. 54].

Taking the evidence from all seven areas into consideration, the prehistoric Americans undoubtedly practiced head flattening more extensively and devoted more ingenuity to its development than any other group of comparable size in the world.

## Dental mutilation

The front teeth are conspicuous elements in a person's appearance. Not surprisingly, therefore, peoples of the past in different parts of the world – Japan, Southeastern Asia, Africa and America – frequently altered their teeth for aesthetic or other reasons. In general, the process consisted either of filing away parts of the enamel, mainly along the occlusal border, or of drilling holes into the labial surfaces for inlaying foreign substances of contrasting color. In the Americas the high concentration of recovered examples in Middle America (in practically the same area where head flattening was practiced) and the earliest date assigned to any of them (near the beginning of Ford's Theocratic phase of the

Formative) strongly suggest that this was the custom's place of origin. But at the same time they suggest that the custom had little appeal outside its place of origin.

For many years Javier Romero of the Instituto Nacional de Antropología e Historia in Mexico City has been studying the American examples of mutilation as they turned up in excavations – 1,212 separate teeth as of 1965 [170, 171]. These fall into fifty-nine classes, representing as many different ways in which the tooth

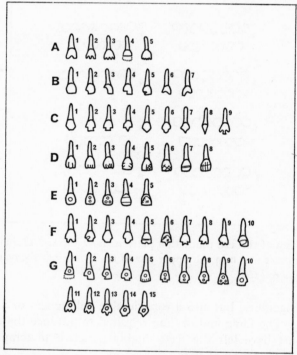

Fig. 23 Classification of 59 different mutilations of the front teeth performed by American Indians. Notches and grooves were made by filing; circular holes for the reception of inlays were made by drilling. After Romero [171]

crowns were altered (fig. 23). The vast majority are known only from Middle America (three are known only from North America and three are known only from South America). In addition, the mutilation of the individual teeth in a single jaw, more commonly upper than lower, was often varied to produce a configuration or pattern (fig. 24). This enhanced the total visual effect. Although many of the recovered jaws are incomplete, Romero could still identify 128 different patterns. Not only does this represent a great

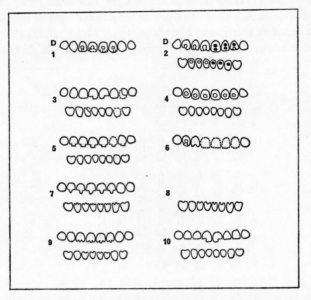

Fig. 24 Ten of the 128 mutilation patterns now known. The lower jaws of nos. 1 and 6 in the upper jaw of no 8 were not recovered. After Romero [169]

deal of ingenuity, but also a considerable willingness to undergo suffering. The filing and drilling required to produce the mutilations must have left the teeth highly sensitive to temperature changes for a period of time.

Technologically speaking, the inlays represent a remarkable accomplishment for people lacking metal cutting tools. Only in America was this stage of the custom reached in prehistoric times. The Middle American Indians drilled a circular hole in the labial surface of a tooth and implanted therein a perfectly-fitting disk of pyrite, jadeite or turquoise. It is thought that they insured the permanence of the inlay by setting it in some sort of cement. In Ecuador, the only other place where this form of mutilation has been found, the Indians used gold for their inlays and set them in large angular-shaped holes.

The custom appeared in Ecuador relatively late – somewhere around AD 500. This is widely accepted as further evidence of long-existing cultural contacts between Ecuador and Middle America. Considering that the custom offered an opportunity to employ gold for personal adornment in a region where gold metallurgy was rapidly developing, one naturally would expect the literature to be full of finds of gold inlays. Quite the contrary is true. A few examples from around Esmeraldas on the north coast of Ecuador are the only ones on record. The four other finds of altered teeth reported from South America (fig. 25) are isolated cases and interpreted as examples of filing. If they are indeed as reported, it is not clear at present how they can be connected with the diffusion of the custom from Middle America.

The few cases reported from North America (fig. 25) are also examples of filing. They occur, however, in places known to have been affected by Mexican influences (Mississippi Valley, Pueblo area). Indeed, some have argued that only individuals bearing the custom on their persons could have transmitted it to these distant points. Significantly, perhaps, most of the finds in the Mississippi Valley have come from the vicinity of the great ceremonial complex in East St Louis known as Cahokia, which was probably founded around AD 700–800 [76].

### Skull surgery

From today's standpoint it is one thing to cut a small hole and/or notch(es) through the enamel of a living tooth, and quite another to cut a large hole through the scalp and bony braincase of a living head – a spectacular surgical procedure known as trephining or trepanning. From the standpoint of a pre-Columbian-Indian surgeon, on the other hand, the distinction may not have been great, either as regards the mechanical procedures used by him or the discomfort, both physical and psychological, felt by his patient. On the technical side, the surgeon must have been sufficiently familiar with accidental scalp cuts to have devised methods for coping with the profuse bleeding that always occurs there. Infection, of course, was beyond his comprehension and something he had to leave to chance. Beyond all this, he would have had no

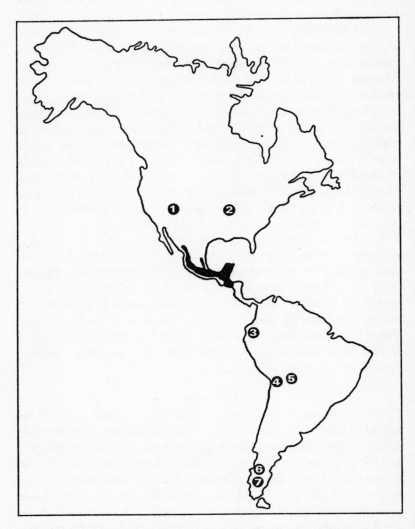

Fig. 25 Middle America stands out in the abundance of finds of prehistoric dental mutilation. Other areas where occasional finds have been made are; (1) Arizona; (2) Illinois; (3) Ecuador; (4) Chile; (5) Bolivia; (6, 7) Argentina. After Romero [172]

difficulty in cutting through the bone of the skull vault, since it is much less dense than enamel. And most crystalline rocks would have provided him with sharp flakes to serve adequately as knives. But it was mainly on the conceptual side that the Indian surgeon was less handicapped than we are today. The British anthropologist Stuart Piggott explains it this way:

The trepidation with which we approach the cerebral operation today is conditioned by our realization of the overwhelming importance of the brain in the vertebrate anatomy, a fact but dimly appreciated until comparatively recent times. It was not so long ago that, in both popular and professional regard, the heart was the seat of courage, the spleen of anger, and that the salient mental characteristics of the individual were located in the various viscera. Small wonder if prehistoric man approached trepanning in the same matter-of-fact way and upon a similar misconception as to the localisation of physiological activities [152, p. 114].

At any rate, in prehistoric Peru trephination was extensively practised and certainly in many cases for therapeutic purposes (plate 17). My estimate of the number of trephined skulls recovered in Peru is around 1,000, a number which may be higher than that for all the rest of the prehistoric world [208]. But the rarity of finds of this nature in other parts of the New World offers a parallel in a reverse way to the distribution of tooth mutilation outside of Middle America. Whereas tooth mutilation was primarily a custom of the northern center of Nuclear America (Mexico), skull surgery was primarily a custom of the southern center of Nuclear America (Peru). The reputed wider distribution of trephination, however, depends on making the distinction between ante- and postmortem bone cutting.

Skull perforations have different meanings according as one takes into account the following two facts: Firstly a hole cut in a skull vault after death for the purpose of obtaining a relic for magical or other uses is not distinguishable from one made shortly before death; and secondly a healed hole in a skull vault resulting from trauma is not distinguishable from a healed trephine opening. Considering how easily such things may be confused, Romero's latest summary of twelve putative examples of trephined skulls from Mexico leaves one with the impression that, in spite of the high development here of the art of dental mutilation, the Mexicans had only just begun to experiment with bone cutting [172]. A like impression results from my summary of twelve putative examples of trephining reported from North America north of Mexico [208].

One of the North American examples came from a site along the Potomac River near Washington, specifically from an ossuary (a pit for reburial after skeletonization) containing over six hundred skulls, together with most of the other bones. Three other ossuaries at the same site raise the number of skulls which I examined to over 1,300. The occurrence in this large sample of a single skull with a healed perforation (and none with an unhealed perforation) does not seem to me to be good evidence of a cultural practice.

By contrast to the few widely scattered examples of trephining in Middle and North America, the one thousand or so undoubted specimens from Peru are concentrated in the central and southern highlands and in one small area of the southern coast (Paracas). As plate 17 shows, the surgical subjects ranged in age from young children to old adults. Indications of fracture – probably the primary reason for the surgery – are seen in many cases. Many of the operations were followed by infection of the bone surrounding the opening and survival left this area intensely scarred. Rather surprisingly, also, when death occurred immediately after the operation, a discolored area is sometimes seen around the unhealed opening in the later recovered skull. The reason for mentioning the changes around the openings is to point out the fact that this area, whether only discolored, or heavily infected, or fully healed and markedly scarred, is always angular in outline – usually triangular, rectangular or pentagonal. This finding suggests to me the possibility that the Indian surgeons had cut away corresponding areas of the scalp before making the trephine openings [206]. Large exposures would have been necessary if the surgeons were to explore the extent of fractures.

This is not to say that the surgical technique of exposing a larger area of skull than was to be opened was always followed in Peru. Many trephined skulls show only one or more round holes completely surrounded by normal bone. Here one must assume that only the bone that was to be cut away was exposed. The most notable example of this kind, preserved in the British Museum (Natural History) in London, has seven healed openings (plate 18). Repeated fractures are impossible as the explanation of such extensive trephining and the alternative is to think of an attempted cure for headache, epilepsy or insanity.

It is noteworthy also that the method used in removing the bone depended on the size of the opening in the scalp. If the opening through the skull wall was of the same size as the opening in the scalp, the bone was scraped away; but if the opening in the scalp was large enough to give the surgeon room for manipulation, he made four canoe-shaped saw cuts at right angles in a tic-tac-toe pattern ('noughts and crosses', for English readers). Probably removal of a section of bone by cutting was speedier than that by scraping. A rarely used method of bone removal consisted of drilling overlapping holes in a circular pattern. Whatever the method used, the patient had to endure it without benefit of anesthesia and with only the help of whatever narcotic effect he could obtain by chewing coca leaves (cocaine). Perhaps the lack of such an effective narcotic elsewhere in the New World is one reason the custom did not spread more widely, in spite of a success rate between fifty-five and sixty per cent. It would seem, however, that as a therapeutic measure trephining developed rather late in Peru. In saying this I am interpreting the evidence from the Necropolis of Paracas on the southern coast, dating from the last few centuries before the beginning of the Christian era, as a manifestation of a cult practice involving corpses.

### Natural lowheadedness

The next subject to be discussed – lowheadedness – is quite unlike the bizarre deliberate body modifications to which we have just given attention; it is a normal variation yielding a definite geographical distribution. The existence of this feature and its distribution has emerged only in the last fifty years as skeletal remains accumulated. Hrdlička, more than anyone else, was responsible for its discovery, since his *Catalogue of Crania* provided the metric data [86, 88].

Although lowheadedness is visible to the trained eye, its degree of expression is best stated by the mean-height index, which is defined in the first footnote of table 13. This index alone clearly separates the Aleuts from the Eskimos, as figure 26 shows. Elsewhere in North America low mean-height indices comparable to those of the Aleuts predominated among the Siouan and other

Plains peoples west of the Mississippi River, among most of the Athapascan peoples of western Canada and western United States, and among the peoples of the southern part of California [196]. Were it not for the presence of head flattening along the Northwest Coast possibly low-headedness would be found in that area also.

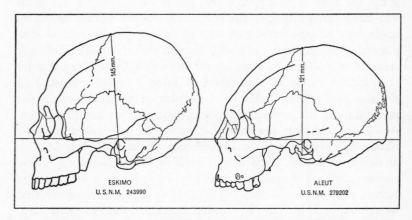

Fig. 26 Comparison of the head heights of two skulls, Eskimo and Aleut, with the same cranial index. The basion-bregma height of the Eskimo exceeds that of the Aleut by 24 mm. and as a result the Eskimo has a mean-height index of 88·4 and the Aleut one of only 74·6. After Stewart [196]

This broad distribution bears out the indications from blood groups and cultural elements that the peoples involved were part of a late population movement out of Asia into the New World. Viewed in reverse, it supports the view that the more peripheral high-headed peoples were older inhabitants.

Middle America has not been studied from this point of view, partly because of the limited skeletal remains available for study and partly because of the presence of artificial deformation in so many of the recovered skulls. But Hrdlička noted the presence of low-headedness in a small series of recent Maya skulls [85].

Lowheadedness appears again in the interior of northern South America and in the far-removed southern tip of South America [197]. It has not been possible so far to make sense of this southern distribution.

## Paleopathology

The point was made in Chapter 3 that the American aborigines entered the historic period (1492) in a fairly healthy state. Study of the skeletal remains from the last part of the prehistoric period tends to confirm this. The name given to studies of this sort – paleopathology – was coined by the bacteriologist Marc Armand Ruffer in the first decade of this century when he was serving as a consultant to the Archaeological Survey of Nubia (Upper Egypt). Yet now, some sixty years later, this science has not advanced notably, largely because few people are qualified to interpret evidence of disease in dried bones. Too little is known, for example, about a widely-distributed abnormal condition of the skull vault, originally called by Hrdlička 'osteoporosis symmetrica' and now more properly called 'hyperostosis spongiosa' [67]. The disease represented is said to be an anemia, but if so, the cause(s) and associated effects are not certainly known.

The evidence for the presence of syphilis in pre-Columbian America is also unsatisfactory and indeed even puzzling. In view of this, and considering that the latest hypothesis on the origin of syphilis makes it an Old World disease (p. 41), a little more needs to be said about the New World evidence from prehistoric times. Before the advent of isotopic dating, many skeletal collections were assumed to be pre-Columbian when actually they were less than five hundred years old. The occurrence of putative syphilitic lesions in populations of this late period could be due, of course, to introduction by Europeans. But can the bone lesions of syphilis be diagnosed with certainty either in late or early populations? Although there are those who claim to be able to do so [107], the fact remains that no means of checking the diagnosis exist at present. Bone is so limited in its response to pathological irritants that not uncommonly several diagnoses are possible for any one set of lesions.

The long bones, particularly the tibiae or shin bones, and the skull vault are the sites of the lesions most commonly attributed to syphilis. Their vulnerability may be due to their subcutaneous locations. Lesions at one or other of these sites, or at both together, generally can be found in decreasing frequencies as one goes back through older and older skeletal assemblages; but there are exceptions. In a survey of this sort which I organized, and in which frontal lesions mainly were emphasized, a collection from the State of Delaware yielded the highest incidence of the lesions in question [217]. The date of the site, however, could not be narrowed within the period AD 1200–1600. The next highest incidence was in an Illinois collection which again could not be dated closer than the period AD 400–1400. By contrast, a large South Dakota collection mainly from the period AD 1600–1800 showed a minimum of lesions, as did the Archaic Indian Knoll collection from Kentucky (around 3350 BC) and the Hawikuh Pueblo collection from New Mexico (AD 1200–1670).

Obviously, the distribution of these lesions is not entirely consistent. The skeletons from a protohistoric site in the Atlantic tide-water region (Delaware) might well show considerable evidence of syphilis because of European contacts. But why then do not those from historic sites in South Dakota visited frequently by French traders show the same thing? And why do lesions like those in the Delaware specimens appear frequently in skeletons from a late prehistoric site in Illinois and rarely in those from a late prehistoric site in New Mexico? Considering the movement of new peoples and cultures up the Mississippi River in late Formative times, could it be that some change in the epidemiological picture followed along? And what produced the bone lesions, if not syphilis? Unfortunately, clear answers to these questions are not yet forthcoming. Until further survey work on the American material is undertaken no one is justified, therefore, in drawing conclusions about the relationship of syphilis in early America to that in the rest of the world.

Turning now to a lesion not caused by infection, spondylolysis, American skeletal remains have contributed notably to an understanding of its etiology. Basically, the term 'spondylolysis' refers to a loss of bony continuity after birth in some part of the neural arch of a vertebra. When the condition is bilateral the arch is a separate bone allowing motion to occur at the new joint between it and the body of the vertebra. Also, since the body of the anomalous vertebra is no longer securely anchored to the adjacent vertebrae above and below, it can move forward and create pressure symptoms. These events, which become more complicated when the intervertebral disks become involved, tend to occur most commonly at the level of the last lumbar vertebra – the so-called 'low back'. This fact seems to reflect the unstable anatomical relationships at this segmental level resulting from man's unique upright posture.

Studies of American Indian skeletons show an incidence of neural arch defects, with or without complications, ranging from six to eight per cent. Most of the world's populations fall into this same range. The Eskimos, and to a lesser extent the Aleuts, however, are exceptions [204]. From 1926 to 1938 the Smithsonian Institution had one or more collecting expeditions in Alaska almost yearly. During that time I handled most of the skeletons from these expeditions that were accessioned in the National Museum (administered by the Smithsonian Institution). In this way I became aware of the fact that the incidence of arch defects among Alaskan natives ranges up to around fifty per cent. I attribute this high incidence to inbreeding. It is now known that mating in most populations is more random than in those of Alaska and, largely as a result, only in certain family lines do arch defects occur. Thus, general skeletal samples of most populations include only a limited number of representatives of the affected family lines. The Alaskan Eskimos, on the other hand, seem to constitute in this respect a grand family line, and as a result every specimen in a skeletal sample is from a member of the affected line.

This brief treatment of American paleopathology must not be interpreted to mean that the subject has equally narrow limits. Many other pathological conditions have been reported, but for one reason or another do not throw much light on the general health status. One of the reasons is the short life expectancy of past times. For example, few Indians survived to the age when most malignancies show up in bones. On the other hand, common afflictions such as wounds, fractures, dental caries and osteoarthritis, even though rather spectacular in certain instances, in no way distinguish Indians from other peoples.

# 10

# Post-Columbian additions to the American population

One of the themes of the foregoing chapters is that a wholly new phase of the peopling of America began in 1492 and is not yet finished. Whereas at some still uncertain but distant time in the past the first man to enter the Western Hemisphere came from Asia, in 1492 the first representative of the new migratory wave arrived on the scene from Europe. Culturally speaking, there was a vast difference between these two forerunners of population movements. The earlier one was a stone-age man travelling on foot; the later one was a Renaissance man sailing in a ship.

By 1492, as we have seen, some of the descendants of the original immigrants had not advanced far culturally, but others had developed the world's third great cultural nucleus. The lag in development reflects the Western Hemisphere's degree of isolation before 1492. As we have seen also, the new immigrants immediately proceeded to demolish the original inhabitants and their cultures as they encountered them. At the same time the new migratory wave began growing at an unprecedented rate until now, only a near half-millennium later, the total population of the Western Hemisphere is approximately five times the highest estimate of the pre-Columbian population and thirty-two times Steward's conservative estimate given in Table 1 (p. 33).

### The contribution of Europe

The progress of European exploration, conquest and colonization outlined in Chapters 5, 6 and 7 indicates the order of arrival in quantity of the several European nationalities involved. The Spanish, of course, were the first on the scene. They became the

POST-COLUMBIAN ADDITIONS TO THE AMERICAN POPULATION

main new population element in the West Indies, Central America, all of South America except Brazil and the southern part of the United States. Brazil was taken over by the Portuguese. Beyond the Spanish holdings in North America, the English and French were the main occupiers, with the Dutch and Swedes playing minor roles. On the other hand, the English, French and Dutch played minor roles in the area of Spanish domination.

The new population elements in the Western Hemisphere grew at different rates. The Spanish colonies discouraged voluntary immigrants of other nationalities, but usually encouraged interbreeding with the local Indians. This limited their growth and economic progress. The Portuguese adopted the same policy and reaped the same results. In North America, by contrast, many colonies were formed initially by peoples in search of religious freedom, a tradition that gradually opened the doors to peoples of other nationalities. As already noted, however, the somewhat liberal attitude of the colonists in this direction did not go hand in hand with encouragement of interbreeding with the Indians. North America, therefore, unlike Central and South America, did not become 'Indianized' to any extent. The avoidance of racial admixture, along with the adoption of a liberal immigration policy, hastened the growth and economic development of eastern North America.

The North American population growth was phenomenal, even after only two centuries of settlement effort. We know just how phenomenal because accurate population figures are available for the most settled part of the area in question. In 1590, just after Sir Walter Raleigh failed in his efforts to establish the Roanoke colony on the coast of what is now the State of North Carolina, the Europe-derived population of all of the continent north of the Spanish holdings was virtually zero. Then during the next two hundred years colonists poured into the country, became unified, and by means of a revolution made themselves politically independent of the home government. At the end of the period (1790) the young United States government conducted its first census, as called for in its constitution (in Europe only Sweden previously had conducted a national census). The United States then consisted of only thirteen states along the Atlantic seacoast, an area of 867,980 square miles. Yet this area was shown by census to contain

3,329,214 people, mostly of European origin. If figures for the Europe-derived population of eastern Canada for the same date were available, a still larger population total could be cited.

The census of 1790 is notable also for yielding information as to the national origins of the individuals enumerated. Although their places of birth were not recorded, their names were. It is thus from inspection of the names that the proportions of the various European nationalities comprising the population of the United States at that time have been worked out. 'In general, 82·1 per cent of the names are English, 7·0 per cent Scottish, 5·6 per cent German, 2·5 per cent Dutch, 1·9 per cent Irish, and all others less than 1 per cent' [199].

## Africa's involuntary contribution

The 1790 census revealed in addition the presence in the United States of a surprisingly large number of African Negroes who had arrived involuntarily as slaves since early in the Colonial Period: 757,208, or nineteen per cent of the total enumeration. These tended to be concentrated in the southern States.

As already mentioned, slave trading became profitable in the New World right from the early part of the 1500s when the Spaniards found the Indians of the West Indies to be unsubmissive to slavery. After these Indians succumbed to the harsh treatment meted out to them by their Spanish masters, or otherwise disappeared, those in charge of the island colonies replaced them with Negro slaves imported from Africa. Much the same thing soon happened along the Caribbean coast of Panama, in Guiana, and along the Atlantic coast of South America, especially in Brazil. Slaves first reached the British North American colonies in 1620 with the settlement of Jamestown. Few slaves reached the more remote New World colonies and thus a Negroid element does not figure to any extent in the populations of most of the present countries bordering on the Pacific.

The records of the slave trade are fragmentary and misleading for many reasons, but chiefly because so much of the trade was carried on in a clandestine fashion. A high proportion of the slaves were carried first to the West Indies and there trans-shipped to other parts of the New World with only rare indications of African origins. Thus, with one exception, the North American colonies (or later States of the Union) received the great majority of their slaves through the West Indian trade. Only South Carolina received slaves in large numbers directly from Africa [49]. In this exceptional case, fortunately, the records often state the part of Africa where each individual shipment originated. By summarizing these records for the years 1733–1807 (63,401 individuals, but still not likely the total number received) Pollitzer [155] was able to show the proportional representation of the different parts of the West African coastal population (fig. 27). East Africans (mainly from Mozambique) also reached South Carolina, but their numbers were less

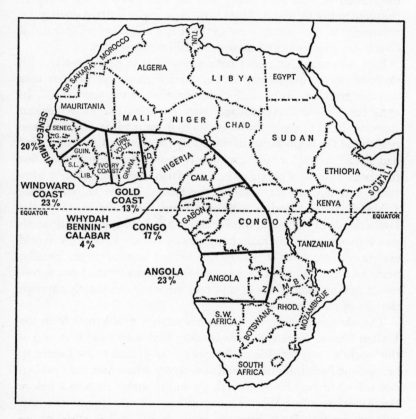

Fig. 27 Map of Africa of the 1946–56 period showing the slave trade area of the west coast divided into six sections and the proportional contribution of each to the slave population of South Carolina. After Pollitzer [155]

than 1 per cent of the total. There is no way of telling how the composition of the South Carolina sample compares with that of the total New World slave population.

Proscription of the slave trade, and eventually of slavery itself, was inevitable, but had to await other developments. The successful outcome of the rebellion against Great Britain by her North American colonies had planted the idea of an independence movement in Brazil and in Spain's American colonies. A good excuse for rebellion in these areas did not come, however, until Napoleon intervened in Spain in 1806, and in 1807 forced the King of Portugal to flee to Brazil. From then on at various times during the remainder of the century most of the major colonies in Central and South America achieved their political independence.

Each emerging American nation now had to deal directly with problems involving its population. And high on the priority lists was the growing world-wide condemnation of the slave trade. In 1794 the United States forbade any participation by American subjects in the slave trade to foreign countries; in 1808 she prohibited the importation of slaves. By then the British Parliament had already passed a bill providing that no vessel should clear out for slaves from any port within the British dominions after 1 May 1807, and that no slave should be landed in the colonies after 1 March 1808. Sweden withdrew from the trade in 1813, the Netherlands in 1814, and the French in 1818. This left the Spanish and Portuguese as the main suppliers of slaves to the New World and they were bought off by the British around 1830. Finally, between 1831 and 1842 these maritime nations worked out agreements among themselves to suppress the trade completely through the use of naval power.

The abolition of slavery became a serious problem only in the United States. Here the slave-holding States seceded and one of the world's most terrible civil wars (1860–5) had to be fought to bring them back into the Union, *sans* slaves. Elsewhere the problem was solved by regular legal methods and in many cases well before the American Civil War. The constitutions of some of the new nations derived from Spanish colonies called for abolition of slavery on a prescribed date. The abolition laws of other new nations called for freeing the slaves gradually, by some such means as a limited apprenticeship, in order to lighten the blow to the slave owners. This was the method used by Great Britain in 1833 for her remaining American colonies (the terminal date of 1840 was voluntarily advanced to 1838). Brazil and Cuba were among the few to hold on to slavery longer than the United States. The terminal date in Brazil was 1888. Cuba went on with a modified form of slavery for a few years longer.

### Immigration in the nineteenth century

Another high-priority population problem facing the new American nations in the nineteenth century involved various human groups seeking asylum from intolerable situations or conditions in their European homelands. The plight of these Europeans had an humanitarian appeal, and at the same time a practical appeal, because of the new-nations' need for more manpower to ensure their continued economic progress and to help preserve their sometimes precarious independence. Also, some of the new nations needed to compensate for the loss of slave labour. From all these standpoints they found the opportunity hard to resist, even though many immigrant groups were coming from other than the traditional parts of Europe.

Looking at the situation from the other side, the European groups seeking to emigrate to the New World generally were impoverished and had to take the cheapest transportation available, namely steerage passage on boats headed for the nearest American ports. In these circumstances, and because opportunities for earning a livelihood appeared especially bright in the United States and Canada, some seventy per cent of the emigration from Europe between 1856 and 1937 – not the whole duration of the movement by any means – ended up in North America. Most of the remainder went to Argentina and Brazil.

Writing in 1947 about the effect of this population movement on the United States, I said:

One of the outstanding phenomena in the field of human biology during the nineteenth century was the rapid population growth of the United States. By 1900 the population of continental United States had increased more than fourteenfold. In Europe, by contrast, France had failed to double its population and Belgium alone had attained a threefold increase. Stating this comparison in another way, at the beginning of the nineteenth century every important European country, even including Spain and Turkey, exceeded the United States in number of inhabitants; whereas now only the USSR has a larger population.

To a considerable extent this remarkable rate of population growth was due to an attendant phenomenon of human biology, remarkable itself for scale, namely immigration. Between 1830 when it got well under way, and soon after 1920 when it had practically ceased, over thirty-eight million immigrants arrived in the United States. This accretion from foreign sources is about equal to the total population of [the United States] in 1870 or to that of France in 1895 [199, p. 315].

Incidental points of interest about this greatly accelerated movement of European peoples into the United States are: the succession of European countries furnishing the immigrants; the fluctuations in the yearly quotas; and the events, either in Europe or in America, responsible for these fluctuations. All three points are summarized in figure 28. I have only one comment on this. With

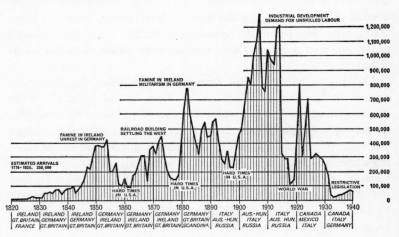

Fig. 28 Graph of the yearly total immigration to the United States from 1820 to 1940. Some of the causes of the fluctuations are indicated and the three leading nationalities in each decade are named. After Stewart [199]

regard to the first point – the varying sources of immigrants in successive decades – it is noteworthy that the majority came from western and northwestern Europe until 1890, after which the majority came from southern and eastern Europe.

The port of entry in the United States for most of the immigrants was New York. Naturally, therefore, there was an initial concentration of each entering nationality in the surrounding area. Later, each tended to migrate to the part of the country which most closely matched the environment and employment possibilities of his homeland. Thus, for example, the Italians are concentrated in the grape-growing parts of New York and California; the Irish are in the urban centers of New York and New England; and the Scandinavians are in the farming communities of Minnesota and Wisconsin.

There is no need here to go into so much detail for Canada, Argentina and Brazil, the only other American nations receiving noteworthy numbers of immigrants in the nineteenth century. For Canada it is sufficient to say that individuals of British ancestry outnumber French-speakers, but together they make up about seventy-five per cent of the population. In order after them are Germans (6 per cent), Ukranians (3 per cent), Italians (2·5 per cent), Dutch (2·5 per cent), Poles (2 per cent) and others (9 per cent). The percentages of foreign-born persons in Canada would be lower were it not for the high rate of emigration of native-born Canadians to the United States during periods of prosperity in the latter country. Census data of 1960–1 from the two countries indicate that just before this time, one native-born Canadian had emigrated to the United States for every sixteen remaining at home.

In Argentina the European-born elements are concentrated in the areas surrounding the port of Buenos Aires. They include, besides Spaniards, mostly Italians and East Europeans (especially Jews). In Brazil the main ports of entry for the immigrants were Rio de Janeiro and Santos. In order of number after Portuguese, the European nationalities represented are: Italians, Germans, Spaniards and Poles. Most of the immigrants were attracted to the four southern States of São Paulo, Paraná, Santa Catarina and Rio Grande do Sul.

## Immigration from Asia

It is one thing to welcome newcomers whose appearance and actions do not seem strange, even though their speech is incomprehensible, and quite another thing to welcome newcomers who are obviously different in all three respects. Marked distinctions of this sort set apart the Negro slaves, of course, from the day of their arrival in the New World and continue to plague their descendants. The Asiatics who emigrated to the Western Hemisphere in the nineteenth and twentieth centuries triggered a similar, but less intense, reaction. Indeed, their presence on the opposite side of the Pacific from their homelands indicates that the need for their services was greater than the Western prejudices against them personally. Probably, if it had been feasible to transport European immigrants willing to do menial work all the way across the continent, Asiatics would have been excluded from the beginning. As it turned out, however, the populations of most of the countries bordering on the Pacific coast of the Americas include a scattering of Asiatics and those of only three countries completely removed from the Pacific have sizeable Asiatic components.

The Chinese were the first to arrive. They began appearing in numbers on the west coast of North America about 1848 following Mexico's transfer of California to the United States and the simultaneous discovery of gold in California. The so-called 'gold rush' led to a rapid population build-up in California and a resulting need for labor, which the Orient was best prepared to supply. The number of Chinese in California climbed rapidly to around 75,000 in 1880, declined to about 30,000 in 1920 and is now back to around 100,000.

The country with the next largest number of Chinese is Peru. The first were admitted in 1849 under contract for extraction of guano, the manure of sea birds found on islands off the coast. After the subsidence of the guano boom, most of the Chinese stayed on in agricultural and other occupations. In 1939 they numbered 16,356.

The Japanese did not accept the early call to fill labor needs in the Western Hemisphere. Instead, they came in of their own accord during the last phase of the great immigration movement. From a zero representation in 1880, their number in California rose to nearly 100,000 in 1930, and to nearly 160,000 in 1960. Likewise in Peru they came mainly in the twentieth century and in somewhat greater numbers than the earlier Chinese. Here they numbered 22,738 in 1939.

By far the largest contingent of Japanese coming to the Western Hemisphere settled in Brazil. Within a period of fifteen years (1925 to 1940) about 200,000, including quite a few from Okinawa, settled in the State of São Paulo and in the Amazon Valley.

Besides the Mongoloid Chinese and Japanese, Asia supplied the Western Hemisphere also with Caucasoid East Indian immigrants. This came about by arrangement within the British colonial empire. The British colonies in America, especially Guiana (now Guyana), were seriously affected by the shortage of plantation labor following the emancipation of Negro slaves in the 1830s. The only successful solution to this problem proved to be the admission of indentured laborers from India and Pakistan. In 1870 the British allowed Dutch Guiana (now Surinam) to participate in this immigration. As a result, East Indians now account for about one-half of the population of Guyana and about one-third of that of Surinam.

*Environmental effects on the immigrants*

In 1907 the Senate of the United States created an Immigration Commission 'to make full inquiry, examination, and investigation . . . into the subject of immigration'. The 'Commission's anthropological investigation [entrusted to Franz Boas in 1908] had for its object an inquiry into the assimilation of the immigrants with the American people as far as the form of the body is concerned' [17, p. 7]. Boas realized, however, that an investigation of such a magnitude was out of the question, and therefore chose only to seek answers to the following two questions: (1) Is there a change in the type of development of the immigrant and his descendants, due to his transfer from his home surroundings to the congested parts of New York? (2) Is there a change in the type of the adult descendants of the immigrant born in this country as compared to the adult immigrant arriving on the shores of our continent? To this end he assembled thirteen assistants and collected five measurements and several observations on 17,821 subjects [75].

Boas' final report appeared in 1911 as volume 38 of the Commission's report series [18]. Most of the collected data is presented in tabular form, with only that on European Hebrews and Sicilians being used to demonstrate the principal finding. The latter is best stated in Boas's own words (p. 5):

In most of the European types that have been investigated the head form, which has always been considered one of the most stable and permanent characteristics of human races, undergoes far-reaching changes coincident with the transfer of the people from European to American soil. For instance, the east European Hebrew, who has a very round head, becomes more long-headed; the south Italian, who in Italy has an exceedingly long head, becomes more short-headed; so that in this country both approach a uniform type, as far as the roundness of the head is concerned. . . .

These results are so definite that, while heretofore we had the right to assume that human types are stable, all evidence is now in favor of a great plasticity of human types, and permanence of types in new surroundings appears rather as the exception than as the rule.

Although Boas' conclusion created a sensation, and he was forced to defend it for nearly thirty years [19], very little effort was made to pursue the lead he had supplied. Nearest to it were the anthropometric studies carried out by Hrdlička in the United States between the years 1910 and 1924 and by Kazimier Stołyhwo in Brazil in 1930 [84, 220]. Hrdlička confined his study to about a thousand so-called 'Old Americans' – 'those [American Whites] whose ancestors on each side of the family were born in the United States for at least two generations; in other words, all those whose parents as well as all four grandparents were born in this country'. By definition, therefore, he eliminated the late immigrants from southern and southeastern Europe and considered mainly the descendants of immigrants from the British Isles. Stołyhwo, on the other hand, journeyed from Poland to Brazil for the purpose of making his study, which was limited to 638 Polish immigrants and their descendants living in the State of Paraná.

The broad metrical description of the Old Americans provided by Hrdlička's study failed to show that this component of the United States population had responded to the local environment with a change in head shape. However, stature did appear to be elevated and this led Hrdlička to say:

The averages [174·4 cm for males; 161·8 cm for females] exceed, by approximately two-thirds of an inch (or 2 cm), those of Americans in general, and even those of the 'native born' . . ., a good proportion of whom are second (or more) generation Americans; and as they hold true for every subdivision of the series, we may regard as established the first fact of importance, which is that in general the Old Americans are the tallest among the American people [84, p. 76].

Stołyhwo's study made no attempt to provide a metrical description of the Brazilian Polish population, and instead simply showed how stature had been affected by the new environment. As summarized in Table 14, most of the Brazilian-born generations

TABLE 14

Average stature of people of Polish descent in Paraná (*Brazil*)*

| Male groups | | Average stature (*mm*) | Female groups | | Average stature (*mm*) |
|---|---|---|---|---|---|
| Fathers born in Poland | | 165·3 | Mothers born in Poland | | 154·1 |
| | 51–63 | 164·2 | | 51–63 | 157·7 |
| | 41–50 | 169·4 | | 41–50 | 156·3 |
| Sons born in | 31–40 | 169·8 | Daughters born in | 31–40 | 159·0 |
| Brazil, aged | 26–30 | 170·6 | Brazil, aged | 26–30 | 159·1 |
| | 21–25 | 171·3 | | 21–25 | 157·4 |
| | 20 | 169·5 | | 20 | 160·1 |

* From Stołyhwo [220], Table 1 modified

are taller than the original Polish-born generation. Inequalities in sample sizes probably account for some of the variations in stature at different ages shown in the table.

A one-time study of a population, such as the foregoing, gives no indication as to whether growth changes between generations – often referred to as secular changes – continue beyond the age span of that population. Only long-range or follow-up studies can indicate the full effect of the environment in this direction. However, comparability in prolonged or successive studies is not easy to achieve, because population samples are seldom selected in the same way over a long time and measurements are usually subject to each investigator's personal error. Granting this, the main support for the existence of secular changes in the body dimensions of the newest Americans comes from the finding in successive generations of a continuing slight increase in average stature – the dimension least subject to measurement error.

Students have provided the most satisfactory population for long-range study of secular change in size. For example, at Harvard University between the years 1880 and 1917 the Department of Physical Education recorded the stature of students engaging in athletics. During the ten years preceding 1880 a college physician recorded student stature. Among the students measured during these forty-seven years were 881 father–son pairs (small series). After 1917 Harvard required medical examinations of all students and the records for an additional fifteen years, combined with the earlier ones, provide another series of some 1,600 pairs (large series). Thanks to the efforts of Gordon T. Bowles, who as a graduate student analyzed the Harvard records, extended secular stature changes have been demonstrated in the Old American population (Tables 15 and 16) [23]. Bowles found a

TABLE 15

Stature of Harvard fathers and sons by age (small series)*

| Age | No. | Fathers Mean ± p.e. | No. | Sons Mean ± p.e. |
|---|---|---|---|---|
| 17 | 32 | 174·2 ± 0·82 | 66 | 176·7 ± 0·52 |
| 18 | 86 | 173·3 ± 0·47 | 170 | 177·8 ± 0·28 |
| 19 | 87 | 173·8 ± 0·43 | 139 | 177·8 ± 0·36 |
| 20 | 49 | 174·5 ± 0·50 | 62 | 177·1 ± 0·53 |
| 21 | 51 | 173·1 ± 0·51 | 19 | 174·6 ± 0·75 |

* From Bowles [23], Table 11, page 18, modified

TABLE 16

Stature of Harvard male students by birth decade (large series)*

| Decade | No. | Mean ± p.e. |
|---|---|---|
| 1856–1865 | 335 | 172·9 ± 0·22 |
| 1866–1875 | 506 | 174·4 ± 0·18 |
| 1876–1885 | 307 | 175·6 ± 0·23 |
| 1886–1895 | 267 | 176·5 ± 0·26 |
| 1896–1905 | 607 | 177·3 ± 0·17 |
| 1906–1915 | 546 | 178·0 ± 0·20 |

* From Bowles [23], Table 21, page 25, modified

similar trend in the records of four New England women's colleges.

Argentina also provides large samples of stature measurements on boys of the same age. This is due to the fact that the local law requires every boy to register for military service upon reaching the age of eighteen. Stature is recorded because acceptance for service depends upon a stated minimum height being exceeded. Fortunately, for the present purpose, two 'classes' born thirty-three years apart (1891 and 1924) have been compared in such a way as to bring out the secular change in size [181]. Figure 29

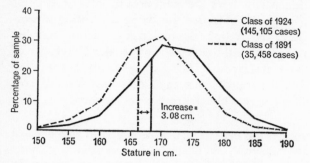

Fig. 29 Frequency polygons showing increase in mean stature in Argentine military registrants of 18 years of age, over a period of 33 years. After Severino-Lopez [181]

summarizes the findings. Although environment undoubtedly has played a role in producing the large increase in stature shown – 3·08 cm – another factor, immigration, may have been just as important. The reason for saying this is that about three-quarters of the 1924 class came from around Buenos Aires and the Plata river system. Not only are the highest statures reported from these regions, but most of the late immigration from Europe settled here. Further analysis would be required to tell whether the secular increase in stature occurred mainly where the immigrants settled. In any case, the situation is not comparable to that described for Harvard University. The latter student population was not much affected by late European immigration and long remained Old American in composition.

Most other anthropometric studies of the Europe-derived American population have been based on more or less random samples, and usually have had as their purpose the determination of size ranges useful in the manufacture of clothing and other products subject to human engineering. Therefore, they have not provided much insight into the nature of the population changes.

One of the exceptions is noteworthy because someone involved thought to inquire into the national extractions of the subjects [25]. The study in question was made towards the end of World War II at an Army Camp in Alabama by request of the Chemical Warfare Service of the United States Army. These circumstances, and the fact that facial dimensions were the main area of interest, suggest that the project had as its objective the sizing and fitting of gas-masks. At any rate, the records on national extraction enabled Alice Brues – a physical anthropologist now at the University of Colorado, but then at Harvard University – to draw from the measurements broader conclusions than otherwise would have been the case. This emerges clearly from her summary:

Regional differences are less marked than those associated with national extraction, but are statistically considerable. Residence in the United States appears to have effected an increase of stature, at least in the shorter European stocks, with a corresponding slight decrease in cephalic index: certainty on this point is prevented by ignorance of selective factors in immigration. Differences in national extraction between different areas of the United States are found to be consider-able, reflecting the historical sequence of migrations. The physical differences of the various regions appear to be primarily determined by the distribution of the various European stocks which settled them [25, p. 480].

*American Negroes and anthropometric studies of race crossing*
Most of our present knowledge of American Negro physique is based on two monumental anthropometric studies carried out independently and almost simultaneously in the early part of this century [46, 74]. The organizers of these studies – Charles B. Davenport of the Carnegie Institution of Washington's Cold Spring Harbor (New York) Station, and Melville J. Herskovits of Northwestern University in Evanston, Illinois – recognized the fact that, as Herskovits put it, 'in the American Negro population there exists what practically amounts to a laboratory condition for the study of race crossing' [74]. Since, of course, this condition is widespread, the investigators could work in different localities: Davenport and Steggerda in Jamaica and Herskovits in the United States (east of the Mississippi River and south of a line connecting St Louis and New York City). Also, they approached the subject

somewhat differently: the former more from the genetical side and the latter more from the anthropological side. I will briefly summarize the main points of each of these studies in turn.

The Jamaican population sample consisted of 370 individuals (197 males and 173 females) with the two sexes divided about equally between three genetical classes: Blacks, Browns and Whites.

Black denotes an individual whose genetic constitution, so far as it is possible to ascertain, is that of a pure African Negro. The term is thus applied in Jamaica. Brown indicates a hybrid – sambo, mulatto, quadroon or more complex cross. This term is sometimes thus applied in Jamaica. Whites have a genetic constitution of an European as nearly as can be ascertained [46].

In 1926–7 when the study was made about 76·9 per cent of the Jamaican population was Black, 18·3 per cent Brown, 1·7 per cent White, and 3·0 per cent 'other' (mainly Asiatics).

The sample of measurements from the Jamaican study presented in Table 17 shows the relatively shorter trunk, longer extremities,

TABLE 17

Means of selected measurements on Jamaicans
by genetical classes and sex*

| Measurement | Blacks | | Browns | | Whites | |
|---|---|---|---|---|---|---|
| | No. | Mean ± p.e. | No. | Mean ± p.e. | No. | Mean ± p.e. |
| | | *Males* | | | | |
| Stature | 54 | 170·6 ± 0·62 | 93 | 170·2 ± 0·47 | 50 | 172·7 ± 0·66 |
| Span | 50 | 180·4 ± 0·88 | 93 | 180·7 ± 0·59 | 50 | 177·3 ± 0·93 |
| Sitting height | 51 | 88·0 ± 0·37 | 93 | 87·7 ± 0·25 | 50 | 91·7 ± 0·31 |
| Leg length | 53 | 92·6 ± 0·45 | 91 | 92·3 ± 0·34 | 48 | 92·0 ± 0·41 |
| Interpupillary distance | 51 | 70·6 ± 0·30 | 93 | 69·0 ± 0·28 | 48 | 65·1 ± 0·30 |
| Nasal breadth | 51 | 45·8 ± 0·26 | 93 | 42·6 ± 0·24 | 50 | 34·9 ± 0·24 |
| | | *Females* | | | | |
| Stature | 51 | 158·3 ± 0·59 | 72 | 158·7 ± 0·49 | 50 | 160·5 ± 0·60 |
| Span | 49 | 165·7 ± 0·58 | 69 | 165·2 ± 0·68 | 50 | 162·1 ± 0·69 |
| Sitting height | 50 | 82·1 ± 0·29 | 72 | 83·0 ± 0·27 | 50 | 85·2 ± 0·31 |
| Leg length | 30 | 85·4 ± 0·42 | 21 | 86·0 ± 0·53 | 6 | 81·6 ± 0·92 |
| Interpupillary distance | 49 | 66·7 ± 0·33 | 72 | 66·2 ± 0·27 | 49 | 62·6 ± 0·29 |
| Nasal breadth | 50 | 40·7 ± 0·27 | 72 | 38·8 ± 0·25 | 49 | 32·3 + 0·26 |

* From Davenport and Steggerda [46]. All means, except those for interpupillary distance and nasal breadth, are in centimeters

wider interpupillary distance and broader nose of the Blacks, traits which clearly differentiate them from the Whites. As for the measurements themselves, the means for the Browns are closer to those for the Blacks than to those for the Whites. From measures of variability not given here 'It appears that in those traits in which the Whites and Blacks differ genetically, the Browns are, in general, especially variable' [46].

Herskovits' series, representing the combined measurements of five investigators working between the years 1915 and 1926, includes, besides children, 1,893 adults (962 males and 931 females) [74]. Apparently the only rule regarding admission to the series was that the individual be regarded, by himself or others, as a sociological Negro. This means that all degrees of racial crossing – mainly between West Africans, Europeans and American Indians – were represented fairly randomly. The main evaluation of the amount of crossing was through genealogies going back at least through the grandparents. By this means Herskovits determined that 'only about 20 to 25% of American Negroes are of unmixed African stock' [73].* Although about one-quarter to one-third of the American Negroes studied claimed partial American Indian ancestry, this mixture 'took place so long ago, and was of such small quantity when compared with the amount of White crossing which took place, that it is biologically of small moment'.

As analyzed genealogically, omitting individuals claiming American Indian ancestors, the measurements tend to grade between Negro and White according to amount of mixture. Herskovits believed that the gradations confirmed the essential validity of the genealogies. In any event, four of the six measurements selected to illustrate the results of the Davenport and Steggerda study (Table 17) are also included in the Herskovits study and hence are used here (Table 18), both for comparison with the former study and for illustration of the results of the latter study. Note, however, that different criteria were used for the selection of the Blacks (or unmixed Negroes) in the two studies, and that the two White series represent immigrants from different parts of Europe.

* Using a broader genetic approach, D.F.Roberts has placed the European element in the general Negro population of the United States at twenty per cent [168].

### Skin-color inheritance

Neither of these major studies on race crossing explored the mode of inheritance of skin color, one of the more distinguishing characters of the racial groups involved in the crossing. Probably this was due to the fact that a seemingly satisfactory hypothesis already had been developed by Davenport as far back as 1913 [45]. His hypothesis grew out of the observation that in Negro–White crosses the $F_2$ generation exhibits increased color variability over

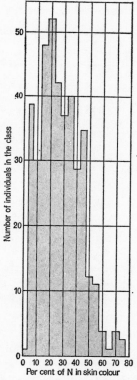

Fig. 30 Polygon of frequency of each grade of N (black) in skin color of Negro–White crosses in Bermuda. After Davenport [45]

the $F_1$ generation. Suspecting that this differential variability indicated the existence of color segregation, he constructed a frequency polygon for black pigmentation (N) obtained with a color top in a population sample from Bermuda (fig. 30), and found five separate peaks in the color range. Since one (double) inheritance factor – gene pair – will account for only three such color peaks or segregations in a population, he stated his hypothesis thus (p. 13): 'There are two (double) factors (A and B) for black pigmentation in the full-blooded negro of the west coast of Africa, and these are separately inheritable.'

TABLE 18

Means (and p.e.) of selected measurements to show
the effect of Negro–White crossing: Males*

*Genealogical divisions†*

| Measure-ment | N | NNW | NW | NWW | W |
|---|---|---|---|---|---|
| Stature | (102) | (115) | (87) | (23) | (727) |
|  | 170·4 ± 0·38 | 170·4 ± 0·43 | 171·7 ± 0·43 | 172·2 ± 0·99 | 174·3 ± 0·14 |
| Sitting | (102) | (115) | (87) | (23) | (727) |
| height | 87·3 ± 0·20 | 88·1 ± 0·18 | 88·4 ± 0·24 | 89·1 ± 0·45 | 91·8 |
| Inter- | (108) | (125) | (93) | (29) | (100) |
| pupillary | 68·1 ± 0·20 | 66·4 ± 0·22 | 66·4 ± 0·24 | 64·6 ± 0·39 | 63·4 ± 0·28 |
| distance |  |  |  |  |  |
| Nasal | (109) | (129) | (95) | (30) | (247) |
| breadth | 43·4 ± 0·18 | 41·3 ± 0·20 | 40·0 ± 0·21 | 37·5 ± 0·48 | 36·1 ± 0·14 |

* From Herskovits [74]

† N = Unmixed Negro (22·0 per cent); NNW = more Negro than White (24·8 per cent); NW = about same amount of Negro and White (16·7 per cent); NWW = more White than Negro (9·3 per cent); W = unmixed White for comparison (mostly from Hrdlička [84])

For a better understanding of figure 30 and of the further expression of the hypothesis in Table 19, the color-top method of skin-color determination needs explanation. The top is essentially a spinning disk designed to blend black (N), red (R), yellow (Y) and white (W) sectors in different proportions according as more or less of each is exposed. When, on spinning the top (usually after many unsuccessful attempts to get the right combination of colors), a match is obtained between the blended color and the selected skin surface, the percentages of N, R, Y and W are recorded. In the Bermuda Negro population used by Davenport in developing his hypothesis the percentages of N obtained in this way ranged from near 0 to 78. Many have complained about the obviously considerable subjectivity involved in this operation, but in the present instance the likelihood of the color segregation being attributable to this factor seems remote. Nevertheless, a different method of skin-color determination has now led to a different hypothesis, as we will see next.

Another geneticist who became interested in the inheritance of skin color was the late R. Ruggles Gates. He studied all sorts of race crossings, but finally concentrated on American Negroes. For

## TABLE 19

### Classification of skin color in race crosses on the basis of the two-factor hypothesis*

| Factors (Gene pairs) | Geno-types† | Phenotypes | Rel. freq. | % of N in offspring‡ | Popular names (Jamaica) |
|---|---|---|---|---|---|
| Both absent | aabb | White | 1:16 | 0–11 | 'Pass for White' Mustifine Mustifee Octoroon |
| One present | Aabb | Light colored | 4:16 | 12–25 | Quadroon |
| Two present | AaBb | Medium colored (F1) | 6:16 | 26–40 | Mulatto |
| Three present | AABb | Dark colored | 4:16 | 41–55 | Mangro, Sambo |
| All four present | AABB | Black | 1:16 | 56–78 | Negro |

* From Davenport [45], Table 7, page 14, modified

† Capital letters (A, B) indicate presence of the factor, lower case letters (a, b) absence of the factor

‡ N = black, one of three colors comprising skin color as determined by the Bradley color top. The ranges of percent were derived from figure 30

this last phase of the study he discarded the color top and substituted a color chart of his own devising. The chart, used as a frontispiece in one of his books [60], consists of nine color blocks representing Gates' selection of the same number of 'persons spread as equally as possible within the whole range of skin-color variations'. Each skin color was first matched on canvas by an 'experienced artist' and then reproduced in colored inks on paper. Color block no. 1 represents the 'blackest [skin color] that could be found,' whereas no. 9 represents the skin color of a white person – Gates himself. Only the first eight blocks were used in the study of Negro–White crosses.

Initially Gates judged each color block to represent a discrete unit of melanin pigment. While matching skin colors with the chart, however, he decided that nos. 2 and 3 represent different tones rather than different degrees of melanin. He decided, there-fore, to combine them (2,3). On the other hand, he found that certain individuals had skin colors falling between pairs of color blocks, particularly nos. 3–4, 6–7 and 7–8. Accordingly, he recorded these individuals as 3·5, 6·5 and 7·5. In addition, he experienced difficulty in telling whether the skin color of some individuals matched color blocks 4, 5 or 6, and hence he treated such cases as a single group (4,5,6). With these adjustments, he was still able to fit all cases into eight color units as follow (with the dashes separating the units): 1 – 2,3 – 3·5 – 4,5,6 – 6·5 – 7 – 7·5 – 8.

When you segregate skin color into eight instead of five units as Davenport did, how do you explain this genetically? The answer is that you propose a three-(double)-factor hypothesis and thereby go one better than Davenport. Gates did just this, and explained it as follows:

From studies of a number of . . . families in which one parent was white and one or both parents near white, it was concluded that there are two factors (S and T), each of which produces a small amount of melanin in the skin, S producing more than T. Combinations of these will produce most of the lighter intermediate skin colors. The darker pigmentations are determined by a third factor, R, which probably produces at least twice as much melanin as S and T combined. We thus arrive at a con-dition in which the genes are weighted for pigment production as follows: R = 6, S = 2, T = 1. These relationships are set forth in [Table 20]. While the actual values assigned to the genes are hypo-thetical, the evidence seems clear, for instance, that T produces very little melanin and R a much greater amount [61, p. 23].

Without going into further detail, I think it is obvious that Gates' color chart affords a different sort of opportunity for sub-jectivity than does the color top. If one sets out by dividing the skin-color range of a population into eight parts, one can surely assign every member of the population to one or another of them and end up with just as many segregations as were predetermined. By contrast, the color top, while demanding a subjective reading, yields only percentages of the component colors and gives no advance indication of the distributional peaks that represent segregation.

My criticism of Gates' hypothesis emphasizes a repeated com-plaint throughout this book, namely, that investigations of the separate components of the American population have been belated, incomplete and sometimes unsatisfactory. Although only selected examples of such investigations – usually those which I regard as particularly significant – have been cited, their limitations should be apparent from the accounts given of them. Clearly, those

TABLE 20

Classification of skin colors in Negro–White crosses
on the basis of the three-factor hypothesis*

| Color blocks (Phenotypes) | Genotypes† | Color blocks (Phenotypes) | Genotypes† |
|---|---|---|---|
| # 1 | RRSSTT = 18<br>RRSSTt = 17<br>RRSStt = 16⎱<br>RRSsTT = 16⎰<br>RRSsTt = 15 | # 4, 5, 6 | RrssTt = 7<br>Rrsstt = 6⎱<br>rrSSTT = 6⎰<br>rrSSTt = 5<br>rrSStt = 4⎱<br>rrSsTT = 4⎰ |
| # 2, 3 | RRSstt = 14⎱<br>RRssTT = 14⎰<br>RRssTt = 13<br>RRsstt = 12⎱<br>RrSSTT = 12⎰ | # 6·5 | rrSsTt = 3 |
|  |  | # 7 | rrSstt = 2⎱<br>rrssTT = 2⎰ |
| # 3·5 | RrSSTt = 11<br>RrSStt = 10⎱<br>RrSsTT = 10⎰<br>RrSsTt = 9<br>RrSstt = 8⎱<br>RrssTT = 8⎰ | # 7·5 | rrssTt = 1 |
|  |  | # 8 | rrsstt = 0 |

* From Gates [61], figure 10, page 26, modified

† Capital letters (R, S, T) indicate presence of the factor, lower case letters (r, s, t) absence of the factor. Values assigned to the factors are: R = 6, S = 2, T = 1. Thus, the formula RRSSTt = 6 + 6 + 2 + 2 + 1 + 0 = 17

relating to American Negroes are not exceptional in these regards. Much more information about American Negroes is needed, particularly as to the ways in which they have responded to the New World environment considered in its widest sense. Today, however, many American Negroes very likely would not submit at all, or certainly not as willingly as in the past, to genealogical questioning and physical examination, the reason being their growing alarm about the possibility of racist purposes motivating these procedures. And they could justify this stand, unfortunately, by citing a propagandist named Carleton Putnam who, in a recent book – not the only one of its kind – classes all differences between Negroes and Whites as innate and characterizes the environmental explanation of any of these differences as the fiendish conception of a socially 'out-group' of anthropologists led by Franz Boas [160].

The numerous accounts of Boas' contributions in the field of anthropology in the foregoing chapters should leave little doubt that he approached the problem of explaining physical differences between human groups in an unbiased and objective manner. This being the case, his conclusions in favor of the environment as the primary cause of these differences can readily withstand malicious accusations. This is not to say, however, that the problem can be considered solved and that further research along this line would be a waste of time; it is to say only that man's very nature makes it extremely difficult to find convincing support for any other explanation.

### *Group differences in atherosclerosis*

An example from a different field – medicine – will show how difficult it is sometimes to distinguish between what is innate and what is acquired. I have in mind a disease commonly referred to as 'hardening of the arteries'. The technical term is atherosclerosis. During the time of racial segregation in the United States, Charity Hospital in New Orleans had separate entrances and facilities for Whites and Negroes. This led to the observation that these two groups had different amounts of atherosclerosis: Whites more than Negroes. To get at the causes of this difference a team of investigators at Louisiana State University School of Medicine in New Orleans set up an International Atherosclerosis Project, the object being to assemble autopsy records on a wide geographical basis.

Table 21, taken from one of a number of articles comprising a summary report on the Project, dramatizes the 'racial' aspect of the findings [226]. A few more details of the collecting program add to the impressiveness of the tabulated figures. Cooperating pathologists in the fourteen countries involved secured a total of 23,207 sets of coronary arteries and aortas from consecutive autopsied persons in the years 1960 to 1965. From this total, 13,084 (15 to 64 years of age) were selected for analysis on the basis of four categories of non-cardiovascular causes of death (accidents, cancer, infections and miscellaneous). In addition, objective criteria were established for quantifying the abnormal changes in the lining tissue (intima) of the vessels. The smallest sample for any group numbered 260.

### TABLE 21

Ranking of American and other racial groups according to their susceptibility to coronary and aortic atherosclerosis *

| Location (Listed in decreasing order of susceptibility) | White | White–Negro | Negro | White–Indian | White–Asiatic |
|---|---|---|---|---|---|
| New Orleans (US) | 18·3† | | | | |
| Oslo (Norway) | 17·8 | | | | |
| Durban (S. Africa) | 14·6 | | | | |
| New Orleans (US) | | 14·5 | | | |
| Manila (Phil.) | | | | | 12·8 |
| Caracas (Venez.) | | | | 12·1 | |
| São Paulo (Brazil) | 10·8 | | | | |
| Puerto Rico (W.I.) | 9·6 | | | | |
| Jamaica (W.I.) | | 9·5 | | | |
| Cali (Colombia) | | | | 9·1 | |
| Puerto Rico (W.I.) | | 8·8 | | | |
| Lima (Peru) | | | | 8·5 | |
| Costa Rica (C.A.) | 8·4 | | | | |
| Santiago (Chile) | 8·2 | | | | |
| Mexico | | | | 7·9 | |
| São Paulo (Brazil) | | 7·4 | | | |
| Bogotá (Colombia) | | | | 6·7 | |
| Guatemala (C.A.) | | | | 6·5 | |
| Durban (S. Africa) | | | 6·2‡ | | |

* From Tejada et al. [226], Table 5, page 519, modified
† Unweighted mean of percentage of intimal surface involved with raised atherosclerotic lesions. The complicated computation of this percentage, involving different areas of the vessels, different age groups, and the two sexes, is explained in Table 4, page 519, of the original publication
‡ Bantu

The main thing to note in Table 21 is that generally Whites have more atherosclerosis than the White–Negro crosses and the latter more than the White–Indian crosses. Unfortunately, the Bantu are not representative of the African Negroes brought to the Western Hemisphere, and the Filipinos of Manila are not representative of the Asiatics most closely related to the American Indians. Note, too, that where there are White and White–Negro groups from the same locality (New Orleans, São Paulo and Puerto Rico) the Whites show the higher figure. But why should the White group of New Orleans have almost twice as much atherosclerosis as that of Puerto Rico? Why should the White–Negro group in New Orleans have twice as much atherosclerosis as that of São Paulo? Can anyone say that the differences are due to race when such factors as nutrition, occupation and climate are not taken into account? For that matter, how do you objectively quantify the lifetime effect that nutrition, occupation and climate have had on a dead man? Obviously, there are still questions regarding the physical differences between the Neo-Americans that remain unanswered.

# 11

# Projections

I have entitled this final chapter 'projections' rather than 'predictions' because the former word conveys more the idea of reading the future in a scientific manner, not that this is always possible. I also could have used the word 'trajectories' and thereby implied the courses of events now beyond control. Having carried the ramifications of the subject up to the present from a still vague point thousands of years in the past, the momentum necessarily carries them a little way beyond actual events. Yet, as we have seen, man can change the course of events very rapidly. How close, therefore the trajectories or projections will prove to be to the true course of events only time will tell.

### Quantitative plots

The uncertainty about future events deviating from projections based on past events is well illustrated by Raymond Pearl's statistical efforts to foretell the ultimate limit of the population of the United States. Using census records – an unusually reliable form of information about population growth – he and his colleagues at Johns Hopkins University in Baltimore fitted logistic curves to the decennial counts, first from 1790 to 1910 [150], and then from 1790 to 1940 [151]. Figure 31 shows the first curve with the census figures for 1920, 1930 and 1940 added. The projection here is for a leveling off of the population at about 197 millions around the year 2100. Figure 32 shows the second curve as adjusted to fit better the census figures for 1920, 1930 and 1940. The projection here is for a leveling off of the population at about 184 millions around the year 2100. How much in error this projection was is indicated by the census figures for 1950, 1960 and 1970 which I have added.

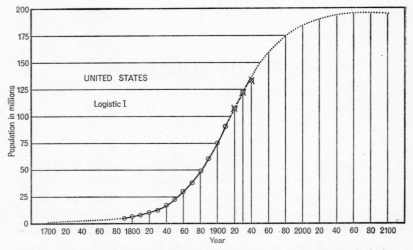

Fig. 31 First logistic curve fitted to the census counts (plain circles) from 1790 to 1910 inclusive. The dashed portion of the curve includes added census counts (crossed circles) from 1920 to 1940, which indicate the need for a better fitting curve. This need led to the second logistic curve shown in fig. 32. After Pearl *et al.* [151]

Pearl was well aware of the limitations of his projections and was careful to qualify them as follows:

. . . it is a basic postulate of the logistic theory of population growth that any particular population can be expected to continue to follow in its later growth the same logistic curve that it has followed in its earlier growth *only* if there has been no serious or cataclysmic alteration of the conditions (climatic, geological, biological, economic or social) under which its earlier growth has taken place [151, p. 487].

Among the unanticipated changing conditions were the increased birth rate and decreased immigration following World War I. Since then, of course, there has been another World War, wars involving Americans in Korea and Vietnam, and the introduction of 'the pill' as a contraceptive. On balance, however, these changes have not held down the population and the rate of growth, which already exceeds the projections and still shows no signs of leveling off.

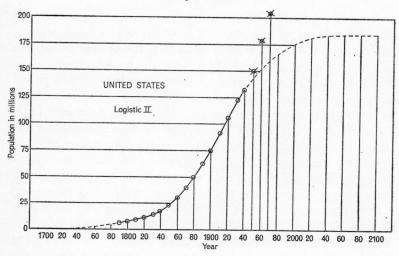

Fig. 32 Second logistic curve fitted to census counts (plain circles) from 1790 to 1940 inclusive. Subsequent census counts (crossed circles) have been added to show that this curve no longer fits. After Pearl *et al.* [151, modified]

The population of mainland United States now represents about ninety per cent of that of all of North America north of Mexico, an area which can be considered roughly half of that of the entire Western Hemisphere. In this sense the southern half consists of Mexico, Central America, the West Indies and South America. Judging from population estimates, these two halves of the hemisphere also may have been equal in total populations some time in the 1960s [3]. My qualification here takes into consideration two factors importantly influencing the estimates: the higher birth rate in South America as compared with North America (38 versus 18 births per 1,000 population), and the lesser accuracy in population enumeration in the southern half of the hemisphere. Presumably, therefore, if dependable census figures were available for all the countries in the southern half of the hemisphere, one could plot a growth curve resembling that for the United States, but ascending more steeply of late. Presumably, too, the rate of increase in this largely Catholic area will continue until religious proscriptions against contraception give way and the birth rate diminishes.

The Mongoloid element, embracing mainly the descendants of the aboriginal inhabitants, now in all degrees of racial mixture, places second to the Caucasoid element in the present population of the Western Hemisphere. Population figures for the American Indians vary in reliability from country to country and from period to period, especially in the places where mixture was intensive from the beginning of settlement, which means primarily Latin America. Again, therefore, the trends are best indicated in the censuses of the United States. These sources show that in 1860 the American Indians were only 0·1 per cent of the total population – probably their nadir; that seventy years later (1930) they were increasing in numbers slowly (0·3 per cent of the population); and that by the end of the next thirty years (1960) they were increasing at a much more rapid rate (2·9 per cent of the population). The 1970 census extends this figure to about 4·0 per cent. Considering that American Indians once constituted the entire population of the area presently represented by the first forty-eight States, the trend toward their complete elimination appears now to be definitely reversed. They can be expected to continue to increase in the sociological sense, which means an increase also in the degree of racial admixture.

The Negroid element, likewise now highly mixed, places third in the hemisphere and well below the others. The census figures for the Negroes in the United States go back, as already stated, to 1790. Figure 33 suggests that the proportion of Negroes in the total population at that time (19·3 per cent) may well represent the highest point in the relationship (zenith), with the nadir (9·7 per cent) not being reached until 1930. Figure 33 shows that after the trend reversed itself the proportion increased to 10·5 in 1960 and to 11·2 in 1970. Like the Indians, the Negroes can be expected to continue increasing in the sociological sense, and especially as repugnance against this most conspicuous type of union diminishes.

The nature of the available information permits one to say more about populations in the quantitative sense than in the qualitative sense. Although some of the census questions get at the characteristics of the population – chiefly economic status – they touch on the physical attributes of the subjects enumerated only as regards sex and age. One can argue that questions on at least stature and weight, if made a part of the census, would not only yield broad insight into population quality, but would supply anthropometric data of great practical value, since human size must be taken into account in so many connections. Understandably, however, these

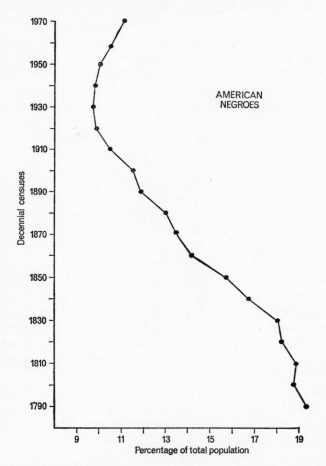

Fig. 33 Changing proportions of Negroes in the total population of the United States as reported in the decennial censuses.

questions have not yet been included in a census and probably never will be. Only if the answers were obtained in the form of careful measurements, would their reliability ever be established. Also, aside from the impracticability of measuring everyone, probably a high proportion of the population would regard the procedure as an invasion of privacy.

As an alternative to the census approach to the entire population, the proposal has been made to utilize the census organization and approach to identify a small but statistically adequate sample of the population for measurement in a separate operation. Although this scheme is attractive, it would be very expensive to carry out, because it would involve the training of many people in standardized measuring techniques and the transporting of them to many places. Nevertheless, it seems to me that eventually the overwhelming size of the American population and the pressing need for its better management will require the collection of this sort of qualitative information.

### Qualitative changes

As matters now stand, projections of the qualitative changes in the American population perforce must rest on slim evidence. The secular change in stature that Bowles studied at Harvard University (p. 214) was carried forward to 1965 by a current professor there, Albert Damon, and judged by him to have run its course [42]. But the evidence consists of four generations of only twelve families (85 subjects: 12 fathers, 24 sons, 30 grandsons and 19 great-grandsons). Probably this finding should not be interpreted to mean that the process is also now inactive in the general population, which includes a great many less favored groups. I expect, therefore, that the Europe-derived population at large will continue slowly to increase in stature for a few more generations.

Nothing is known on this score about the American Negroes, but the process of hybridization, coupled with increasing improvements in health and nutrition, should be producing an even more marked change of the same sort in them. Developments along this line among Indians are even more of a mystery.

Damon's study revealed a remarkable up-turn in body weight in his fourth Harvard generation [42]. This may not be typical, or it may mean only that modern Americans are tending more than ever to over-eating. It should be noted in this connection that many of the North American Indians now living on reservations are much fatter than their ancestors who lived a more active life. In any event, body weight is a characteristic which fluctuates with age, degree of activity and the available food supply. The accelerating urbanization which marks the modern way of life should militate against a slimmer waistline.

Secular changes in size and shape amount to so little in the long run that a trained eye could not detect them if presented with two batches of photographs taken of, say, eighteen-year-old Harvard students in 1850 and in 1950. On the other hand, the changes that come with race crossing tend to result promptly, as we have seen, in features intermediate between those of the parent races. In this respect, a random sample of reservation Indians photographed in 1950 might appear noticeably different – i.e., somewhat less Indian – from one photographed in 1850 on the same reservation. I feel certain, however, that in most parts of Latin America, where the Whites and Indians have been crossing for over four hundred years, a comparison of the same sort would not reveal such apparent changes as those in North America. In Latin America, if anywhere in the Western Hemisphere, a new American type may have emerged. Although they have now backed off from the idea, in 1950 the North American anthropologists Carleton Coon, Stanley Garn and Joseph Birdsell were willing to recognize a 'Ladino' race in the phenotypic sense – i.e., on the basis of gross appearance [41].

These same authors also went so far in 1950 as to recognize the 'North American Colored' as a phenotypic race. In view of the great amount of segregation of physical features still evident in this group, I see such a race as barely emerging. If it were possible to look for changes in the North American Negroes through a century of time in the way described above for the other American groups, the findings might or might not be positive, depending on locality. This qualification is necessary because of the great amount of internal migration that has taken place in the United States since the Civil War. The exodus from the South that started after the war ended has led now to a great increase in all degrees of mixture in the northern cities, with a residue of less-mixed groups left behind [241].

What I am getting at is that physical change in the American population, although seemingly more evident in the last couple of centuries, is still a slow process. The dramatist Israel Zangwill, who early in this century characterized America as 'the great

Melting-pot, where all races of Europe are melting and re-forming', created through his hyperbole an impression of speed – of a process rapidly approaching completion [242]. Only in the social sense is this true; social evolution outruns biological evolution. And, of course, this applies also to the racial elements in the American melting-pot other than those from Europe.

The American population at large will continue to change physically as its component elements experience and react to the diminishing degrees of isolation. Throughout this book the concept of isolation – continent from continent, people from people, culture from culture – has been the key to the unfolding story. The continuance of isolation helped create the aboriginal Americans; the reduction of isolation went far towards bringing about their destruction and at the same time the creation of the Neo-Americans. Now, just as important as the reduction of isolation is the advancement of technology, which has reached an unparalleled height. As a result of their good fortune in this direction, the Neo-Americans have an opportunity beyond that granted before to any other people to manage their destiny, but whether they will do so successfully none of the projections from past events foretells.

# Appendix

Scales for converting centimeters into inches *

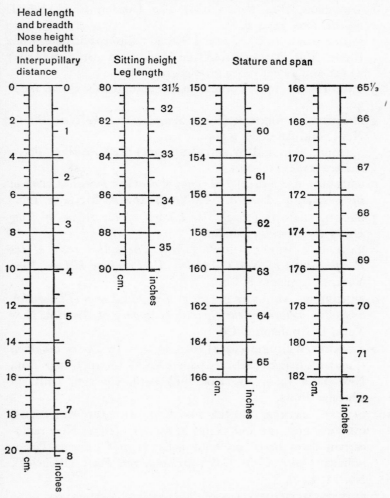

Head length
and breadth
Nose height
and breadth
Interpupillary
distance

Sitting height
Leg length

Stature and span

# References

1 ANDERSON, DUANE C. (1966) The Gordon Creek burial, *SWest. Lore* **32**: 1–9.

2 ANONYMOUS (1962) New and revised radio-carbon dates from Brazil, *Mus. News* (W.H.Over Mus., State Univ. S. Dak.) **23** (11 and 12): 4 pages (mimeographed).

3 ANONYMOUS (1966) Population size and growth, *Popul. Index* **32**: 160–8.

4 ARCINIEGAS, GERMAN (1955) *Amerigo and the New World.* New York, Alfred A. Knopf.

5 ARNOLD, J.R. and W.F.LIBBY (1951) Radio-carbon dates, *Science* **113**: 111–20.

6 ASHBURN, P.M. (1947) *The ranks of death; a medical history of the conquest of America.* New York, Howard-McCann, Inc.

7 BACON, FRANCIS (1622) *The historie of the reigne of King Henry the Seventh.* London.

8 BANCROFT, HUBERT HOWE (1876) *The native races of the Pacific States of North America. V. Primitive history.* New York, D.Appleton & Co.

9 BANDELIER, ADOLPHE F. (1893) *The gilded man (El dorado), and other pictures of the Spanish occupancy of America.* New York, D.Appleton & Co.

10 BENNETT, WENDELL (1951) Introduction. In *The civilizations of ancient America* (Selected papers XXIX Intern. Congr. Am., New York 1949, Sol Tax, Ed.) 1–16. Chicago, Univ. of Chicago Press.

10a BERGER, RAINER, REINER PROTSCH, RICHARD REYNOLDS, CHARLES ROZAIRE and JAMES R. SACKETT (1971) New radiocarbon dates based on bone collagen of California Paleoindians, *Contr. Univ. Calif. archaeol. res. Facil.* (Berkeley), No. 12: 43–9.

11 BIRKET-SMITH, KAJ (1959) The earliest Eskimo portraits, *Folk, Copenhagen,* **1**: 5–14.

12 BOAS, FRANZ (1891) Second general report on the Indians of British Columbia, *Rep. Br. Ass. Advant Sci.* (Leeds, 1890), **60**: 562–715 (see pages 647–55 for section on deformed crania).

13 BOAS, FRANZ (1894) The anthropology of the North American Indian, *Mem. int. Congr. Anthrop.* (Chicago, 1893), pages 37–49.

14 BOAS, FRANZ (1895) Zur Anthropologie der nordamerikanischen Indianer, *Z. Ethnol.*, **27**: 366–411.

15 BOAS, FRANZ (1899) Anthropometry of Shoshonean tribes, *Am. Anthrop.* n.s. **1**: 751–8.

16 BOAS, FRANZ (1901) A.J.Stone's measurements of natives of the North-west Territories, *Bull. Am. Mus. nat. Hist.* **14**(6): 53–68.

17 BOAS, FRANZ (1911) Abstract of the report on changes in bodily form of descendants of immigrants, Senate Doc. 747, 61st Congr., 3rd ses. Washington, Government Printing Office.

18 BOAS, FRANZ (1911) Changes in bodily form of descendants of immigrants (Final report), Senate Doc. 208, 61st Congr., 2nd ses. Washington, Government Printing Office.

19 BOAS, FRANZ (1940) Changes in bodily form of descendants of immigrants, *Am. Anthrop.* **42**: 183–9.

20 BORAH, WOODROW and SHERBURNE F. COOK (1963) The aboriginal population of central Mexico on the eve of the Spanish conquest, *Ibero-Am.* **45**: 160 pages.

21 BORDIER, A. (1877) Les Esquimaux du Jardin d'Acclimatation, *Mém. Soc. Anthrop. Paris*, 2e sér., **1**: 448–61.

22 BOWDITCH, HENRY P. (1877) *The growth of children.* Boston.

23 BOWLES, GORDON TOWNSEND (1932) *New types of Old Americans at Harvard, and at eastern women's colleges.* Cambridge, Mass., Harvard Univ. Press.

24 BOYD, WILLIAM C. (1950) *Genetics and the races of man.* Boston, Little, Brown & Co.

25 BRUES, ALICE (1946) Regional differences in the physical characteristics of an American population, *Am. J. phys. Anthrop.* **4**: 463–80.

26 CALLEN, E.O. (1967) Analysis of the Teohuacan coprolites. In *Report of the Tehuacan Archaeological–Botanical Expedition*

(Douglas S. Byers, Ed.) I, 261–89. Austin, Univ. of Texas Press.

27 CALLEN, E.O. and T.W.M.CAMERON (1960) A prehistoric diet revealed in coprolites, *New Scient.* **8**: 35–40.

28 CAMPBELL, JOHN M. (1963) Ancient Alaska and paleolithic Europe, *Anthrop. Pap. Univ. Alaska* **10**(2): 29–49.

29 CANDELA, P.B. (1942) The introduction of blood group B into Europe, *Hum. Biol.* **14**: 413–43.

30 CAPPS, STEPHEN R. (1934) Notes on the geology of the Alaska Peninsula and Aleutian Islands, *Bull. U.S. geol. Surv.* **857-D**: 141–53.

31 CHAGNON, N.A., J.V.NEEL, L.WEITKAMP, H.GERSHOWITZ and M.AYRES. (1970) The influence of cultural factors on the demography and pattern of gene flow from the Makiritare to the Yanomama Indians, *Am. J. phys. Anthrop.* **32**: 339–50.

32 CHARD, CHESTER S. (1963) The Old World roots: Review and speculations, *Anthrop. Pap. Univ. Alaska* **10**(2): 115–21.

33 CHARD, CHESTER S. (1969) Archeology of the Soviet Union, *Science* **163**: 774–9.

34 CHERVIN, ARTHUR (1907) *Anthropologie bolivienne. II. Anthropometrie.* Paris.

35 CLAFLIN, WILLIAM H., JR. (1931) The Stalling's Island mound, Columbia County, Georgia, *Pap. Peabody Mus.* **14**(1): 47 pages.

36 COLLINS, HENRY B., JR. (1932) Caries and crowding in teeth of the living Alaskan Eskimo, *Am. J. phys. Anthrop.* **16**: 451–62.

37 COLUMBUS, CHRISTOPHER (1892) Extracts from the log or journal of the first voyage. In *The Voyages of Christopher Columbus* (Transl. from Navarrete by M.F.Vallette) 18–165. New York, United States Catholic Historical Society.

38 COMETTO, C.S. (1931) Contribución al estudio del desarrollo físico de los niños argentinos, etc., *Archos argent. Pediat.* **2**: 55–63.

39 COOK, S.F. (1946) Human sacrifice and warfare as factors in the demography of pre-colonial Mexico. *Hum. Biol.* **18**: 81–102.

40 COON, CARLETON S. (1965) *The living races of man.* New York, Alfred A. Knopf.

41 COON, C.S., STANLEY M.GARN and JOSEPH B.BIRDSELL (1950) *Races; a study of the problems of race formation in man.* Springfield, Ill., Charles C. Thomas.

42 DAMON, ALBERT (1968) Secular trend in height and weight within Old American families at Harvard, 1870–1965, *Am. J. phys. Anthrop.* **29**: 121 (Abstract).

43 DANIEL, GLYN (1968) One hundred years of Old World prehistory. In *One hundred years of anthropology* (J.O.Brew, Ed.) 54–93. Cambridge, Mass., Harvard Univ. Press.

44 DARWIN, CHARLES (1871) *Journal of researches into the natural history and geology of the countries visited during the voyage of H.M.S. Beagle round the world.* New York, D.Appleton & Co.

45 DAVENPORT, CHARLES B. (1913) Heredity of skin color in Negro–White crosses. *Publs Carnegie Instn* **188**: 106 pages.

46 DAVENPORT, C.B. and MORRIS STEGGERDA (1929) Race crossing in Jamaica, *Publs Carnegie Instn* **395**: 516 pages.

47 DE TERRA, HELMUT, JAVIER ROMERO and T.D.STEWART (1949) Tepexpan man, *Publs Anthrop. Viking Fund* **11**: 160 pages.

48 DOBYNS, HENRY F. (1966) An appraisal of techniques [for estimating aboriginal American populations] with a new hemispheric estimate, *Curr. Anthrop.* **7**(4): 395–416.

49 DONNAN, ELIZABETH (1935) Documents illustrative of the history of the slave trade to America. IV. The border colonies and the southern colonies, *Publs Carnegie Instn* **409**: 719 pages.

50 DUCKWORTH, W.L.H. and B.H.PAIN (1900) An account of some Eskimo from Labrador, *Proc. Camb. phil. Soc.* **10**: 286–91. (Reprinted in 1904 in *Studies from the Anthropological Laboratory, the Anatomy School, Cambridge* (W.L.H.Duckworth, Author and Ed.) **34**: 268–73; see 196–7 for corrections. Cambridge, Univ. Press.)

50a DUNBAR, CARL O. and KARL M. WAAGE (1969) *Historical geology.* 3rd. ed. New York, London, Sydney, Toronto, John Wiley & Sons, Inc.

51 DUNN, FREDERICK L. (1965) On the antiquity of malaria in the western hemisphere, *Hum. Biol.* **37**: 385–93.

52 DURÁN, DIEGO (1867) *Historia de las Indias de Nueva-Espana y Islas de Tierra Firme* (José F. Ramirez, Ed.) I. Mexico, Impr. de J.M.Andrade y F.Escalante.

53 EHRENREICH, PAUL (1897) *Anthropologische studien über die Urbewohner Brasiliens vornehmlich der Staaten Matto Grosso, Goyaz und Amazonas (Purus-Gebiet).* Braunschweig.

54 EWERS, JOHN C. (1965) The emergence of the Plains Indians as the symbol of the North American Indian, *Rep. Smithson. Instn* (1964), 531–44.

55 FERGUSON, THOMAS STUART (1958) *One fold and one shepherd.* San Francisco, Books of California.

56 FERRIS, H.B. (1916) The Indians of Cuzco and the Apurimac, *Mem. Am. anthrop. Ass.* **3**: 56–148.

57 FORD, JAMES A. (1969) A comparison of Formative cultures in the Americas; diffusion or the psychic unity of man, *Smithson. Contr. Anthrop.* **11**: 213 pages.

58 FRY, GARY F. and JOHN G. MOORE (1969) *Enterobius vermicularis*: 10,000-year-old human infection, *Science* **166**: 1620.

59 GARCIA, GREGORIO (1729) *Origen de los Indios de el Nuevo Mundo,* etc. 2ª impresión. Madrid, Francisco Martinez Abad.

60 GATES, R. RUGGLES (1949) *Pedigrees of Negro families.* Philadelphia, The Blakiston Co.

61 GATES, R. RUGGLES (1953) Studies in interracial crossing. II. A new theory of skin color inheritance, *Int. anthrop. ling. Rev.* **1**: 15–67.

62 GLADWIN, HAROLD S. (1947) *Men out of Asia; with a foreword by Earnest A. Hooton.* New York, Whittlesey House.

63 GOLDER, F. A. (1922–5) *Bering's voyages.* 2 vol. New York, American Geographic Society.

64 GOLDSTEIN, M.S. (1943) *Demographic and bodily changes in descendants of Mexican immigrants, with comparable data on parents and children in Mexico.* Austin, Institute of Latin-American Studies, Univ. of Texas.

65 HACKETT, C.J. (1963) On the origin of the human treponematoses (pinta, yaws, endemic syphilis and venereal syphilis), *Bull. Wld Hlth Org.* **29**: 1–41.

66 HAMMEL, H.T. (1963) Effect of race on response to cold. *Fedn Proc. Fedn Am. Socs exp. Biol.* **22**: 795–800.

67 HAMPERL, H. and P. WEISS (1955) Ueber die spongiöse Hyperostose an Schädeln aus Alt-Peru, *Virchows Arch. path. Anat. Physiol.* **327**: 629–42.

68 HANSEN, SØREN (1886) Contributions à l'anthropologie des Groënlandais orientaux. *Bull. Soc. Anthrop. Paris*, sér. 3, **9**: 609–19.

69 HAYNES, C. VANCE, JR. (1968) Geochronology of man–mammoth sites and their bearing upon the origin of the Llano complex. Paper presented at the symposium on Pleistocene and Recent environments of the central Plains, Univ. of Kansas, Lawrence, 25 October. 36 pages (mimeographed).

70 HAYNES, C. VANCE, JR. (1969) The earliest Americans, *Science* **166**: 709–15.

71 HEIZER, ROBERT F. and SHERBURNE F. COOK (1952) Fluorine and other chemical tests of some North American human and fossil bones, *Am. J. phys. Anthrop.* **10**: 289–303.

72 HEIZER, ROBERT F. and LEWIS K. NAPTON (1969) Biological and cultural evidence from prehistoric human coprolites, *Science* **165**: 563–8.

73 HERSKOVITS, MELVILLE J. (1927) The physical form and growth of the American Negro, *Anthrop. Anz.* **4**: 293–316.

74 HERSKOVITS, MELVILLE J. (1930) *The anthropometry of the American Negro.* (Columbia Univ. Contr. Anthrop. XI.) New York, Columbia Univ. Press.

75 HERSKOVITS, MELVILLE J. (1943) Franz Boas as physical anthropologist, *Mem. Am. anthrop. Ass.* **61**: 39–51.

75a HEYERDAHL, THOR (1971) The voyage of Ra II, *Nat. geogr. Mag.* **139**(1): 44–71.

76 HOLDER, PRESTON, and T.D. STEWART (1958) A complete find of filed teeth from the Cahokia mounds in Illinois, *J. Wash. Acad. Sci.* **48**: 349–57.

77 HOPKINS, DAVID M. – Ed. (1967) *The Bering land bridge.* Stanford, Calif., Stanford Univ. Press.

78 HRDLIČKA, ALEŠ (1900) *Anthropological investigation of 1000 white and colored children, etc.* New York and Albany.

79 HRDLIČKA, ALEŠ (1907) Skeletal remains suggesting or attributed to early man in North America, *Bull. Bur. Am. Ethnol.* **33**: 113 pages.

80 HRDLIČKA, ALEŠ (1908) Physiological and medical observations among the Indians of southwestern United States and northern Mexico, *Bull. Bur. Am. Ethnol.* **34**: 460 pages.

81 HRDLIČKA, ALEŠ (1910) Contribution to the anthropology of

Central and Smith Sound Eskimo, *Anthrop. Pap. Am. Mus. nat. Hist.* **5**(2): 177–280.

82 HRDLIČKA, ALEŠ (1912) Early man in South America, *Bull. Bur. Am. Ethnol.* **52**: 405 pages.

83 HRDLIČKA, ALEŠ (1913) A search in eastern Asia for the race that peopled America, *Smithson. misc. Collns* **60**(30): 10–13.

84 HRDLIČKA, ALEŠ (1925) *The Old Americans.* Baltimore, The Williams & Wilkins Co.

85 HRDLIČKA, ALEŠ (1926) The Indians of Panama; their physical relation to the Mayas, *Am. J. phys. Anthrop.* **9**: 1–15.

86 HRDLIČKA, ALEŠ (1927) Catalogue of human crania in the United States National Museum collections: The Algonkin and related Iroquois; Siouan, Caddoan, Salish and Ashaptin, Shoshonean, and Californian Indians, *Proc. U.S. natn. Mus.* **69**(5): 127 pages.

87 HRDLIČKA, ALEŠ (1930) Anthropological survey in Alaska, *Rep. Bur. Am. Ethnol.* **46**: 19–374.

88 HRDLIČKA, ALEŠ (1931) Catalogue of human crania in the United States National Museum collections: Pueblos, southern Utah Basket-Makers, Navaho, *Proc. U.S. natn. Mus.* **78**(2): 95 pages.

89 HRDLIČKA, ALEŠ (1933) The Eskimo of the Kuskokwim, *Am. J. phys. Anthrop.* **18**: 93–145.

90 HRDLIČKA, ALEŠ (1935) The Pueblos; with comparative data on the bulk of the tribes of the Southwest and northern Mexico. *Am. J. phys. Anthrop.* **20**: 235–460.

91 HRDLIČKA, ALEŠ (1937) Early man in America: What have the bones to say? In *Early man as depicted by leading authorities at the international symposium at the Academy of Natural Sciences, Philadelphia, March 1937* (George Grant MacCurdy, Ed.) 93–104. Philadelphia, J.B.Lippincott Co.

92 HRDLIČKA, ALEŠ (1942) Crania of Siberia, *Am. J. phys. Anthrop.* **29**: 435–73.

93 HRDLIČKA, ALEŠ (1945) *The Aleutian and Commander Islands and their inhabitants.* Philadelphia, Wistar Institute of Anatomy & Biology.

94 HUDSON, E.H. (1958) *Non-venereal syphilis; a sociological and medical study of bejel.* Edinburgh, E. & S.Livingstone, Ltd.

95  HURT, WESLEY R., JR. (1960) The cultural complexes from the Lagoa Santa region, Brazil, *Am. Anthrop.* **62**: 569–85.

96  HURTADO, ALBERTO (1932) Respiratory adaptation in the Indian natives of the Peruvian Andes. Studies at high altitude, *Am. J. phys. Anthrop.* **17**: 137–65.

97  HYADES, PAUL et JOSEPH DENIKER (1891) *Mission scientifique du Cap Horn, 1882–83.* VII (Anthropologie, Ethnographie). Paris.

98  IDELL, ALBERT (1957) *The Bernal Díaz chronicles: The true story of the conquest of Mexico.* New York, Doubleday & Co.

99  IMBELLONI, JOSÉ (1950) Cephalic deformations of the Indians in Argentina, *Bull. Bur. Am. Ethnol.* **143**(6): 53–5.

100  INGSTAD, HELGE (1964) Vinland ruins prove Vikings found the New World, *Natn. geogr. Mag.* **126**: 708–34.

101  IRVING, WASHINGTON (1961) *Astoria, or anecdotes of an enterprise beyond the Rocky Mountains.* 2 vols. Philadelphia, J.B.Lippincott Co.

102  JEFFERSON, THOMAS (1802) *Notes on the State of Virginia.* 9th American ed. Boston.

103  JENNESS, DIAMOND (1928) Ethnological problems of Arctic America. In *Problems of polar research* (W.L.G.Joerg, Ed.) 167–175. New York, American Geographical Society.

104  JOCHELSON, WALDEMAR (1933) History, ethnology and anthropology of the Aleut, *Publs Carnegie Instn* **432**: 91 pages.

105  KANASEKI, TAKEO, TADAAKI HARADA and KIYOTAKA ASAKAWA (1955) On the skeletal remains excavated from the Goryo shell-mound, Shimomashiki-gun, Kumamoto-Prefecture, *Q. Jl Anthrop. Kyushu* **2**: 93–163.

106  KAPLAN, BERNICE A. (1949) The fourth summer seminar in physical anthropology, *Yearb. phys. Anthrop.* **4**: 22–39.

107  KERLEY, E.R. and W.M.BASS (1967) Paleopathology: Meeting ground for many disciplines, *Science* **157**: 638–44.

108  KINGSBOROUGH, EDWARD KING, VISCOUNT (1831–48) *Antiquities of Mexico.* 9 vols. London, Robert Havell and Colnaghi, Son & Co.

109  KLUCKHOHN, CLYDE and DOROTHEA LEIGHTON (1947) *The Navaho.* Cambridge, Mass., Harvard Univ. Press.

110  KROEBER, A.L. (1915) Frederick Ward Putnam, *Am. Anthrop.* **17**: 712–18.

111 KROEBER, A.L. (1939) Cultural and natural areas of native North America, *Univ. Calif. Publs Am. Archaeol. Ethnol.* **38**: 242 pages.

112 KRONE, R. (1906) Die Guarrany-Indianer des Aldeamento do Rio Itariri im Staate von São Paulo in Brasilien, *Mitt. anthrop. Ges. Wien* **36**(N.F. **6**): 130–46.

113 LA HITTE, CHARLES DE et HERMAN TEN KATE (1897) Notes ethnographiques sur les Indiens Guayaquis et description de leurs caractères physiques, *An. Mus. La Plata*, Sec. Antrop. **2**: 36.

114 LAS CASAS, FRAY BARTOLOME (1951) *Historia de las Indias* (Ed. by Augustin Millares Carlo, with an introduction by Lewis Hanke). 3 vols. Mexico, Fondo de Cultura Económica.

115 LASKER, GABRIEL W. (1952) An anthropometric study of returned Mexican emigrants. In *Indian tribes of aboriginal America* (Selected Pap. XXIX Int. Congr. Am., New York 1949, Sol Tax, Ed.) 242–6. Chicago, Univ. of Chicago Press.

116 LAUGHLIN, WILLIAM S. (1949) The physical anthropology of three Aleut populations: Attu, Atka, and Nikolski. Doctoral thesis, Harvard Univ.

116a LAUGHLIN, WILLIAM S. (1967) Human migration and permanent occupation in the Bering Sea area. In *The Bering Land Bridge* (David M. Hopkins, Ed.) 409–450. Stanford, Calif., Stanford University Press.

117 LEHMANN-NITSCHE, ROBERT (1904) Études anthropologiques sur les Indiens Takshik (groupe Guaycuru) du Chaco Argentin, *Revta Mus. La Plata* **11**: 261–314.

118 LEHMANN-NITSCHE, ROBERT (1908) Estudios antropológicos sobre los Chiriguanos, Chorotes, Matacos y Tobas (Chaco Occidental), *An. Mus. La Plata*, 2ª ser. **1**: 53–149.

119 LYELL, SIR CHARLES (1849) *A second visit to the United States of America*. 2 vols. New York, Harper & Brothers.

120 MACNEISH, R.S. (1969) *First annual report of the Ayacucho Archaeological–Botanical Project.* Andover, Mass., Phillips Acad, R.S.Peabody Found. for Archaeol.

121 MACNEISH, R.S., R.BERGER and REINER PROTSCH (1970) Megafauna and man from Ayacucho, highland Peru, *Science* **168**: 975–7.

122 MANOUVRIER, LEON (1883) Sur les Araucans du Jardin d'Acclimatation, *Bull. Soc. Anthrop. Paris*, sér. 3, **6**: 727–32.

123 MARTIN, P.S. and H.E.WRIGHT, JR. (1967) Pleistocene extinctions; the search for a cause, *Conf. int. Ass. quartn. Res.* (Boulder-Denver, Colorado, 1965) **7**(6): 453 pages.

124 MATSON, G. ALBIN (1970) Distribution of blood groups [in Mexico and Central America]. In *Handbook of Middle American Indians*, vol. 9 (T.D.Stewart, Ed.) 105–47. Austin, Univ. of Texas Press.

125 MAY, HERBERT G. and BRUCE M. METZGER – Eds. (1965) The Oxford annotated Bible with the Apocrypha. Rev. standard version. Oxford, University Press.

126 MEGGERS, BETTY J., CLIFFORD EVANS and EMILIO ESTRADA (1965) Early Formative period of coastal Ecuador; the Valdivia and Machalilla phases, *Smithson. Contr. Anthrop.* **1**: 235 pages.

127 MENDES CORRÊA, A.A. (1925) O significado geneológico do 'Australopithecus' e do crânio de Tabgha e o arco antropofilético índico, *Trabhs Soc. port. Antrop. Etnol.* **2**(3): 249–86.

128 MILLS, C.A. (1942) Climatic effects on growth and development with particular reference to the effects of tropical residence, *Am. Anthrop.* **44**: 1–13.

129 MOORE, CLARENCE B. (1916) Some aboriginal sites on Green River, Kentucky, *J. Acad. nat. Sci. Philad.* **16**: 431–87.

130 MOORE, JOHN G., G.F.FRY and E.ENGLERT, JR. (1969) Thorny-headed worm infection in North American prehistoric man, *Science* **163**: 1324–5.

131 MORSE, DAN (1961) Prehistoric tuberculosis in America, *Am. Rev. resp. Dis.* **83**: 489–504.

132 MOSTNY, GRETA (1957) La momia del cerro El Plomo, *Boln Mus. nac. Hist. nac. Chile* **27**(1): 118 pages.

133 MOURANT, A.E., ADA C.KOPEĆ and KAZIMIERA DOMANIEWSKA-SOBCZAK (1958) *The ABO blood groups: Comprehensive tables and maps of world distribution.* Springfield, Ill., Charles C. Thomas.

134 MOVIUS, HALLAM L. JR. (1949) Lower paleolithic archaeology in southern Asia and the Far East. In *Studies in physical anthropology. No. 1, Early man in the Far East* (W.W.Howells, Ed.) 17–81. American Association of Physical Anthropologists.

135 MÜLLER-BECK, HANSJÜRGEN (1967) On migrations of hunters across the Bering land bridge in the upper Pleistocene. In *The Bering land bridge* (David M. Hopkins, Ed.) 373–408. Stanford, Calif., Stanford Univ. Press.

136 MUMFORD, A.A. and M.YOUNG (1923) The interrelationships of the physical measurements and the vital capacity, *Biometrika* **15**: 109–33.

137 MUNIZAGA, JUAN R. (1965) Skeletal remains from sites of Valdivia and Machalilla phases, *Smithson. Contr. Anthrop.* **1**: 219–34.

138 NEEL, JAMES V. (1970) Lessons from a 'primitive' people, *Science* **170**: 815–22.

139 NEEL, J.V. and F.M.SALZANO (1967) Further studies on the Xavante Indians. X. Some hypotheses-generalizations resulting from these studies, *Am. J. hum. Genet.* **19**: 554–74.

140 NEEL, J.V., F.M.SALZANO, P.C.JUNQUEIRA, F.KEITER and D. MAYBURY-LEWIS (1964) Studies on the Xavante Indians of the Brazilian Mato Groso, *Am. J. hum. Genet.* **16**: 52–140.

141 NEEL, J.V., A.H.P.ANDRADE, G.E.BROWN, W.E.EVELAND, J. GOOBAR, W.A.SODEMAN, JR., G.H.STOLLERMAN, E.D.WEINSTEIN and A.H.WHEELER (1968) Further studies of the Xavante Indians. IX. Immunologic status with respect to various diseases and organisms, *Am. J. trop. Med. Hyg.* **17**: 486–97.

142 NEEL, J.V., W.M.MIKKELSEN, D.L.RUCKNAGEL, E.D.WEINSTEIN, R.A.GOYER and S.H.ABADIE (1968) Further studies of the Xavante Indians. VII. Some observations on blood, urine and stool specimens, *Am. J. trop. Med. Hyg.* **17**: 474–85

143 NEWMAN, MARSHALL T. (1953) The application of ecological rules to the racial anthropology of the aboriginal New World, *Am. Anthrop.* **55**: 311–27.

144 NEWMAN, MARSHALL T. (1960) Adaptations in the physique of American aborigines to nutritional factors, *Hum. Biol.* **32**: 288–313.

145 NEWMAN, MARSHALL T. (1969) Control data for determining biological effects of the food supplement program at Vicos, Peru, *Am. J. phys. Anthrop.* **31**: 265 (Abstract).

146 NEWMAN, MARSHALL T. and CARLOS CALLAZOS CH. (1957) Growth and skeletal maturation in malnourished Indian boys

from the Peruvian Sierra, *Am. J. phys. Anthrop.* **15**: 431 (Abstract).

147 NISWANDER, J.D., F.KEITER and J.V.NEEL (1967) Further studies on the Xavante Indians. II. Some anthropometric traits of the Xavantes of Simões Lopes, *Am. J. hum. Genet.* **19**: 490–501.

148 OAKLEY, KENNETH (1964) *Frameworks for dating fossil man.* Chicago, Aldine Publishing Co.

149 OGATA, TAMOTSU (1970) Physical changes in man during the Jomon period of Japan in accordance with the climatic and geological alterations, *Int. Congr. anthrop. ethnol. Sci.* (Tokyo, 1968) I: 95–7.

150 PEARL, RAYMOND and LOWELL J.REED (1920) On the rate of growth of the population of the United States since 1790 and its mathematical representation, *Proc. natn. Acad. Sci. U.S.A.* **6**: 275–88.

151 PEARL, RAYMOND, LOWELL J.REED and JOSEPH F.KISH (1940) The logistic curve and the census of 1940, *Science* **92**: 486–8.

152 PIGGOTT, STUART (1940) A trepanned skull of the Beaker period from Dorset and the practice of trepanning in prehistoric Europe, *Proc. prehist. Soc.* n.s. **6**: 112–32.

153 PÍO CORRÊA, MANOEL, JR. (1962) La vida y la obra del Mariscal Rondón, *Am. indig.* **22**: 247–55.

154 PITTARD, EUGÈNE (1901) Contribution à l'étude anthropologique des Esquimaux du Labrador et de La Baie d'Hudson, *Bull. Soc. neuchâtel. Géogr.* **13**: 158–76.

155 POLLITZER, W. S. (1958) The Negroes of Charleston (S.C.); a study of hemoglobin types, serology, and morphology, *Am. J. phys. Anthrop.* **16**: 241–63.

156 POLO, MARCO (1926) *The book of Ser Marco Polo, etc.* (Sir Henry Yule, Transl. and Ed.) 2 vols. Third ed. rev. by Henri Cordier. London, J. Murray.

157 POULSEN, KNUD (1909) Contribution to the anthropology and nosology of the East-Greenlanders, *Meddr Grønland* **28**(4): 131–50.

158 PRATT, DALLAS (1969–70) Discovery of a world: Early maps showing America, *Antiques Mag.* **96**: 900–6, **97**: 128–34.

159 PRESCOTT, WILLIAM H. (1874) *History of the conquest of Peru.* Philadelphia, J.B.Lippincott Co.

160 PUTNAM, CARLETON (1967) *Race and reason*. Washington, D.C., Public Affairs Press.

161 QUINN, D.B. (1961) The argument for the English discovery of America between 1480 and 1494, *Geogrl J.* **127**: 277–85.

162 RANKE, KARL ERNST (1906–7) Anthropologische Beobachtungen aus Zentralbrasilien, *Abh. bayer. Akad. Wiss.* **24**(1): 1–148.

163 RASMUSSEN, KNUD (1927) *Across Arctic America. Narrative of the Fifth Thule Expedition*. New York, G.P.Putnam's Sons.

164 REED, DWAYNE, GEORGE BROWN, ROSALIE MERRICK, JOHN SEVER and ELMER FELTY (1967) A mumps epidemic on St George Island, Alaska, *J. Am. med. Ass.* **199**: 113–17.

165 RITCHIE, WILLIAM A. (1932) The Lamoka Lake site; the type station of the Archaic Algonkin period in New York, *Res. & Trans. N.Y. State Archaeol. Ass. Rochester* **7**(4): 79–134.

166 RITCHIE, WILLIAM A. (1969) *The archaeology of New York State*. Rev. ed. Garden City, N.Y., The Natural History Press.

167 RIVET, PAUL (1957) Les origins de l'homme Américain. Paris, Gallimard.

168 ROBERTS, D.F. (1955) The dynamics of racial intermixture in the American Negro – some anthropological considerations, *Am. J. hum. Genet.* **7**: 361–7.

169 ROMERO, JAVIER (1958) Mutilaciones dentarias prehispanicas de México y América en general, *Instituto nac. Antrop. Hist.*, Ser. Invest., **3**: 326 pages

170 ROMERO, JAVIER (1960) Ultimos hallazgos de mutilaciones dentarias en México, *An. Inst. nac. Antrop. Hist.* **12**: 151–215.

171 ROMERO, JAVIER (1965) Recientes adiciones a la colección de dientes mutilados, *An. Inst. nac. Antrop. Hist.* **17**: 199–256.

172 ROMERO, JAVIER (1970) Dental mutilation, trephination, and cranial deformation [in Middle America]. In *Handbook of Middle American Indians*, vol. 9 (T.D.Stewart, Ed.) 50–67. Austin, Univ. of Texas Press.

173 ROSENBLAT, ÁNGEL (1945) *La poblacion indígena de América, desde 1492 hasta la actualidad*. Buenos Aires, Ed. Institución Cultural Española.

174 ROSHOLT, JOHN N., JR. (1962) Pleistocene dating with Th and Pa isotopes, *McGraw-Hill Yb Sci. Technol.*, page 196.

175 ROUMA, GEORGES (1933) *Quitchouas et Aymaras. Étude des populations autochtones des Andes boliviennes.* Bruxelles.

176 ROUSE, IRVING (1948) The Arawak, *Bull. Bur. Am. Ethnol.* **143**(4): 507–46.

177 ROWE, JOHN HOWLAND (1946) Inca culture at the time of the Spanish conquest, *Bull. Bur. Am. Ethnol.* **143**(2): 183–330.

178 SAMUELS, R. (1965) Parasitological study of long-dried fecal samples, *Mem. Soc. Am. Archaeol.* **19**: 175–9.

179 SAPPER, KARL (1924) Die Zahl und die Volksdichte der indianischen Bevölkerung in America vor der Conquista und in der Gegenwart, *Proc. Int. Congr. Am.* (The Hague, 1924) **21**(1): 95–104.

180 SELTZER, CARL C. (1933) The anthropometry of the Western and Copper Eskimos, based on data of Vilhjalmur Stefansson, *Hum. Biol.* **5**: 313–70.

181 SEVERINO LÓPEZ, JUAN (1948) La talla de enrolamiento en la Argentina. Investigación sobre la clase 1924, *An. Inst. étnico nac. B. Aires* **1**: 123–83.

182 SITTIG, OTTO (1896) Compulsory migrations in the Pacific Ocean. *Rep. Smithson. Instn.* (to July 1895), pages 519–35.

183 SKELTON, R.A., THOMAS E. MARSTON and GEORGE D. PAINTER (1965) *The Vinland map and the Tartar relation.* New Haven, Yale Univ. Press.

184 SMITH, JOSEPH, JR. – Transl. (1921) *The Book of Mormon.* Salt Lake City, Utah, The Church of Jesus Christ of Latter-day Saints.

185 SMITH,W., R.WOODBURY and N.F.S.WOODBURY (1966) The excavation of Hawikuh by Frederick Webb Hodge: Report of the Hendricks-Hodge Expedition, 1917–23, *Contr. Mus. Am. Indian* **20**: 336 pages.

186 SNOW, CHARLES E. (1948) Indian Knoll skeletons of site Oh2, Ohio County, Kentucky. *Univ. Ky Rep. Anthrop.* **4** (no. 3, pt. 2): 371–555.

187 SPINDEN, H.J. (1917) The origin and distribution of agriculture in America, *Proc. int. Congr. Am.* (Washington, 1915) **19**: 269–76.

188 SPUHLER, J.N. (1950) Genetics of three normal morphological variations: Patterns of superficial veins of the anterior thorax,

peroneus tertius muscle, and number of vallate papillae, *Symp. quant. Biol.* **15**: 175–89.

189 SPUHLER, JAMES N. (1951) Some genetic variations in American Indians. In *Papers on the physical anthropology of the American Indian* (William S. Laughlin, Ed.) 177–202. New York, The Viking Fund, Inc.

190 STARR, FREDERICK (1902) The physical characters of the Indians of southern Mexico, *Univ. Chicago decenn. Publs.* **4**: 53–109.

191 STEENSBY, H.P. (1910) Contributions to the ethnology and anthropogeography of the Polar Eskimos, *Meddr Grønland* **34**(7): 253–406.

192 STEWARD, JULIAN H. (1949) The native population of South America, *Bull. Bur. Am. Ethnol.* **143**(5): 655–68.

193 STEWARD, JULIAN H. – Ed. (1946–59) Handbook of South American Indians, 6 vols. *Bull. Bur. Am. Ethnol.* **143**.

194 STEWART, C.A. (1922) The vital capacity of the lungs of children in health and disease, *Am. J. Dis. Child.* **24**: 451–96.

195 STEWART, T.D. (1936) Anthropometric nomenclature. I. The cephalic (length–breadth) index, *Am. J. phys. Anthrop.* **22**: 97–140.

196 STEWART, T.D. (1940) Some historical implications of physical anthropology in North America, *Smithson. misc. Collns* **100**: 15–50.

197 STEWART, T.D. (1943) Distribution of cranial height in South America, *Am. J. phys. Anthrop.* **1**: 143–55.

198 STEWART, T.D. (1946) A reexamination of the fossil human skeletal remains from Melbourne, Florida, *Smithson. misc. Collns* **106**(10): 1–28.

199 STEWART, T.D. (1947) Anthropology and the melting pot, *Smithson. Rep. 1946*, pages 315–44.

200 STEWART, T.D. (1948) The true form of the cranial deformity originally described under the name 'tête trilobée,' *J. Wash. Acad. Sci.* **38**: 66–72.

201 STEWART, T.D. (1949) The development of the concept of morphological dating in connection with early man in America, *SWest. J. Anthrop.* **5**: 1–16.

202 STEWART, T.D. (1950) Deformity, trephining and mutilation in

South American Indian skeletal remains, *Bull. Bur. Am. Ethnol.* **143**(6): 43–52.

203 STEWART, T.D. (1951) Antiquity of man in America demonstrated by the fluorine test, *Science* **113**: 391–2.

204 STEWART, T.D. (1953) The age incidence of neural-arch defects in Alaskan natives, considered from the standpoint of etiology, *J. Bone Jt Surg.* **35-A**: 937–50.

205 STEWART, T.D. (1953) Skeletal remains from Zaculeu, Guatemala. In *The ruins of Zaculeu, Guatemala* (R.B.Woodbury and A.S.Trick, Eds.) 295–311. Richmond, Va., The William Byrd Press.

206 STEWART, T.D. (1956) Significance of osteitis in ancient Peruvian trephining, *Bull. Hist. Med.* **30**: 293–320.

207 STEWART, T.D. (1956) Skeletal remains from Xochicalco, Morelos. In *Estudios antropológicos publicados en homenaje al Doctor Manuel Gamio.* 131–55. Mexico.

208 STEWART, T.D. (1958) Stone age skull surgery: A general review, with emphasis on the New World, *Smithson. Rep. 1957*, pages 469–91.

209 STEWART, T.D. (1960) A physical anthropologist's view of the peopling of the New World, *SWest. J. Anthrop.* **16**: 259–73.

210 STEWART, T.D. (1960) The Chinook sign of freedom: A study of the skull of the famous chief Comcomly, *Smithson. Rep. 1959*, pages 463–76.

211 STEWART, T.D. (1960) Skeletal remains from Venado Beach, Panama: Cranial deformity, *Actas Congr. int. Am.* (San José, Costa Rica, 1958) **33**(2): 45–54.

212 STEWART, T.D. (1965) The problem of analyzing the height of the cranial vault. In *Homenaje a Juan Comas en su 65 aniversario.* II, pages 356–66. Mexico.

213 STEWART, T.D. (1969) Laguna Beach man re-examined in the light of direct $C_{14}$ dating, *Am. J. phys. Anthrop.* **31**: 255 (Abstract).

214 STEWART, T.D. (Manuscript) Human skeletal remains from Dzibilchaltun, Yucatan; with a review of cranial deformity types in the Maya region. 50 pages.

215 STEWART, T.D. – Ed. (1970) *Physical anthropology.* Volume 9 of *Handbook of Middle American Indians* (Robert Wauchope, Gen. Ed.). Austin, Univ. of Texas Press.

216 STEWART, T.D. and MARSHALL T. NEWMAN (1951) An historical résumé of the concept of differences in Indian types, *Am. Anthrop.* **53**: 19–36.

217 STEWART, T.D. and LAWRENCE G. QUADE (1969) Lesions of the frontal bone in American Indians, *Am. J. phys. Anthrop.* **30**: 89–110.

218 STEWART, T.D. and ALEXANDER SPOEHR (1952) Evidence on the paleopathology of yaws, *Bull. Hist. Med.* **26**: 538–53.

219 STEWART, T.D. and H.V. WALTER (1955) Fluorine analysis of putatively ancient human and animal bones from Confins Cave, Minas Gerais, Brazil, *An. Congr. int. Am.* (São Paulo, 1954) **31**(2): 925–37.

220 STOŁYHWO, K. (1932) Körpergrösse, ihre Vererbung und Abhängigkeit von dem neuen Milieu bei den polnischen Emigranten in Paraná (Brasilien), *Verh. Ges. phys. Anthrop.* **6**: 94–106.

221 STRONG, WILLIAM DUNCAN (1951) Cultural resemblances in Nuclear America; parallelism or diffusion? In *The civilizations of ancient America* (Sel. Pap. XXIX Int. Congr. Am., New York 1949, Sol Tax, Ed.) 271–9. Chicago, Univ. of Chicago Press.

222 STURTEVANT, WILLIAM C. (1960) The significance of ethnological similarities between southeastern North America and the Antilles, *Yale Univ. Publs Anthrop.* **64**: 58 pages.

223 SULLIVAN, LOUIS R. (1925) Anthropometry of the Siouan tribes, *Anthrop. Pap. Am Mus. nat. Hist.* **23**: 81–174.

224 SWADESH, MORRIS, with comments by GEORGE I. QUIMBY, HENRY B. COLLINS, EMIL W. HAURY, GORDON F. EKHOLM and FRED EGGAN (1954) Time depths of American linguistic groupings, *Am. Anthrop.* **56**: 361–77.

225 TAYLOR, DOUGLAS (1938) The Caribs of Dominica, *Bull. Bur. Am. Ethnol.* **119**: 109–60.

226 TEJADA, CARLOS, J.P. STRON, M.R. MONTENEGRO, *et al.* (1968) Distribution of coronary and aortic atherosclerosis by geographic location, race, and sex, *Lab. Invest.* **18**: 509–26.

227 TEN KATE, HERMAN (1905) Matériaux pour servir à l'anthropologie des Indiens de la République Argentine, *Revta Mus. La Plata* **12**: 33–57.

228 TOCHER, J.F. (1902) Note on some measurements of Eskimo of Southampton Island, *Man* 2(115): 165–7.

229 TROTTER, MILDRED and GOLDINE C. GLESER (1958) A re-evaluation of estimation of stature based on measurements of stature taken during life and of long bones after death, *Am. J. phys. Anthrop.* 16: 79–123.

230 ULLOA, ANTONIO DE (1944) *Noticias americanas. Entretenimiento físico-histórico sobre la América meridional y la septentrional oriental, etc.* Ed. Nova. Buenos Aires.

231 VIRCHOW, RUDOLF (1878) Eskimos, *Z. Ethnol.* 10 (*Verh. berl. Ges. Anthrop. Ethnol. Urgesch.*, pages 185–8).

232 VIRCHOW, RUDOLF (1880) Eskimos von Labrador, *Z. Ethnol.* 12 (*Verh. berl. Ges. Anthrop. Ethnol. Urgesch.*, pages 253–74).

233 WALTER, H.V., A.CATHOUD and ANIBAL MATTOS (1937) The Confins man – a contribution to the study of early man in South America. In *Early man as depicted by leading authorities at the International Symposium at the Academy of Natural Sciences, Philadelphia, March 1937* (George Grant MacCurdy, Ed.) 341–8. Philadelphia, J.B.Lippincott Co.

234 WEBB, WILLIAM S. (1946) Indian Knoll, site Oh2, Ohio County, Kentucky, *Univ. Ky Reps Anthrop. Archaeol.* 4(no. 3, pt. 1): 115–365.

235 WEBB, WILLIAM S. and CHARLES E. SNOW (1945) The Adena people (with chapter on Adena pottery by James B. Griffin), *Univ. Ky Reps Anthrop. Archaeol.* 6: 369 pages.

236 WEIDENREICH, FRANZ (1939) On the earliest representatives of modern mankind recovered on the soil of East Asia, *Peking nat. Hist. Bull.* 13(3): 161–74.

237 WEISBACH, A. (1878) *Körpermessungen verschiedener Menschenrassen.* Berlin.

238 WENDORF, FRED, ALEX D. KRIEGER and CLAUDE C. ALBRITTON (1955) *The Midland discovery; a report on the Pleistocene human remains from Midland, Texas (With a description of the skull by T.D.Stewart).* Austin, Univ. of Texas Press.

239 WILLEY, GORDON R. (1960) New World prehistory, *Science* 131(3393): 73–85.

240 WILSON, THOMAS (1895) On the presence of fluorine as a test for the fossilization of animal bones, *Am. Nat.* 29: 301–17, 439–56, 719–25.

241 WORKMAN, P.L., B.S.BLUMBERG and A.J.COOPER (1963) Selection, gene migration, and polymorphic stability in a US White and Negro population, *Am. J. hum. genet.* **15**: 429–37.

242 ZANGWILL, ISRAEL (1914) *The melting-pot: A drama in four acts.* New and rev. ed. New York, Macmillan Co.

# Index

255